An Anthology of

NEW YORK POETS

An Anthology of

Drawings by *JOE BRAINARD*

NEW YORK POETS

Edited by RON PADGETT
and DAVID SHAPIRO

VINTAGE BOOKS

A Division of Random House   New York

Acknowledgment is hereby extended to the following publishers for permission to reprint from copyrighted material:

City Lights Books: From *Lunch Poems,* by Frank O'Hara. Copyright © 1964 by Frank O'Hara.

Columbia University Press: From *Spring in This World of Poor Mutts,* by Joseph Ceravolo. Copyright © 1968 by Joseph Ceravolo. From *Highway to the Sky,* by Michael Brownstein. Copyright © 1969 by Michael Brownstein.

Corinth Books: From *Many Happy Returns,* by Ted Berrigan. Copyright © 1969 by Ted Berrigan. From *White Country,* by Peter Schjeldahl. Copyright © 1968 by Peter Schjeldahl.

Doubleday & Company, Inc.: "February" and "Freely Espousing" Copyright © 1960 by Donald Allen; "Fabergé," "A Reunion," "Roof Garden" Copyright © 1964 by Société Anonyme d'Editions Literature et Artistiques; "A White City" Copyright © 1965 by The Modern Poetry Association; "Almanac," "A Man in Blue," "Stun," "Today" Copyright © 1966 by James Schuyler; "Poem (How about . . .)" Copyright © 1968 by The Poetry Project, St. Mark's Church in-the-Bowery; "Buried at Springs," "December," "Earth's Holocaust," "Going," "Ilford Rose Book," "The Master of the Golden Glow," "Milk," "Salute," and 3/23/66," from *Freely Espousing,* by James Schuyler.

E. P. Dutton & Co., Inc.: From *Poems From Deal* by David Shapiro. Copyright © 1969 by David Shapiro. From *The Double Dream of Spring* by John Ashbery. Copyright © 1970 by John Ashbery.

Grove Press, Inc.: From *The Pleasures of Peace and Other Poems,* by Kenneth Koch. Copyright © 1969 by Kenneth Koch. From *Thank You and Other Poems,* by Kenneth Koch. Copyright © 1962

Acknowledgments

Thanks to Bob Cornfield, Joe LeSueur, Ted Wilentz, Bennett Sims, Christopher Cerf, Edith Epstein, Renée Neu, Joe Brainard, Bill Berkson, Arthur A. Cohen, Kenneth Koch and Ted Berrigan.

FRANK O'HARA
1926–1966

"I too walk'd the streets of Manhattan island . . ." WHITMAN

"I did everything with that great mad joy you get when you return to New York City . . ." KEROUAC

Contents

CLARK COOLIDGE

KENWARD ELMSLIE

LEWIS MAC ADAMS

JOHN ASHBERY

ED SANDERS

Preface

Putting this anthology together has been a great pleasure, calling into play the usual range of problems, aesthetic and moral, which every editor with a conscience faces, continually, to offset his presumptuousness. Who knows why we selected whom we did? Does knowing a poet help you understand his work any better? We happen to know almost all the poets in this book (there is one we have still to meet), and most of these poets know each other as well. Obviously, as editors we're going on the assumption that these acquaintances and friendships, these sharings of tastes and affections, are going to go a long way toward giving this book a sense of solidarity. It would be facile as well as misleading to see these poets as forming a "School," to pass them off as a literary movement. Fortunately, most poets of any interest these days are so enlightened that they automatically reject, in their lives and work, the unhealthy idea of being part of a literary movement. Like water off a duck's back, such abstractions roll back into nothingness.

Are New York poets new realists, or dissociated from any sympathy for the wretched of the earth? Are they drifting into a penumbra? Or do their sleek attractive surfaces glide by in the light? Have they freshened up the diatribe? Have any of their collaborations produced beautiful corpses? Are New York poets a diploma elite that buries its children? Are they merely tasting the ripest apple on the table, in the air? Is it a *dérèglement de tous les sens*? Or has it become, peculiarly Americanized, only a "leaving-out business," a taking-away process? Have they generated a whole vocabulary of forms, a new sestina, new

] xxix

collages, cut-ups? Is it "deep gossip"? Why have the old copula been expunged?

Perhaps we do protest too much, but this is to prepare ourselves for the gruesome possibility of the "New York School of Poets" label, one which has been spewed forth from time to time by some reviewers, critics and writers either sustained by provincial jealousy or the bent to translate everything into a manageable textbookese. Very few of the poets in this anthology were born in New York City, but many of them live here, and of these, many plan to leave, temporarily or otherwise. There is even a contingent which John Ashbery once referred to as the "*soi-disant* Tulsa School." The fact remains that New York has remained for all of them a fulcrum they continue to use in order to get as much leverage as possible in literature, a city where they met and continued their lives together, whether they came from Cleveland or Newark or Cincinnati or Providence or Tulsa. And although the New York School tag is an alarmingly useless one, it does remind one that many of these poets met in schools, at Harvard, Columbia, N.Y.U. or the New School, sometimes as undergraduates taught by Delmore Schwartz or in poetry workshops taught by Kenneth Koch, Bill Berkson or Frank O'Hara. The crisscrossing of friendships is surprising and inspiring, like telling someone to see a certain movie and, incredibly, they too like (or hate) it.

Once we had made our selection of which poets to invite to our anthology (which we did, not without disagreement) and after we had invited them, we went a step further by asking the poet to select from his own work a sizable body of poems he himself liked a lot, the idea being to have everyone included happy with the eventual selection. An equal advantage consisted in what we feel to be the poet's ability to judge his own work, since judging one's own work is as much of being a poet as writing it in the first place. This procedure also lightened our work load and made this, we hope, a more personal book, with as little editorial intervention as possible. In other words, we have tried to publish twenty-seven little books in one big volume. We were both delighted with the outcome because we feel that every poet made a first-rate selection of his own work. In only a few cases have we had to ask permission to include a poem the poet had omitted. Continuing this agreement between us and the other poets was our agreement with each other as to which poems to use, a concurrence which reassured us that taste still exists (good and bad), if we want it.

When we had very nearly finished our selections of particular poems, we began to think about the editorial paraphernalia which ordinarily accompanies such anthologies, in the back, afterthoughts. We quickly decided that manifestoes and statements on poetics were in this case unnecessary. Besides, most of the poets in this book would probably decline, with a smile, the invitation to write anything as eternal as a manifesto. In addition to this reticence, most of us would recall Frank O'Hara's Personism manifesto with a gleeful shudder, realizing that it is a hard piece to top and that it in many ways speaks for us all:

PERSONISM: A MANIFESTO *

Everything is in the poems, but at the risk of sounding like the poor wealthy man's Allen Ginsberg, I will write to you because I just heard that one of my fellow poets thinks that a poem of mine that can't be got at one reading is because I was confused *too*. Now, come on. I don't believe in god, so I don't have to

* Reprinted from *Yugen*.

make elaborately sounded structures. I hate Vachel Lindsay, always have, I don't even like rhythm, assonance, all that stuff. You just go on your nerve. If someone's chasing you down the street with a knife you just run, you don't turn around and shout, "Give it up! I was a track star for Mineola Prep."

That's for the writing poems part. As for their reception, suppose you're in love and someone's mistreating (mal aimé) you, you don't say, "Hey, you can't hurt me this way, I *care!*" you just let all the different bodies fall where they may, and they always do may after a few months. But that's not why you fell in love in the first place, just to hang onto life, so you have to take your chances and try to avoid being logical. Pain always produces logic, which is very bad for you.

I'm not saying that I don't have practically the most lofty ideas of anyone writing today, but what difference does that make? they're just ideas. The only good thing about it is that when I get lofty enough I've stopped thinking and that's when refreshment arrives.

But how can you really care if anybody gets it, or gets what it means, or if it improves them. Improves them for what? for death? Why hurry them along? Too many poets act like a middle-aged mother trying to get her kids to eat too much cooked meat, and potatoes with drippings (tears). I don't give a damn whether they eat or not. Forced feeding leads to excessive thinness (effete). Nobody should experience anything they don't need to, if they don't need poetry bully for them, I like the movies too. And after all, only Whitman and Crane and Williams, of the American poets, are better than the movies. As for measure and other technical apparatus, that's just common sense: if you're going to buy a pair of pants you want them to be tight enough so everyone will want to go to bed with you. There's nothing metaphysical about it. Unless, of course, you flatter yourself thinking that what you're experiencing is "yearning."

Abstraction in poetry, which Allen recently commented on in *IT IS*, is intriguing. I think it appears mostly in the minute particulars where decision is necessary. Abstraction (in poetry, not in painting) involves personal removal by the poet. For instance, the decision involved in the choice between "the nostalgia *of* the infinite" and "the nostalgia *for* the infinite" defines an attitude towards degree of abstraction. The nostalgia *of* the infinite representing the greater degree of abstraction, removal, and negative capability (as in Keats and Mallarmé). Personism, a movement which I recently founded and which nobody yet knows about, interests me a great deal, being so totally opposed to this kind of abstract removal that it is verging on a true abstraction for the first time, really, in the history of poetry. Personism is to Wallace Stevens what *la poésie pure* was to Béranger. Personism has nothing to do with philosophy, it's all art. It does not have to do with personality or intimacy, far from it! But to give you a vague idea, one of its minimal aspects is to address itself to one person (other than the poet himself), thus evoking overtones of love without destroying love's life-giving vulgarity, and sustaining the poet's feelings towards the poem while preventing love from distracting him into feeling about the person. That's part of personism. It was founded by me after lunch with LeRoi Jones on August 27, 1959, a day in which I was in love with someone (not Roi, by the way, a blond). I went back to work and wrote a poem for this person. While I was writing it I was realizing that if I wanted to I could use the telephone instead of writing the poem, and so Personism was born. It's a very exciting movement which will undoubtedly have lots of adherents. It puts the poem squarely between the poet and the person, Lucky Pierre style, and the poem is correspondingly gratified. The poem is at last between two persons instead of two pages. In all modesty, I confess that it may be the death of literature as we know it. While I have certain regrets, I am still glad I got there before Alain Robbe-Grillet did. Poetry being quicker and surer than prose, it is only just that poetry finish literature off. For a time people thought that Artaud was going to accomplish this, but actually, for all its magnificence, his polemical writings are not more outside literature than Bear Mountain is outside New York State. His relation is no more astounding than Dubuffet's to painting.

What can we expect of Personism? (This is getting good, isn't it?) Everything, but we won't get it. It is too new, too vital a movement to promise anything. But it, like Africa, is on the way. The recent propagandists for technique on the one hand, and for content on the other, had better watch out.

FRANK O'HARA
9/3/59

We have maintained a biographical section, less out of vanity than the desire to give the facts about a rather large number of poets who remain, for the most part, unknown nationally. The same goes for the bibliographical notes, which are intentionally detailed.

Perhaps it is not our place to try to say very much about these poets, and it is certainly not our desire. What abilities we might or might not have as editors probably do not extend to articulate or meaningful abstraction. In other words, it's not our territory. F. S. C. Northrop, discussing the function and future of poetry, says, "(It is) to start afresh with the immediacy of experience as it has forced the scientist to new and more adequate theory and, in terms of this theory, to make articulate a new philosophy joining the theoretic and aesthetic component of reality, thereby defining a new meaning for human existence and hence a new morality, which it will be the privilege of some Dante of the future to express metaphorically and embody aesthetically in the feelings and emotions of men." We will content ourselves by saying that you might find any kind of poem in this anthology; that is, there never has been any kind of hard and fast notion of how a person ought to write. If he wanted to write a sonnet he could do so without feeling that someone might look at him sideways, even if his sonnet did have fifteen lines, or fifteen thousand lines. The freedom to work with traditional forms and syntax, and the freedom to work with them freely, to use them as the Muse dictated, or to ignore them altogether, is one of the most cheerful things about these poets; with them, the idea of opposing the tradition of the old to the tradition of the new is positively ludicrous.

Here we must emphasize the limits of this book. It is not a collection of poems about New York, nor is it a collection of poets writing about New York—we don't think any of them would agree as to what New York even is—nor is it even a collection of all the good poets living and/or writing in and/or about New York. For instance, the marvelous work of Charles Reznikoff has not been included here because he has not been felt very widely as an influence. Allen Ginsberg has of course been felt very strongly as an influence and a man, either positively or negatively, but he is such a poet of the open cosmos that we felt including him here would have been a shameless appropriation. There are some good poets in New York City whose work is very unlike the present selection, and it could not be included either. Likewise, there are some young and interesting poets showing the influence of those in this volume, but the end of the book had to come at some point, and when that point came, there were some cruelly cut off. The point is that we do not in any way wish to pass judgment on poets not included, at least not with this volume. Finally, it should be said that we both like each poet included, and that in a few cases there were poets we could not convince each other about.

The poets are arranged in a manner we hope sufficiently disguised as to suggest no particular order, since we wished to make no particular point by putting them in this sequence. We especially did not wish to suggest any lineage or historical arrangement.

As for the order of the poems, each poet was invited to arrange them as he wished. Some wished to and did, some were not especially excited about it and did also, some expressed neutrality, interested to see what we would do. When this occurred we arranged the poems in no discernible order. This is, after all, a Random House book.

For which we suggested an incredible number of titles, all of them useless, among which were The Heavenly Humor, Very Good Poems, Great Feats of Harmony, Great Feet of Hominy, Loomings, Ugly Ellipses, An Agreement of Poets, Malign Machinations, Shasta Daisies, Up Against the Wall, Fear Among the Legs of a Chair, Poetry With-

out Fear, Lyrical Bullets, Pansies Freaked with Jet,
Fleurons and Tailpieces, The Understatement of the Year,
Alarming Upheavals, La Meilleure Choix de Poèmes, Of
Manhattan the Son, Treed Again, A Museum of Modern
Poetry, Magic City, Goodbye to Strange Phantoms,
Moving Ramps, City Lights, etc. But wit has its end,
and we came to that end.

Ron Padgett and David Shapiro

New York City, June, 1968

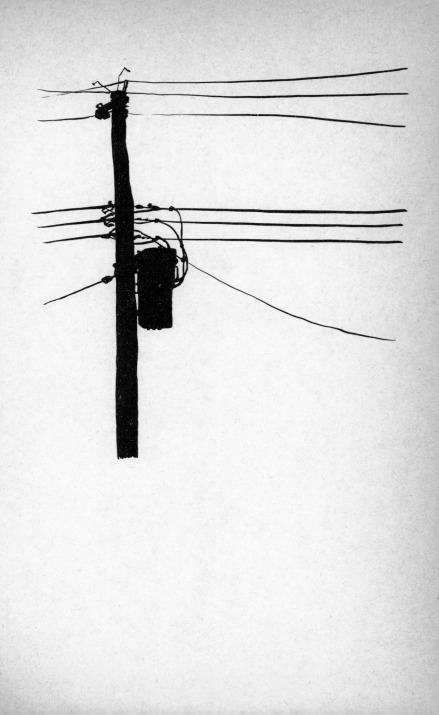

JAMES
SCHUYLER

Salute

Past is past, and if one
remembers what one meant
to do and never did, is
not to have thought to do
enough? Like that gather-
ing of one of each I
planned, to gather one
of each kind of clover,
daisy, paintbrush that
grew in that field
the cabin stood in and
study them one afternoon
before they wilted. Past
is past. I salute
that various field.

An Almanac

Shops take down their awnings;
women go south;
few street lamp leaners;
children run with leaves running at their backs.

In cedar chests sheers and seersuckers displace flannels and wools.

Sere leaves of the Scotch marigolds;
crystals of earth melt;
the thorn apple shows its thorns;
a dog tracks the kitchen porch;
wino-hobos attempt surrender to warm asylums.

Caged mink claw;
gulls become pigeons;
snow bends the snow fence.
Heavy food;
rumbling snow ploughs.

Seats in the examination hall are staggered.
The stars gleam like ice;
a fragment of bone;
in the woods matted leaves;
a yellowish shoot.
A lost key is found;
storm windows are stacked on the beams of the garage.

A Reunion

> *"Week after week glided away in the
St. Clare mansion . . ."* HARRIET BEECHER STOWE

You will like their upstairs
papered with wrappers off Blue Goose oranges.
You will like their grandmother.
They keep up her grave.
You may get to like them.

A White City

My thoughts turn south
a white city
we will wake in one another's arms.
I wake
and hear the steam pipe knock
like a metal heart
and find it has snowed.

February

A chimney, breathing a little smoke.
The sun, I can't see
making a bit of pink
I can't quite see in the blue.
The pink of five tulips
at five p.m. on the day before March first.
The green of the tulip stems and leaves
like something I can't remember,
finding a jack-in-the-pulpit
a long time ago and far away.
Why it was December then
and the sun was on the sea
by the temples we'd gone to see.
One green wave moved in the violet sea
like the U.N. Building on big evenings,
green and wet
while the sky turns violet.

A few of the almond trees
had a few flowers, like a few snowflakes
out of the blue looking pink in the light.
A gray hush
in which the boxy trucks roll up Second Avenue
into the sky. They're just
going over the hill.
The green leaves of the tulips on my desk
like grass light on flesh,
and a green copper steeple
and streaks of cloud beginning to glow.
I can't get over
how it all works in together
like a woman who just came to her window
and stands there filling it
jogging her baby in her arms.
She's so far off. Is it the light
that makes the baby pink?
I can see the little fists
and the rocking-horse motion of her breasts.
It's getting grayer and gold and chilly.
Two dog-size lions face each other
at the corners of a roof.
It's the yellow dust inside the tulips.
It's the shape of a tulip.
It's the water in the drinking glass the tulips are in.
It's a day like any other.

Roof Garden

tubs of . . .
         memory
for a moment
      won't supply a name
               not portulacas
                     (". . . she had on her
                        new dressmaker dress and
                        spectator pumps . . .")
petunias
      tubs of pink petunias
a gray roof
       black when it's hot
light grays today
         green tubs of punctured glow
             before a glowing wall
all the walls reflecting light
at six on a summer evening
              the petunias shimmer in a breeze
a long, long time ago
            petunias
adorable, sticky flower

Freely Espousing

a commingling sky

      a semi-tropic night
      that cast the blackest shadow
      of the easily torn, untrembling banana leaf

or Quebec! what a horrible city
so Steubenville is better?
            the sinking sensation
when someone drowns thinking, "This can't be happening to me!"
the profit of excavating the battlefield where Hannibal whomped the
                                                            Romans
the sinuous beauty of words like allergy
the tonic resonance of
pill when used as in
"she is a pill"
on the other hand I am not going to espouse any short stories in which
        lawn mowers clack.
No, it is absolutely forbidden
for words to echo the act described; or try to. Except very directly
as in
bong. And tickle. Oh it is inescapable kiss.
Marriages of the atmosphere
are worth celebrating
                where Tudor City
catches the sky or the glass side
of a building lit up at night in fog
"What is that gold-green tetrahedron down the river?"
"You are experiencing a new sensation."

        if the touch-me-nots
        are not in bloom
        neither are the chrysanthemums

the bales of pink cotton candy
in the slanting light
                are ornamental cherry trees.
                The greens around them, and
                the browns, the grays, are the park.

It's. Hmm. No.
        Their scallop shell of quiet
        is the S.S. *United States.*

It is not so quiet and they
are a medium-size couple who
when they fold each other up
well, thrill. That's their story.

Fabergé

"I keep my diamond necklace in a pond of sparkling water
for invisibility.

"My rubies in Algae Pond are like an alligator's adenoids.

"My opals—the evening cloud slipped in my pocket and I
felt it and vice versa.

"Out of all the cabs I didn't take (a bit of a saver) I paved
a street with gold. It was quite a short street, sort of a doll
house cul-de-sac.

"And there are a lot of other pretties I could tell about—
ivory horses carved inside bone dice; coral monkeys too tiny
to touch; a piece of jade so big you might mistake it for the
tundra and a length of chalcedony as long as the Alcan Highway which is the Alcan Highway. It is solidified liquid
chalcedony.

"Here, just for you, is a rose made out of a real rose and
the dew drop nestled in a rosy petal that has the delicate five
o'clock shadow fuzz—blue—is not a tear. I have nothing to
cry about now I have you."

December

Il va neiger dans quelque jours
FRANCIS JAMMES

The giant Norway spruce from Podunk, its lower branches
bound,
this morning was reared into place at Rockefeller Center.
I thought I saw a cold blue dusty light sough in its boughs
the way other years the wind thrashing at the giant ornaments
recalled other years and Christmas trees more homey.
Each December! I always think I hate "the over-commer-
cialized event"
and then bells ring, or tiny light bulbs wink above the entrance
to Bonwit Teller or Katherine going on five wants to look at all
the empty sample gift-wrapped boxes up Fifth Avenue in
swank shops
and how can I help falling in love? A calm secret exultation
of the spirit that tastes like Sealtest egg-nog, made from milk
solids,
Vanillin, artificial rum flavoring; a milky impulse to kiss and be
friends.
It's like what George and I were talking about, the East West
Coast divide: Californians need to do a thing to enjoy it.
A smile in the street may be loads! you don't have to undress
everybody.
"You didn't *visit* the Alps?"
"No, but I saw from the train they were black
and streaked with snow."
Having and giving but also catching glimpses
hints that are revelations: to have been so happy is a promise
and if it isn't kept that doesn't matter. It may snow
falling softly on lashes of eyes you love and a cold cheek
grow warm next to your own in hushed dark familial December.

A Man in Blue

Under the French horns of a November afternoon
a man in blue is raking leaves
with a wide wooden rake (whose teeth are pegs
or rather, dowels). Next door
boys play soccer: "You got to start
over!" sort of. A round attic window
in a radiant gray house waits like a kettle drum.
"You got to start. . . ." The Brahmsian day
lapses from waltz to march. The grass,
rough-cropped as Bruno Walter's hair,
is stretched, strewn and humped beneath a sycamore
wide and high as an idea of heaven
in which Brahms turns his face like a bearded thumb
and says, "There is something I must tell you!"
to Bruno Walter. "In the first movement
of my Second, think of it as a family
planning where to go next summer
in terms of other summers. A material ecstasy,
subdued, recollective." Bruno Walter
in a funny jacket with a turned up collar
says, "Let me sing it for you."
He waves his hands and through the vocalese-shaped spaces
of naked elms he draws a copper beech
ignited with a few late leaves. He bluely glazes
a rhododendron "a sea of leaves" against gold grass.
There is a snapping from the brightwork
of parked and rolling cars.
There almost has to be a heaven! so there could be
a place for Bruno Walter
who never needed the cry of a baton.
Immortality—
in a small, dusty, rather gritty, somewhat scratchy
Magnavox from which a forte

drops like a used Brillo Pad?
Frayed. But it's hard to think of the sky as a thick glass floor
with thick-soled Viennese boots tromping about on it.
It's a whole lot harder thinking of Brahms
in something soft, white and flowing.
"Life," he cries (here, in the last movement),
"is something more than beer and skittles!"
"And the something more
is a whole lot better than beer and skittles,"
says Bruno Walter,
darkly, under the sod. I don't suppose it seems so dark
to a root. Who are these men in evening coats?
What are these thumps?
Where is Brahms?
And Bruno Walter?
Ensconced in resonant plump easy chairs
covered with scuffed brown leather
in a pungent autumn that blends leaf smoke
(sycamore, tobacco, other),
their nobility wound in a finale
like this calico cat
asleep, curled up in a bread basket,
on a sideboard where the sun falls.

Stun

If you've ever been in a car
that was hit by a train
whang
(a tearing like metal shears)

flip   spin
       "Why I'm perfectly OK!"
this streaming blood
a euphoric sweat of thanksgiving
and later

a hunk of scrap iron
just there on the turnpike
for no reason
flies up and
whang
it goes on your new underneath
well, it's like you were thrown
grabbed by the scruff of the neck
head over heels right into Proust's steamy cup
just another crumb
of scalloped cookie
odious and total memory
                (of the cells, no doubt)
in prickle-green, speed-lashed
Massachusetts

Today

July 26th, 1965

The bay today breaks
in ripples of applause.
The wind whistles.
Spruce and bright-leaved birch
at the edge
are flat yet plump

as letters with "see enclosures."
A gull mews, the mailboat toots,
the wind rises and pours with a noise like water
and spills black jazz
from spiked brown seed cups of red columbine.
The wind takes with it
a wrack of voices: "the who?"
and unintelligible shapes of phrases
or one scrape: hickory on cement.
Across the bay today
a white house smaller than a thumbnail moon
shines like the light
it shows at night, a star
or sun of kerosene.
The barn swallows from the eaves
are up to something, maybe
showing their fledglings how to do it, scything
an insect harvest from the air.
Round and brown as rabbit droppings,
seed pods of blue-eyed grass
bobble and split along the seams:
so big for so small a flower.
A sailboat scuds,
a poplar tugs at roots
in soil a scurf on rock.
Everything chuckles and creaks
sighs in satisfaction
reddens and ripens in tough gusts of coolness
and the sun smites

3/23/66

It's funny early spring weather, mild and washy,
the color of a head-cold.
The air rushes. Branches
are going nowhere, like the ocean,
spring salt unstopping sinuses. Winter salt doesn't.
Everything just sitting around: a barn without eaves,
a dumpy cottage set catty-corner
on its lot, a field with a horse in it.
A plane goes over, leaving its wake,
an awakening snore. A truck
passes, perceived as a quick shuffle
of solitaire cards. And the poor old humpy lawn
is tufted with Irish eyebrows of onion grass.
A chill on the nape smells frowsty
the spring no more awake
than a first morning stretch
and no more asleep. Growing
and going, in sight and sound, as the fire last night
looked out at us reading *Great Expectations* aloud
and fled up the chimney.

Buried at Springs

There is a hornet in the room
and one of us will have to go
out the window into the late
August mid-afternoon sun. I
won. There is a certain challenge

in being humane to hornets
but not much. A launch draws
two lines of wake behind it
on the bay like a delta
with a melted base. Sandy
billows, or so they look,
of feathery ripe heads of grass,
an acid-yellow kind of
goldenrod glowing or glowering
in shade. Rocks with rags
of shadow, washed dust clouts
that will never bleach.
It is not like this at all.
The rapid running of the
lapping water a hollow knock
of someone shipping oars:
it's eleven years since
Frank sat at this desk and
saw and heard it all
the incessant water the
immutable crickets only
not the same: new needles
on the spruce, new seaweed
on the lowtide rocks
other grass and other water
even the great gold lichen
on a granite boulder
even the boulder quite
literally is not the same

II

A day subtle and suppressed
in mounds of juniper enfolding
scratchy pockets of shadow
while bigness—rocks, trees, a stump—

stand shadowless in an overcast
of ripe grass. There is nothing
but shade, like the boggy depths
of a stand of spruce, its resonance
just the thin scream
of mosquitoes ascending.
Boats are light lumps on the bay
stretching past erased islands
to ocean and the terrible tumble
and London ("rain persisting")
and Paris ("changing to rain").
Delicate day, setting the bright
of a young spruce against the cold
of an old one hung with unripe cones
each exuding at its tip
gum, pungent, clear as a tear,
a day tarnished and fractured
as the quartz in the rocks
of a dulled and distant point,
a day like a gull passing
with a slow flapping of wings
in a kind of lope, without
breeze enough to shake loose
the last of the fireweed flowers,
a faintly clammy day, like wet silk
stained by one dead branch
the harsh russet of dried blood.

"Earth's Holocaust"

It's time again.
Tear up the violets
and plant something more difficult to grow.
Everything a little cleaner, a little more ugly:
cast cement tubs of malevolent ageratums,
and: "Your grandmother baked
and froze that pie. We saved it
for a special occasion." Codicils
don't add up to much when there's nothing to leave:
a bedroom, stretching from Portland
to Richmond stunningly furnished in
French motel provincial. On the brighter side
plastic seaweed has proved
an unqualified success. As have ready-glued scrapbooks
which if out of style
still epitomize. In this one
is your first matchbook cover,
an advertisement with a misprint,
a pair of bronze baby shoes,
a tinted enlargement of a tintype.
Twins on the up-swing: there are more people.
A regular Shriners' parade of funerals.
But there are not less people.
There are more people
of all sorts, conditions and flavors.
Getting to shake each
by the hand takes time.
Not more though
than abstracting the grain of dust
from each raindrop. Starfish
have no sense of time, at all.

Going

In the month when the Kamchatka bugbane
finally turns its strung out hard pellets white
and a sudden drench flattens the fugitive
meadow saffron to tissue paper scraps
and winds follow that crack and bend without breaking
the woody stems of chrysanthemums so the good of not disbudding
shows in lower smaller flights of metallic pungency,
a clear zenith looks lightly dusted and fades to nothing
at the skyline, shadows float up to lighted surfaces
as though they and only they kept on the leaves
that hide their color in a glassy shine.
A garnering squirrel makes a frantic chatter at a posse of cats
that sit and stare while their coats thicken. Days
are shorter, more limpid, are like a kiss
neither dry nor wet nor on the lips
that sends a light shock in rings
through all the surface of the skin. Early, in the middle
of the afternoon, the light slants
into rooms that face south-west: into this room
across a bookcase so the dead-brown gold-stamped
spines look to be those to take down now:
Hodge and His Masters, The Cereals in America.
If a leaf of gold were beaten to transparency,
and all that here roots and extrudes were tarnished silver
and blackened bronze—bumped and brushed against
here and there into highlights—
were seen through it by the wind-flickered quick-setting sun,
October would look no different than it looks

The Master of the Golden Glow

An irregular rattle (shutters) and
a ferule tapped
on a blackboard—or where you come from
do they say chalkboard?—anyway it's not any sort of pointer
it's a sash facing west
wood and glass drummed on by autumn tatters.
Say, who are you
anyway? "I think we may have met before.
God knows I've heard enough about you."
That largest maple—
half its leaves an undreamt of butter:
if only safflower oil
were the color of its name
the way olive oil is. "Why,
don't you *like* butter?"
The doctor's youngest son
paddles the canoe while he (the doctor) casts
for mud-flavored carp in the long brackish pond:
Agawam, meaning lake. Lake Pond,
Pond Lake, Lake Lake, Pond Pond,
its short waves jumping up and down
in one place with surplus energy to spend.
Somewhere, out of the wind,
the wind collects a ripe debris.
"I'll tell you who I am: someone
you never met
though on a train you studied a boil on my neck
or bumped into me
leaving a late late party
               'Sorry'
or saw throwing bones in the ocean
for an inexhaustible retriever."

The wind drops. The sky darkens
to an unfathomable gray
and through hardware cloth one
leaf is seen to fall
describing the helixes of conch shell cores
gathered in summer, thrown out in autumn.
More litter, less clutter.

Ilford Rose Book

Thank you for your letter
and its extenuations. "He
said to tell them it is they
not he who said
a drawing can be illustrationy."
Another night. The grass
yellower. And the elms close in.
Flaming gray to the west
a blinding shadow. Dusty Easter
eggs, an ashtray no one
will wash, Dad
with all his buttons on
back in the watch fob days.

Milk

Milk used to come in tall glass, heavy and uncrystalline as frozen melted snow. It rose direct and thick as horse-chestnut tree trunks that do not spread out upon the ground even a little: a shaft of white drink narrowing at the cream and rounded off in a thick-lipped grin. Empty and unrinsed, a diluted milk ghost entrapped and dulled light and vision.

Then things got a little worse: squared, high-shouldered and rounded off in the wrong places, a milk replica of a hand made Danish wooden milk bat. But that was only the beginning. Things got worse than that.

Milk came in waxed paper that swelled and spilled and oozed flat pieces of milk. It had a little lid that didn't close properly or resisted when pulled so that when it did give way milk jumped out.

Things are getting better now. Milk is bigger—half a gallon, at least—in thin milky plastic with a handle, a jug founded on an oblong. Pick it up and the milk moves, rising enthusiastically in the neck as it shifts its center of weight. Heavy as a breast, but lighter, shaping itself without much changing shape: like bringing home the milk in a bandana, a neckerchief or a scarf, strong as canvas waterwings whose strength was only felt dragged under water.

On the highway this morning at the go-round about where you leave New Hampshire, there had been an accident. Milk was sloshed on the gray-blue-black so much like a sheet of early winter ice you drove over it slowly, no matter what the temperature of the weather that eddied in through the shatterproof glass gills. There were milk-skins all around, the way dessert plates look after everyone has left the table in the Concord grape season. Only bigger, unpigmented though pretty opaque, not squashed but no less empty.

Trembling, milk is coming into its own.

Poem

How about an oak leaf
if you had to be a leaf?
Suppose you had your life to live over
knowing what you know?
Suppose you had plenty money

"Get away from me you little fool."

Evening of a day in early March,
you are like the smell of drains
in a restaurant where *paté maison*
is a slab of cold meat loaf
damp and wooly. You lack charm.

CLARK
COOLIDGE

Fed Drapes

FELL FAR BUT THE BARN (came) up & smacked me
Who're you, bleedin? Fled.
Blat in back of a Victrola Car
is so red is such that sun
fell in the rushes & pen bear appear

the white wrong numeral on the wall
can't take it off with the clock
                down with the clock it . . .
                        way
on the board-couch with brass, kindergarten clench joints
backed violet rip into the gas valve
it hemmed & snowed

        the wrong way
            remnant face
                rubber
        the pucker

Mangrove in Crome

gas sigh invert balk
caball ants too
    trunk
        if so, in case, sat soon
sump, pro
        down
    lump, lung, in toe, if is
saturday flirt
          sank echo chiming dreg, it
sank down dream so, concert your so self sue, if

Benny's charts so pipe bark, kids cramp
back trudging allergic, stamp snapping
           fired
shark 'lastic keeled in, ramp dun bird so?
whiskered die & plectrum
    roll of ouvre   (Premium)
         clatter punt & echo

shoot   shot   shout

                  scup

Movies

obsidian lasher, partly   pip oversmokes

                                 in gym it

    pristine in boards setting and then cows

               very   the snout

     then there   very send howler call tunes

    squandering very squirrel limit

                         Baby

                              bound

                   Blue-ing snakes

   grass it film

                  guess filter varies

  the, um, a snooze

              − − − − −

Prentiss March: gulch, mist, "Gosh!", hyphen
ledge it glow harm, in variant, rye, rust
tumble hex an echo, last, landing sown stash on
burnt, barn & stools, caitiff, larcency, England, Euglena
in trip, middle onion & stand, "Varmint!", pipe, thrush
arc opens & puddle, side cap, buck & wing-nut, sediment

              − − − − −

             a looseness

High Pitched Whale

left from   gay behind private
                    it is it   of hip it
    in have made   two one shifts
                    drivel agony   also over
    belief health over   remember
        him   riders of there   color whole is
                but is it in the are also awkward
    going of face   put kind on
                    the out the   walls touch
        it out it in   does flowers
                    get with a grain   the was the
            faintly color   out out clear   sense
    image   as a in office   position prints
    image
                            beautiful as own
            last than   go dear
        straps   screen her where here
                main chin this   overpapers
        the as car   flowers work
                    sect to photo   soft whole sifts
                            but
        out go subtle   limp funny orange
                in been men   impulse to basis
        color thing out   star shown?
    to as   go is a two   to by in a the
            and are if is a   the this   the the is it

The Hammer

chocolate, pained, vaned, hysterical, box
laps retreat
but Carlisle cold & the heaven
fats but bold sour sun picks
sits traits of bed & hold-it
pipes vaunt all hell, making
it marking loss pulpish starring
pirates
    dove love?
coal fuss
    make crimp
lad loss
it pikes & repeater badness
milestone's mess guardian
throb spill crome the lands
hard band core of it flips
bicycle Surinam & rights cross to it lip
odd light clods bounce
floor at hung wrongs
might crisis
    kin strung?
don't dope ten nut to donut
on pall around skull sign pill
the droll waves Canuck to fend
for dust shelf slap its slot
the dull aids aim damage collapse
clock strut's drainage imagine
dull out coats the hole
charging charming
     lucks loose in streaks
film doll rind bender
    slaps hasps soon

the fall value cents
                              slow tacks do clasp
the matter screw line batter
bats
              yes
sign inflate & dam
same?   signs brash case bright & stand it back rage
blackness curls onion tines
binds of kite am Appian snort
lighten lakes
                              fell flew
stalactites cough thin fright dial

moon silent mike breasts
paper sign gloaming contest
coal avenue mirror lump pea
Styrene damage arena

                    gong

arette simple TV freights
mallow
              range pump
hashee in a bloat of flight

         gong

steam end

end

Styro

quite is high
quatic
deliverance rates   dial   3
in ex
trees palling steins ing
snail of it, acrid, the dumps
the "sill row"
to knees smoke
sir fins
drub in minnow the illicit of haunt (bite)
crust, stub, crayon, chives
Galatea dumbing hard
cawl o'wrist it?
nubs
(Nile)
an green   and ever attack
styrene mistachio dubloon
rack sun correct ratchet
Dumbo in   size
sign or hone win
gold when aft
whom   whine
it, state

lark bender hair air
    tooth
          nothing
               tin
           agate knock furs lock hitch tape crayon napkin sock
air mint   rams   to kelp bed   wrap
                 noggins
paper flower boiler wall   strain
            knit edge
                 grapple air filer
     tack stands
         air
           oil mile roll hitcher   air
              fader
       mole awl scants miler air descender
                 parts
             topaz
        blacks
  air pile socks clamp axis hole
        tiger air motes
      boreal armature

Ghost

meat bubble when in
else which twine else
measure, whelming if
wanted once

dumb, early fits
whence number, dent
top or
owl none oat

storm wants
tropes
          train nor ounce
horn coal condor
which left
          crane outs

ice

ounce code orange
a
     the
            ohm
trilobite trilobites

          prune acrylic whose
                dives
     marls pays loops watts
        lock mix deem
                        white apart
          sass

by   a   I

        of   to

on   no

we   or   by

a   I   of

        to   on

no   we   or

listene
secting
erences

miliari
ontempt
opposit

compani
bilitie
pontane

nerousl
ercussi
ndition

aluable
rievabl
fluence

berness
ionalis
deliber

KENWARD
ELMSLIE

The Dustbowl

The Harvey Girls invaded Kansas that spring of the famine
nudged by sweet memories of cornfields in the snow.
Okie weeders. Stranded in the orchards. Huts. Silos.

Ah, the times they had——huts——racing down avenues
of rattly stalks, droopy and sere, oooo-eeee! roughhousing
in jeans and poke bonnets until the laundry basin

announced supper (thwacked) beans and jello (thwacked)
followed by coupling in the sheds. Alas that winter of the famine
there were no sheds, and still they stayed, sullen

girls of the south, squinting at yellow skies
out of verboten shacks. Alas that summer of the famine
they breakfasted on leaves from gullies

and the air tasted of acorns, ah, the meadows smelled of vanilla.
Alas that winter of the famine, their men lay down on the highways,
and their women lay down with them, and felt the hot truck wind.

Alas ladies in the cities, clutching their scalloped hankies,
oiled up the icy sidewalks in the violent dusk
and hitching up their leathern garments, fell and sued.

Taxes. Caverns. Cereal. Vegetable. Simple gestures
(entering attics, bikes wobbling, dogs sunning)
lurched into something checkerboard, with every piece

outsized, gummed to attract the police.
The Harvey Girls slept until came the spring of the glut.
   Thrumming, the weed machines released an ebony menace.

   That summer of the glut, the fields were like monsters in heat,
and the Harvey Girls, freckled and worn, smiled at the northern mistral
   and headed on mules for the mountains, that autumn of the glut.

Experts at Veneers

   "In Montana, claws skim through the dawn,
   herders just saddle up, yes that's it!
   But then, they gulp hiccough pills in the highschools,
   not to skip one ambiance in the tunnel of fun."

That symbiosis in the garden says to adventure.
The jelly on the daffodil will mildew by July,
and the orange result if the birds come by
will suffice as our capitol, won't it?
   And I was there, and I was there.

Here we are, in what seems to be an aerial predicament.
The Government certainly looks handsome in the mackerel sky,
awaiting wind fungus, beribboned in *its* way, goodbye.
Blackamour stump, how luminous you'll be.
   And I was there, and I was there.

History of France

Wind, cold, rain.
Then came the sky person:
a pale empress.

Today is beautiful—
such lively girls!
A sharp-cornered stone hovers.

Ah, rigid acceptance!
Money buys everything
except walls between people.

The empire in the rain
with the muzzled atmosphere
stopped us at the border.

Striped barriers! Oafs!
And beyond, men in swimsuits shout,
"Art, make us free."

Another plaintive morning
full of chickens, dust, and buoys.
The sea keeps re-beginning . . .

Lobster claws in the pine forests
betoken an illogical sea
which sings: I *know*, I *know*.

Sticky tar and plastic messes
clarify the alliance of judge and guide.
True democracy need never exist.

Not only need, but never will.
Think of cliffs. Think of peacocks.
And the salty skiffs of the colonels.

Withdrawing rooms come next——perfumed earphones
for the young people: it's the Divine Sarah.
Wooden leg sounds bump about the divans.

"Secrecy in the provinces,
a journey under a waterfall——
these won't test your manhood, Robert."

A pretty woodwind, and thrushes.
They say the dormers fly open
to admit sweet-faced aristocrats.

And the maids dump out the cakes,
the pretty bush designs on the main course,
while everyone hides letters in hollow trees.

The party includes the lady with the map-shaped face,
the boyish man, the chess-playing lifeguard;
how they love the French summers recently.

The cleverer towns have crested yellow parks,
nice and oblong with ferns and pebble deer,
and on these the old sweet lovers loll (the wasps).

Underneath them, musical flushing,
tunnels to the ocean,
and bloated hairy sea creatures.

We have never (bump) sat on (bump) rocks,
the women facing west,
and watched the Atlantic and Pacific sunset,

the men tucked into blankets,
the children tucked in too,
and the old people in the cars.

Well done! You see, the cities
have erected spangled circus nets
or are they nests?

Into them (keep whirring, pap factories)
ocean souvenirs fall, misty bitchy things,
so the boulevards get more usage.

Now, in the mountain gravel pits,
the workers wear scoopy hats,
in which they smuggle out the granules.

But in the mauve valleys,
such attractive colleges.
All built on animal cemeteries, alas.

In winter, they pack 'em solid,
come spring, to Hans and Ivan's amazement,
but now——he reaches the valuables:

fountains of exposed beasts and breasts,
lottery tickets in the sluices,
to prevent the acids from seeping through.

In the warehouses, racketeers
daydream of that sky person,
the pale empress.

At lunchtime, they take it out,
the tongue-shaped wooden box;
today is beautiful.

Shirley Temple Surrounded by Lions

In a world where kapok on a sidewalk looks like an "accident"
—innards—would that freckles could enlarge, well, meaningfully
into kind of friendly brown kingdoms, all isolate,
with a hero's route, feral glens,
and a fountain where heroines cool their mouths.

Scenario: an albino industrialiste, invited to the beach at noon
(and to such old exiles, oceans hardly teem with ambiguities)
by a lifeguard after her formulae, though in love—
"Prop-men, the gardenias, the mimosa need anti-droopage stuffing."
Interestingly slow, the bush and rush filming.

Hiatus, everyone. After the idea of California sort of took root,
we found ourselves in this cookie forest; she closed the newspaper,
groped past cabanas, blanched and ungainly.

The grips watched Marv and Herm movies of birds tweeting,
fluttering around and in and out an old boat fridge, on a reef,
    when eek, the door——or was it "eef"——
    "Shirl" said the starling, end of——

The janitors are watching movies of men and women ruminating.
Then a cartoon of two clocks, licking. Chime. Licking, chime.
    Then a?
After that, photos of incinerators in use moved families more than
the candy grass toy that retches. Dogs. For the dressers, *"Mutations"*,
about various feelers. For the extras, movies of revenge that last.

This spree *has* to last. "Accept my pink eyes, continual swathing,"
Shirley rehearsed. "Encase me in sand, then let's get kissy."
Do children have integrity, i.e., eyes? Newsreels, ponder this.
How slow the filming is for a grayish day with its bonnet
bumping along the pioneer footpath, pulled by——here,
                         yowly hound.

Work Room

On the spool pedestal
   (Sag Harbor visit #2:
   glass rolling-pin place)

the silver Buddha hand
         to the right of the *HICKORY ELASTIC*
         printed in yellow lettering
         19th Century mystery wood-and-glass box
            (visit #2 to Blue Door
            which I idly re-arrange as Blue *D'or*)
         converted into Postcard Area

   and the gingham curtain
   (keep going)

   trees outside
   (keep going)

   a segment of lake

gesturing STOP
except the fingers bend back
and the forefingers and thumb touch
too delicately to signal anything bossy
     (my writing god)

today seems karma-prone
or as an old diary might put it:
good weather for work

Another Island Groupage

the bunks in the bogus square
twittered with skeletal birds
we ate the Spear People syrup pears
and listened for "twin" words

the past has gotten blurrier
insecticides ate up the sampler
Ganymede and his worrier
open onto (as if catapulted) an ampler

vista: gismo, curtain, gismo:
(gismo) pronouncing weedier "rothier"
(curtain) Alabama notions like Quiz Mo'
(gismo) the three mirrors of the clothier

and now angelic cranes must swing the maidens
into retentive and shadowy valley hugs
The Britishers in the Spade Inns
will take tea gingerly, muffling the "ugs"

manifested behind the curtain
after wither discussions (swans and swans)
they let the vigorous dirt in
the bonbons and herbs and second bonbons

bleary-mouthed they gulp the water
(girls in their mouths) nectar
and buy the partitions of the park daughter
metalling them to protect her

when tantrums are sung to motherly saints
(re the policy of the rain police)
a black rock avalanche repaints
the persiflage of the victim's "Greece"

Flaming Creatures

From the tug the shore crops are merely blurry wilderness
much as in chase dreams of dogs, stones have smells
volatile as cities in a holiday mood
where getting on and off platforms cones the night's events.
We on the tug recall death in the trees,
parachutists gliding down to mined branches, all seen in
    mirrors.

The Narrows was the end of our white adolescence.
The Mauve Shadow, the whale comedian,
flicked over surfaces all its own,
with membranes like balloons left in the sun,
in search of a shrivelled event, or shrivelled events.
For the oldsters, toys expire compulsively.
The stewardess says in an outfield (it)
a recognizable fire was lit.

Feathered Dancers

Inside the lunchroom the travelling nuns wove
sleeping babies on doilies of lace.
A lovely recluse jabbered of bird lore and love:
      "Sunlight tints my face

          and warms the eggs outside
          perched on filthy columns of guilt.
          In the matted shadows where I hide,
          buzzards moult and weeds wilt. "

Which reminds me of Mozambique
in that movie where blacks massacre Arabs.
The airport runway (plane never lands, skims off) is
      bleak——
scarred syphillitic landscape——crater-sized scabs——

painted over with Pepsi ads——
as in my lunar Sahara dream——giant net comes out of sky,
encloses my open touring car. Joe slumps against Dad's
emergency wheel turner. Everyone's mouth-roof dry.

One interpretation. Mother hated blood!
When the duck Dad shot dripped on her leatherette lap-robe,
dark spots not unlike Georgia up-country mud,
her thumb and forefinger tightened (karma?) on my ear-lobe.

Another interpretation. Motor of my heart stalled!
I've heard truckers stick ping-pong balls up their butt
and jounce along having coast-to-coast orgasms, so-called.
Fermés, tous les jardins du Far West, I was taught——tight shut,

so you can't blame them. Take heed, turnpikes.
Wedgies float back from reefs made of jeeps: more offshore
    debris.
Wadded chewy depressants and elatants gum up footpaths.
    Remember Ike's
"Doctor-the-pump-and-away-we-jump" Aloha Speech to the
    Teamsters? "The—"

he began and the platform collapsed, tipping him onto a traffic
                                                        island.
An aroused citizenry fanned out through the factories that day
to expose the Big Cheese behind the sortie. Tanned,
I set sail for the coast, down the Erie and away,

and ate a big cheese in a café by the docks,
and pictured every room I'd ever slept in:
toilets and phone-calls and oceans. Big rocks
were being loaded, just the color of my skin,

and I've been travelling ever since,
so let's go find an open glade
like the ones in sporting prints
(betrayed, delayed, afraid)

where we'll lie among the air-plants
in a perfect amphitheatre in a soft pink afterglow.
How those handsome birds can prance,
ah . . . unattainable tableau.

Let's scratch the ground clean,
remove all stones and trash,
I mean open dance-halls in the forest, I mean
where the earth's packed smooth and hard. Crash!

It's the Tale of the Creation. The whip cracks.
Albatrosses settle on swaying weeds.
Outside the lunchroom, tufts and air-sacs
swell to the size of fruits bursting with seeds.

White Attic

The white attic rests
among dripping trees

with unrolling tunnels
and trembling luggage

around were dens
all kinds of dens

and dazzling fruit
to weary the wind

the sun would end
and we'd smoke among the trees

our wary arms
tenderly relaxed

the urn faces a tree
of unequal height

when it came I grew
moved to two rooms in town

where I reach out at night
and bat the far air

Circus Nerves and Worries

When that everybody's legal twin Mrs. Trio
enters the casino, I expect personal disaster.
Out of next winter's worst blizzard I'm convinced
into the lobby and up the ladder she'll hustle
holding that squeaky velvet purse to one ear.
Placing one green and black peppermint-striped chip
gingerly on zero, zero it is. Which is when I fall dead.
In my shower while soaping. This very next year.

Goony intuition? Well, once in April at the Cafe Jolie
pointblank she asked, this terror at time in your eyes,
wouldn't crossing a river help? How about now?
Give up my innocence hunt, I exclaimed,
intimacies with failure, all my 'sudden magic' hopes?
And today came this dream about moths, I lied,
mouthing, yes wisdoms. Only how to read their lips? Tell me!
                                                        Tell me!
I dream about vines, she said. Thank you and *ciao*.

Yesterday I looked at my body. Fairly white.
Today fairly white, the same. No betterment.
Why can't I feel air? Or take in mountains?
I lose my temper at pine needles, such small stabs.
Breezes scratch me (different from feeling)
and I long to breathe water. Agenda tomorrow:
Cable her care of casino TIME TERROR GONE
STOP SEAWEED DREAM GREAT STOP (actually, a lie)

Florida Hillocks

the fecund plantation
the damp areas of the squatters
the valuable ocean bushes
seed pearls in the ancestral mouth safe
    drop noiselessly in the mammy apron

follow this guilty yellow instrument
bury it in the orchid swamp
out of insane attic windows
prophetic widows will gesture
    put jonquils—crotches—haunches—

the winter garden above the gazebo
is suffering from cellar blight
awful mushrooms spell out our names
oranges in the river squeeze against the piles
   jewelled hirelings have stolen all the gates

bugs attached to strings (our toys)
form immediate mosaics
of roses drying, of the boy's pillow,
of lithe janitors, of seed pearls dropping
   down the well of the fecund plantation

Duo-tang

   Laundry so near the ocean bothered Frank.
The lack of medicine on the shelves
   also confused his emotional stance.

   A moth fluttered against his leg.
A gust of wind made his Pepsi keen
   as its foam trickled down inside.

   A banana boat on a horizon otherwise blank
passed over a time-piece buried in valves
   over which sea-growths stirred. Grant's

Tomb. Cleopatra's Needle. The Hague.
He flipped the pages of the travel magazine
and wondered if Monsieur had lied.

Tomorrow, he'd go to the bank,
shop for some unguents and skin salves,
and finish The Castles' book on the dance.

The Hesitation Waltz! How vague
the past seemed: static scene after static scene.
He watched the retreating tide

and patted his belly. The sun sank.
Monsieur and J. were off by themselves.
He took off his pants.

He was too proud to beg.
He lay down and thought of Jean.
The sheet had dried.

TED
BERRIGAN

Words for Love

for Sandy

Winter crisp and the brittleness of snow
as like make me tired as not. I go my
myriad ways blundering, bombastic, dragged
by a self that can never be still, pushed
by my surging blood, my reasoning mind.

I am in love with poetry. Every way I turn
this, my weakness, smites me. A glass
of chocolate milk, head of lettuce, darkness of clouds at one o'clock obsess me.
I weep for all of these or laugh.

By day I sleep, an obscurantist, lost
in dreams of lists, compiled by my self
for reassurance. Jackson Pollock   Rene'
Rilke   Benedict Arnold   I watch
my psyche, smile, dream wet dreams, and sigh.

At night, awake, high on poems or pills
or simple awe that loveliness exists, my lists
flow differently. Of words bright red
and black, and blue. Bosky. Oubliette. Dis-
servered. And O, alas

Time disturbs me. Always minute detail
fills me up. It is 12:10 in New York. In Houston
it is 2 p.m. It is time to steal books. It's
time to go mad. It is the day of the apocalypse
the year of parrot fever! What am I saying?

Only this. My poems do contain
wilde beestes. I write for my Lady
of the Lake. My god is immense, and lonely
but uncowed. I trust my sanity, and I am proud. If
I sometimes grow weary, and seem still, nevertheless

my heart still loves, will break.

LXXVI

I wake up back aching from soft bed Pat
gone to work Ron to class (I
never heard a sound) it's my birthday. I put on
birthday pants birthday shirt go to ADAM's buy a
pepsi for breakfast come home drink it take a pill
I'm high. I do three Greek lessons
to make up for cutting class. I read birthday book
(from Joe) on Juan Gris real name José Vittoriano
Gonzáles stop in the middle read all
my poems gloat a little over new ballad quickly skip old
sonnets imitations of Shakespeare. Back to books. I read
poems by Auden Spenser Pound Stevens and Frank O'Hara.
    I hate books.
             I wonder if Jan or Helen or Babe
ever think about me. I wonder if Dave Bearden still
dislikes me. I wonder if people talk about me
secretly. I wonder if I'm too old. I wonder if I'm fooling
myself about pills. I wonder what's in the icebox. I wonder
if Ron or Pat bought any toilet paper this morning

Personal Poem #7

for John Stanton

It is 7:53 Friday morning in the Universe
New York city to be somewhat exact
I'm in my room wife gone working Gallup
fucking in the room below
                              had 17½ miligrams desoxyn
last night 1 Miltown, read Paterson, parts
1 & 2, poems by Wallace Stevens & How Much Longer
Shall I Be Able To Inhabit The Divine Sepulchre
(John Ashbery). Made lists of lines to
steal, words to look up (didn't). Had steak & eggs
with Dick while Sandy sweetly slept.

At 6:30 woke Sandy
fucked til 7 now she's late to work & I'm still
high. Guess I'll write to Bernie today
and Tom. And call Tony. And go out at 9 (with Dick)
to steal books to sell, so we can go
to see A NIGHT AT THE OPERA.

Personal Poem #8

It's 5:03 a.m. on the 11th of July this morning
and the day is bright gray turning green   I can't stop
loving you says Ray Charles   and I know exactly
what he means because the Swedish policeman in the
next room is beating on my door demanding sleep
and not Ray Charles and bluegrass   does he know
that in three hours I go to court to see if the world

will let me have a wife   he doesn't of course it wouldn't
occur to him   nor would it occur to him to write
"scotch-tape body" in a notebook but it did occur to
John Stanton alias The Knife Fighter age 18 so why
are my hands shaking I should know better

XXXVI

after Frank O'Hara

It's 8:54 a.m. in Brooklyn it's the 28th of July and
it's probably 8:54 in Manhattan but I'm
in Brooklyn I'm eating English muffins and drinking
pepsi and I'm thinking of how Brooklyn is New
York city too how odd I usually think of it as
something all its own like Bellows Falls like Little
Chute like Uijongbu
                          I never thought on the Williams-
burg bridge I'd come so much to Brooklyn
just to see lawyers and cops who don't even carry
guns taking my wife away and bringing her back
                                                            No
and I never thought Dick would be back at Gude's
beard shaved off long hair cut and Carol reading
his books when we were playing cribbage and
watching the sun come up over the Navy Yard
across the river
                      I think I was thinking when I was
ahead I'd be somewhere like Perry street erudite
dazzling slim and badly loved
contemplating my new book of poems
to be printed in simple type on old brown paper
feminine marvelous and tough

LI

Summer so histrionic, marvelous dirty days
is not genuine   it shines forth from the faces
littered with soup, cigarette butts, the heavy
is a correspondent   the innocence of childhood
sadness graying the faces of virgins aching
and everything comes before their eyes
to be fucked, we fondle their snatches but they
that the angels have supereminent wisdom is shown
they weep and get solemn etcetera
from thought   for all things come to them gratuitously
by their speech   it flows directly and spontaneously
and O I am afraid! but later they'll be eyeing the butts of
                                                        the studs
in the street rain flushing the gutters bringing from Mem-
                                                        phis
Gus Cannon gulping, "I called myself Banjo Joe!"

LII

for Richard White

It is a human universe: & I
is a correspondent   The innocence of childhood
is not genuine   it shines forth from the faces
The poem upon the page is as massive as Anne's thighs
Belly to hot belly we have laid
                         baffling combustions

are everywhere   graying the faces of virgins
aching to be fucked   we fondle their snatches
and O, I am afraid!   The poem upon the page
will not kneel   for everything comes to it
gratuitously   like Gertrude Stein to Radcliffe
Gus Cannon to say "I called myself Banjo Joe!"
O wet kisses, death on earth, lovely fucking in the poem
      upon the page,
you have kept up with the times, and I am glad!

LIII

The poem upon the page is as massive as
Anne's thighs   belly to hot belly we have laid
Serene beneath feverous folds, flashed cool
in our white heat   hungered   and tasted   and
Gone to the movies   baffling combustions
are everywhere!   like Gertrude Stein at Radcliffe,
Patsy Padgett replete with teen-age belly!   every-
one's suddenly pregnant and no one is glad!
O wet kisses, the poem upon the page
Can tell you about teeth you've never dreamed
Could bite, nor be such reassurance! Babies are not
Like Word Origins and cribbage boards   or dreams
of correspondence!   Fucking is so very lovely
Who can say no to it later?

LV

*"Grace to be born and live as
variously as possible"* FRANK O'HARA

Grace to be born and live as variously as possible
White boats   green banks   black dust   atremble
Massive as Anne's thighs upon the page
I rage in a blue shirt at a brown desk in a
Bright room sustained by a bellyful of pills
"The Poems" is not a dream   for all things come to them
Gratuitously   In quick New York we imagine the blue
                                                            Charles
Patsy awakens in heat and ready to squabble
No Poems she demands in a blanket command   belly
To hot belly we have laid   serenely white
Only my sweating pores are true in the empty night
Baffling combustions are everywhere! we hunger and
                                                            taste
And go to the movies   then run home drenched in flame
To the grace of the make-believe bed

LXX

after Arthur Rimbaud

Sweeter than sour apples flesh to boys
The brine of brackish water pierced my hulk
Cleansing me of rot-gut wine and puke
Sweeping away my anchor in its swell
And since then I've been bathing in the poem
Of the star-steeped milky flowing mystic sea
Devouring great sweeps of azure green and

Watching flotsam, dead men, float by me
Where, dyeing all the blue, the maddened flames
And stately rhythms of the sun, stronger
Than alcohol, more great than song,
Fermented the bright red bitterness of love
I've seen skies split with light, and night,
And surfs, currents, waterspouts; I know
What evening means, and doves, and I have seen
What other men sometimes have thought they've seen

LXXII A Sonnet for Dick Gallup

July 1963

The logic of grammar is not genuine   it shines forth
From The Boats   We fondle the snatches of virgins
                          aching to be fucked
And O, I am afraid!   Our love has red in it   and
I become finicky as in an abstraction!
                                (. . . but lately
I'm always lethargic . . .   the last heavy sweetness
through the wine . . .)
                    Who dwells alone
                    Except at night
(. . . basted the shackles the temporal music the spit)
    Southwest lost doubloons rest, no comforts drift on
dream smoke
              (my dream   the big earth)
On the green a white boy goes   to not
Forget   Released by night (which is not to imply
Clarity   The logic is not The Boats   and O, I am not
    alone

LXXIV

> *"The academy of the future*
> *is opening its doors."*   JOHN ASHBERY

The academy of the future is opening its doors
my dream a crumpled horn
Under the blue sky the big earth is floating into "The
                                           Poems."
"A fruitful vista, this, our South," laughs Andrew to his Pa.
But his rough woe slithers o'er the land.
Ford Madox Ford is not a dream. The farm
was the family farm. On the real farm
I understood "The Poems."
                    Red-faced and romping in the wind, I, too,
am reading the technical journals. The only travelled sea
that I still dream of
is a cold black pond, where once
on a fragrant evening fraught with sadness
I launched a boat frail as a butterfly

For You

to James Schuyler

New York's lovely weather hurts my forehead
here where clean snow is sitting, wetly
round my ears, as hand-in-glove and
head-to-head with Joe, I go reeling
up First Avenue to Klein's. Christmas
is sexy there. We feel soft sweaters
and plump rumpled skirts we'd like to try.

It was gloomy being broke today, and baffled
in love: Love, why do you always take my heart away?
But then the soft snow came sweetly falling down
and head in the clouds, feet soaked in mush
I rushed hatless into the white and shining air,
glad to find release in heaven's care.

Bean Spasms

(to George Schneeman)

in praise of thee
the? white dead
whose eyes know:

what are they
of the tiny cloud my brain:
The City's tough red buttons

O Mars, red, angry planet, candy
bar, with sky on top,
"why, it's young Leander hurrying to his death"
what? what time is it, in New York   in these here alps
City of lovely tender hate
and beauty making beautiful
old rhymes?

I ran away from you
when you needed something strong
then I leand against the toilet bowl aack
Malcolm X
I love my brain
it all mine now is
saved not knowing
that &
that happily
being that:

"we kill our selves to propagate our kinde"
yes, that's true   John Donne
        the hair on yr nuts & my
                big blood-filled cock are a part in that
        too

PART 2

                Mister Robert Dylan doesn't feel well today
                That's bad
                This picture doesn't show that
                It's not bad, too
        it's very ritzy in fact
        here I stand I can't stand
        to be thing
        I don't use   atop
                the empire state
                        building
                                & so sauntered out the door
That reminds me of the time
I wrote that long piece about a gangster name of "Jr."
O Harry James! had eyes to wonder but lacked tongue to
                                        praise
                        so later peed under his art
                paused only to lay a sneeze
                                on Jack Dempsey
                        asleep with his favorite Horse
                That remind me of I buzz
                on & off Miro pop
                        in & out a convertible
                minute by minute   GENEROSITY!
    Yes now that the seasons totter in their walk
    I do a lot of wondering about Life   in praise of ladies dead of
& Time plaza(s), Bryant Park by the Public   eye of brow
Library, Smith Bros. black boxes, Times
                Square
                Pirogi, Houses

with long skinny rivers thru them
they lead the weary away
off hey!
I'm no sailor
off a ship
at sea   I'M HERE
& "The living is easy"

It's "HIGH TIME"
& I'm in shapes
of shadow, they
certainly can warm, can't they?
Have you ever seen one?   NO!
of those long skinny Rivers
O well hung, in New York City?
NO! in fact
I'm The Wonderer
& as yr train goes by   forgive me, René   'just oncet'
I woke up in Heaven
He woke, and wondered more; how many angels
on this train huh?   snore
for there she lay
on sheets that mock lust   done that 7 times
been caught
and brought back
to a peach nobody.
To Continue:
Ron Padgett & Ted Berrigan
hates yr brain
my dear
amidst the many other little buzzes
& like, Today, as Ron Padgett might say
is
"A tub of vodka"
"in the morning"

she might reply
and it keeps it up
past icy poles
where angels beg fr doom then zip
ping in-and-out, joining the army
wondering about Life
by the Public Libraries of
Life
No Greater Thrill!
(I wonder)
Now that the earth is changing I wonder what time it's getting
to be
sitting on this New York Times Square
that actually very ritzy, Lauren   it's made of yellow wood or
I don't know something   maybe
This man was my
friend   its been fluffed up
He had a sense for the
vast   doesn't he?
Awake my Angel! give thyself
to the lovely hours   Don't cheat
The victory is not always to the sweet.
I mean that.
Now this picture is pretty good here
Though it once got demerits from the lunatic Arthur Cravan
He wasn't feeling good that day
Maybe because he had nothing on
paint-wise I mean

PART 3

I wrote that
about what is
this empty room   without a heat
in three parts
a white flower
came home wet & drunk   2 pepsis

and smashed my fist thru her window
                              in the nude
    As the hand zips you see
        Old Masters, you can see
            well hung in New York   they grow fast here
            Conflicting, yet purposeful
                    yet with outcry vain!
            Praising, that's it!
you string a sonnet around yr fat gut
        and falling on your knees
                          you invent the shoe
                for a horse. It brings you luck
            while sleeping
                      "You have it seems a workshop nature"
            "Good Lord!"
                          Some folks is wood
            Ron Padgett wd say
            amidst many other little buzzes
        past the neon on & off
                    night & day   STEAK SANDWICH
            Have you ever tried one, Anne?
        "I wonder what time 'its'?
        as I sit on this new Doctor
    NO   I only look at the buildings they're in
as you and he, I mean he & I buzz past
                          in yellow ties   I call that gold

        THE HOTEL BUCKINGHAM
        (facade) is blacker, and taller than last time
is looming over lunch   naked   high time   poem
                                  & I, equal in
                              perfection & desire
    is looming   both eyes   over coffee-cup (white)
                                      nature
            and man: both hell on poetry.
            Art is art and life is
                    "A Monograph on Infidelity"

Oh. Forgive me stench of sandwich
    O pneumonia in American Poetry
Do we have time?   well look at Burroughs
  7 times been caught and brought back to Mars
      & eaten.
"Art is art & Life
is Home," Fairfield Porter said that
      turning himself in
      The night arrives again in red
some go on even in Colorado   on the run
     the forests shake
   meaning:
      coffee the cheerfulness of this poor
         fellow is terrible, hidden in
         the fringes of the eyelids
         blue mysteries' I'M THE SKY!
  The sky is bleeding now
      onto 57th Street
   of the 20th Century
        HORN & HARDART'S
 I'm not some sailor off a ship at sea
I'm the wanderer   (age 4)
    & now everyone is dead
   sinking bewildered of hand, of foot, of lip
  nude, thinking
laughter burnished brighter than hate
         goodbye.
   André Breton said that
      what a shit!
 He's gone!
    up bubbles all his amorous breath
   & Monograph on Infidelity entitled
        The Living Dream

I never again played
            I dreamt that December 27th, 1965
            all in the blazon of sweet beauty's breast
    I mean "a rose"   Do you understand that?
                Do you?
    The rock&roll songs of this earth
    commingling absolute joy AND
    incontrovertible joy of intelligence
                            certainly can warm
                                cant they?
                    and they do.
        Keeping eternal whisperings around
                            (Mr. Macadams writes in
                            the nude: no that's not
    we want to take the underground   me that: then zips in &
    revolution to Harvard!   out the boring taxis, re-
        and yet this girl has   fusing to join the army,
        so much grace   asleep "on the springs"
                    I wonder!   of red GENEROSITY
        Were all their praises simply prophecies
        of this
                the time   NO GREATER THRILL
                                        my friends
        But I quickly forget them, those other times, for what
    are they but parts in the silver lining of the tiny cloud my
    brain drifting up into smoke the city's tough blue top:

            I think a picture always
            leads you gently to someone else
    Don't you? like when you ask to leave the room
            and go to the moon.

Many Happy Returns

to Dick Gallup

It's a great pleasure to
wake "up"
        mid-afternoon

              2 o'clock

          and if thy stomach think not
no matter . . .

        because
        the living
           "it's easy"

          you splash the face &
            back of the neck
        swig pepsi

& drape the bent frame in
        something "blue for going out"

             * * *

you might smoke a little pot, even
        or take a pill

             or two pills

          *

      (the pleasures of prosperity
        tho they are only bonuses

                really)
        and neither necessary nor not

         *

Puerto-Rican girls are terrific!

you have to smile, but you don't
touch, you haven't eaten
yet, & you're too young
to die . . .

&

No, I'm only kidding!
Who on earth would kill
for love?
(Who wouldn't?)

&

Joanne & Jack
will feed you
today
because
Anne & Lewis are
"on the wing" as
but not like
always . . .

& &

Michael is driving a hard bargain
himself
to San Francisco . . .

&

&
Pete & Linda
& Katie and George
Emilio, Elio and Paul
have gone to Maine .   .   .

& & &

Everyone, it seems, is somewhere else.

None are lost, tho.　　At least
　　we aren't!
　　　　　　(GEM'S SPA: corner of 2nd Avenue &
　　　　　　　　　　Saint Mark's Place)

　　　　　　✽

I'm right here
sunlight opening up the sidewalk
opening up today's breakfast "black & white," & I'm about to be

　　　　born again

　　　　　　　　thinking of you
　　　　　　　　　　　　Ted Berrigan

Resolution

The ground is white with snow.
It's morning, of New Year's Eve, 1968, & clean
City air is alive with snow, its quiet
Driving. I am 33. Good Wishes, brothers, everywhere

& Don't You Tread On Me.

HARRY
MATHEWS

The Relics

The Devoted Spy

Where are the brass islands?
There are the brass islands.
Their yellow wheat does not bend, and their peaks
Ring, flat. Their brass ports
Have a stupid glory in thin dusk—
By day, even near-yellow scrap copper
In that drab gold is sweet relief.
Streets are stiff with the wink and clink
Or wired lids, a deaf clatter
Of brass feet that batter brass,
Brass teeth, brass tears,
Brass breasts! In one such city
I found a mop of red rags
But left, my business done. I forget
The color. It is dazzling here to see poppies—
Wild poppies salt the harvest wheat
Like memorial ribbons red among tubas.

The Battle

The sun rose red as parsley
And several ill-sewn drums
Ejected clouds of fish through the grass
Whose nostrils drew a wild smoke.
Beyond was a beach of gunpowder (beautiful:
Its bones small but barbed), but neither
I nor the water could reach it, and gulls
Fell along it with soft harassed explosions
That left lemon-smell and a sound of triangles
In the air, on the bones a whitish moisture.
Sweet things! A few cigarettes

Brought a dozen round, which I assembled
In a matter of years, despite their barbs
And soapishness; and the machine talked
Nonsense, and was uneatable. I decided
To desert, applying the wit left me
To becoming an amateur bomb, and jump
—With some anxiety, for the sea was swarming—
Onto the beach. I arose successful
A sad vibration of tuning forks
To touch some colors, wines, moons,
And laundry boiling in wintriness.

Daffodils, or Theodora's Train

They built the basilica on battered bones and bombed it.
Then it was. Relics and their guards became
A vague dust over puzzled mosaics;
But it is. I miss the pinkeared angels,
And the heartfelt noise of harmoniums at dusk
Interwoven with caterwauls; the garden too
Is grime where the earth fluttered with tearbanes,
Fustre, elgue, and tender paperdews
Sweetening the souls of hot cigars:
Yet why mourn?
The strand is merged mud, shadeless, undrying,
I eat lost eels and fatigued
Field-snakes, my body's my only company,
But the world is whole. When over the ocean
Ashes regretful loom and unfurl
Toward land and evening, the sun flattens them.
I parody dead astronomers who extracted
Dying stars from their slaty wills,
My hands reaping light where black
Ooze divulges her yellow tesserae.

L'Hôpital des Enfants Malades

A day of sudden reminders
Flags snapped in haze,
Buildings shed their fur
And phrases were issued in German
To those who could speak; the others . . .
From the haze a naked girl,
Holy, composed of sponges,
Singing "Put up your mind,
My glamor will teach you trust."
Her swine are around me—"Wait"—
The faithful prunelike children,
"Wait until I recall
The morning when you were invisible
Or until you have grown usual,
Until I know less."

The Ring

    Pierre put the gold in the morning into the ring-machine, and prayed. A sharp mallet swung anxiously in his hands, blades leapt from the agitation of his waiting feet; outside, trucks and cranes wheezed and clanged an aural incense into the tin-colored Paris sky. Paris! city of Jews and Antijews, of smitten children and childcoiffed flat eyes, where the meanness of the winter sun and the meanness of sausage-sellers beat as with their laden rubber chains the dark appetites of yearning—many reflections indited themselves on the casual slices of scrap copper that lay on the cement floor about the machine. The latter, also gray, was powered by twin anonymous engines; bakelite studs, whose double rectangular alignment banded the metal volumes with a uniform of final enclosure, vibrated blurringly sometimes, and when several hours' running had magnified the motor heat, emitted wasps of nostalgic smell. The mallet smashed aimlessly now the copper detritus, now the spread idle kneebones between which it shook. Some substance drifted from the. The telephone rang. "And what did it really mean? and what was it to be borne for? All those who are yet allowed the glory and honor of that glorious happiness, which comes from daring to order for the moment in their lives when they triumphantly love, 'the like for the like'." Next it was time for lunch:

I began the pristine ascent. What if the flanks broke
Upon a depth of frozen honeys? The underskin of
    my forearms
Clutched upon scale. Gray thyme stood stiff in the
    small fissures,
Nameless blue spurts bloomed low; apples, lawns and
    streams
Were known dryness dryer than this wish. My body
    is there,
Not desire, not will: breathing, bruises—no beauty in
    the memory,
But hunger: holding a hot smoothed stone in my fist,
One with the spatial air towards the crest. In the
    dusky cwms
I await rainbow caverns, O forests of erect amber,
Cools of adept obsidian! After the approaches and
    before the last steepness
Was a tilted plane: there the stone roughness was
    muscled—
I looked back, far, lost, content, my calves twitched
From the painful irresistible push, I saw the ascent
    and its excitement;
Afterwards, less. Circular autumn
Will embrace the windy clambered peak. The precious
    ointment
In the flask of caves; and the light allows

A dun shadow under the egglike nacreous ridges.
They did not come after me;
I returned through calm rainy woods. Some rocks as
        loose as milk teeth
Scrambled down and I clung to the grilled cliff with
        my tongue. Were there pools in the cooler heights
For the coming bliss of thirst? Hot boots suck
        upwards
From the boozy mud before a vast and intimate
        splendor
Where earth, stone and shingle were nubile hatchings
In imperial day, with sweat in my mouth,
Sweetness in my lungs

        The pair return.
        There was no hope, yet through dissuasions of
                                buttermetal
        Heaps, themselves, they join
        Where the olive-rank pales in resigned expectancy
        And of sun, in pools of silver dust
        Ascending easily high terrace to terrace
        Over sheepflecked stiles, above the extended sea
        Leaning on its russet stones
        Where the wafted pines acknowledge redemption
        Above pines
        Sky, blue sombrero: the orange ground
        Breaks with sweetwater and old rocks garlanded
        The blue sky mounts?
        The earth is fading orange
        Swims cuprous instigation
        There is too much to say
                                fading bronze messengers
        A sharp musics of loquat leaves
        Observe their flight—both relief and ecstasy
        O my love into the bronze bell
        Steps, or sinking of a celestial tram

Some slight black foliage; fading earth; cliffs are
   of distant bronze
Let all the
The quick bright sea-blue
Pass, pass: Attend the sky,
    they're blue, passionate, invisible,
As your hand places the jar of blue crystals
By the waiting bath.

The Sense of Responsibility

The society in my head
Said the viper in the washrag
Having no creator, requires my love:
"Eton pets who lag in their Latin
At a slow trot, who become of note
Reversing their school-step (as the apple ate Adam),"
And such—innocents whose Eden is need.
Divination without divinity
Affirmed the viper in the twirled spaghetti
Morse-tusks clatter in paleocrystic seas
My absurd blood is thin chrism
For my creatures by default, the default not mine:
I trace the dancing of their secular swarm.

Invitation to a Sabbath

Râles of Easter . . . The sucking . . .
The ghastly gaiety of returning strangers
Inspired a vacuum of enormous tenuity.
There came (it was a day when cracked
Boy was found in a furrow-drain,
Naked, smelling of heavenly smoke,
Chanting red places, cakes, tits,
Wings) a liquescent company, eight
Ladies in plaids among the disbanding mercury,
Four cavaliers in secular chasubles.
Vanished, vanished!
Their milky exhausts, gathered in tearbottles
Of perilous alabaster, illuminate nothing
Made thick. The ash tree stands in the stars.

Comatas

In the snowy yard a baroque thermometer,
Its foot freezing my pale fig-face
In its quicksilver bell, marks zero
On the china backing with a stripe of blue,

Whose top, scalloped as a cipher for waves,
The legend *Océan Atlantique* explains,
For the stripe (which the mercury glass bisects)
Separates *Père Europe* on the left
And Centigrade side from *Notre Fille*
L'Amérique, the Fahrenheit column. Yet the continents
Are not mere persons: but dun elevator-shafts
Mount the parallel gradations, bucolic
In their details—Silenus asleep in the mezzanine
Of Europe, Arcadians in blue jeans on either
Third floor competing transatlantically,
A marsh of nymphs above one, a hive
Of wild bees on the shaft's wall,
The upper floors empty but for a woodland
Mist or smoke through which a woman
Yellowhaired and slim is vaguely naked
On the right—is it for her one wants to
Test the cedar elevator-boxes
That rise with the disintegration of icicles and lace?
If we entered, I must do so in exile and imagine
America (and you, my remembrance) opposite
Through tiered nature zooming towards innocence
Numbered dream of parallel transcendance
Perhaps?
                         your hair muddles
The real and the false in such ambitious copulation
That touching between our straining souls
Each skin with nerveless amorous indifference
Our minds are debauched, and our bodies are balloons—
"The little girls—sighs of tar
I'th'giddy wheat. On hieratic mountains
I raped the bright corpses of dæmons,
Tractors shuttling yellowly below.
O valleys. I examine my exact feet
By Proust. Ladies, have a drink—shadows
Wander in through your children, and swallows

Spin quietly in the tender air."

And now before us the snows are stretched
Still and all the (look!) air's
Gusty music thins; may honeys
Run for him. The ripple of her ribs
Flash like the Var where the bullocks drink
And woven ferns droop from the bank
—In the shade I dream that my quiet singing
Mixes that beauty with itself; and a shadow
Of crows or nymphs speckles the field.

Jack	This one-eared Negro walks round the world in a step
Jacques	This one-eyed Indian's happy when he cries in the dark
Jack	If A follows B, and I you, find "me"
Jacques	If you're after me—who are you?
Jack	How can a hard sleeper sleep with the light on?
Jacques	(They bore me to death with their broad vowels!)
Jack	When was she not a cunning stunt?

The tense of her tendons

Soon

he was ware of a spring, in a hollow land, and the rushes grew
thickly around it, and dark swallowwort, and green maiden-
hair, and blooming parsley, and deergrass spreading through
the marshy land. In the midst of the water the nymphs were
arraying their games, the sleepless nymphs, dread goddesses
of the country people, Eunice, and Malis, and Nycheia, with
her April eyes. And now the boy was holding out the wide-
mouthed pitcher to the water, intent on dipping it, but the
nymphs all clung to his hand, sweetly restraining him, and
they led him to a ferny knoll, where their steps crushed green
smells into the dimming air. Then Amalmé, sacred to herself, lifted from its bed of hairy grass a disc of pink stone,
with her blue hands of peace, and he heard faintly, like a

halfremembered prophecy, the murmur of the soap spring.
Dread Critasta bade him lie down, and she took him by the
left foot, and Garga of the curled breasts by the right, and
plunged him headmost naked into the plangent ooze, and as
he sank into its benign suffocation even to his knees, he
heard the tingling laughter and singing of the nymphs gathered about him in their holy circle, and the deaf padding of
their feet in the itchy grass. When his brain had closed with
morose darkness, and sorrow had filled his heart at the shame
of life, they lifted him roughly out, and their laughter was an
easy barking, and they cleaned the muddy suds from him
with their spit and dried him with fronds of stinging-nettles,
writhing as he was, in the rigorous sheets soiled with his
incontinence; dried and wiped him until he bled, and blood
swelled his transparent gummy skin, and they licked and
flailed him in turn, singing the rapid tangos of that land,
and sucked and scratched his occasional bone, Garga whip-
ping him with her leather dugs, Nanpreia stuffing his mouth
with her acrid springy hair. And when the shame of death
overtook him with a helpless spasm, and Nycheia's hands
dripped his silver semen, came again Critasta with her shears
to slit his seams and skin him deftly: and the bundle of his
skin crackled in the fire that now flamed in the marsh, a fire
of feathers, turds, and grey briers, while the nymphs in their
frenzy shrieked small shrieks of nausea and hunger; and that
smell was dear. Then the boy looked towards the setting sun,
towards the companions he had lately left; and he saw his
General, who had sent hot orders, and a galloper hurtled
back for the horse which opened just as the last light fled up
the hill to its summit and took refuge in the clouds; infantry
appeared, and were pushed in among them and charged
them, and, as night fell, they saw the breakup of the enemy,
who abandoned all their stuff and went streaming up the col
towards the two peaks of Mania, escaping into what they
thought was empty land beyond. You

followed your mother into our orchard,
And with a disdain of years
I watched you pick wet apples.
My twelfth year was on me
When that sight felled and terrible folly undid me.

5

Sever me from my appetent mind,
From the drum's glory, from the Dutch agio
Of dividends, bananas, and Christ's
Prayer, not from seduction not
From the limn of her limbs
                              nor the way
                                   of her waist
From the air of her hair   and the ease of her ears
From the bow of her elbow   and the shoal of her shoulders
From the tucks of her buttocks   and the wreath of her
                                                    breath
From the hot of her heart   and the rain of her brain
From the soul of her soles   and the ash of her lashes
From the I of her eyes   and the fur of her forearm
From the bee of her bite   and the ouch of her touch
From the gum of her gums   and the pins of her nipples
From the musk of her muscles   and the trill of her nostrils
From the flan of her flanks   and the ice of her thighs
From the tug of her tongue in the south of her mouth
From the nave of her navel   and the fangs of her fingers
In the asp of her clasp, from the thump of her thumb
From the spines of her spine   and the rack of her back
From the leap of her lips   and the yank of her ankles
From the blur of her blood   and the bells of her breasts
From the lunge of her lungs   and the he of her hips
From the oh of her throat   and the uvula of her vulva
Yet the mouth of her belly are the heart of her feet

Yet the foot of her belly are the mouth of her heart
Yet the knees of her belly are the foot of her mouth
The hands of her eyes soft hurricanes
                         Seduction
    hrscht!
                    sang

                                        "garden
                    The flowers speak in whispers (I
                    Utter not a sound)

                                                snowing

                    The flowers spoke in whispers and with
                    Concern looked on: 'Do not molest
                    Our sister;
                            you sad and sallow man

Zum

Ha sawaram aoaf beaesarm

Zu zwurmu
Zehe essewearrmm eovv bbeeeezz

Zehea
    zarozaarazinazg zasawazazm zaozof bzaezaezasz
                    bezz
                                    biz
        Desire's everlasting
                            f
                    s

        hairy   w
                              a
 didn'd   oil enema   a
      I'm sorry   a
                                 a
 made him bend over   drool
                              a   a
      "nates"   rubberbelly
 bluntfaced   pubic shave a   a
    20 juicyfruit please   footless
                                       a
 lined the Jews up   I meant   a
    masterhaul   then I can't understand
                          drilled   a
                      1   Sieglinde!

    sorry
             I'm   1
 ptlaarplop   "wherever you are"   the machine   a
                          of——   taste
                                       a
    know thyself   a mass of bloody rubbish
             will never   junior
        enis   a
                    that time you
 brown spots   Mrs. Pemberton   lickle-lickle
                                       a
             kotex mirror   "I love you"
    with his truncheon   would have   a
                  sorry   a
      Tonto?   a
             no underpants?!
 slim knife   a
                   urp   a
 The smell   r
          m
    golden

.   .   .   .

Bells, mud, clouds, despair
My life was hers now she is in it
There are sails, and blue summer, and impossibility
My bonebites soothe in a slush agglomeration
Mercury bubbles ascend: breath
My eyes cast a shadow of her outwards
My meaning confirms her absorbed altitude
The dog's gums yelp silence, silence
Her shadow pierces the dead serenities
The kayakist ignores the dull revelations
Sweet adoration of my dying existence
Little coils of her hair glitter
Verity's bitter nourishing honey
Supine in the pit or snow lake
Neither tressed anadems, nor baccar, nor amomum
"Goodbye, sweetheart, goodbye," she said, "Kenneth"
Immortal bees flit into the snow
Two wraiths face themselves, and lust
Orange snow suspends its collapse
What are you in the Delaware haze, X?
Rises between them in innocent devotion
In the doubled shadow you became I still
Her swimming shadow, the crash—sky!
Burn!

Comatas sang this as dusk came.

The Firing Squad

The mind burns its wafers.
The mind is an impolitic army,
An army, and conceives of a putsch
At the priestly sermon only.
The mind is "perhaps not",
And burns its wafers.
That is one mind; another
Is a wafer. What is blood?
The expendability of soap is not epic
But lyric, for the thighs.
The wafer-mind is not expendable
—The wafer has become mind
To be not burned: the impolitic mind
Must burn itself, not lyric or even . . .
There are certain questions (which
Mind was yours? whose thighs
Require policing? what army merits
Dalliance?) but a wafer
Does not ask them, while the priest
May be dreading his lunch
Or leftover minds.
There are otherwise answers to question
On hot dirty days
When the mind cannot even consume itself
When soap never hardens
When notions of eternity

The putsch of perhaps
Strain in hopeless reckoning
Toward the blanching conviction of wine
And guns: the expended blood
Leaves a change of eyes
Not of minds—enough
To know with mindly satisfaction
Fire is living,
Fire death.

TONY
TOWLE

George Towle

We put our heads here, and see nothing but beautiful yellow
                                                    flowers.
We notice them because they are a different color,
having just come from a green so extraordinary
that we would have been there forever.
Previously we felt the intensity of red,
asea with carnations and tulips. It is no matter
that you are oblivious, you are already there,
fitting into a number of years—
the sun revolves in its glory,
the animals bite the grass;
and when they are fat we will bite them,
chasing them over the hills to work up our appetites.
The bluejay flies overhead, the frog keeps pace with you on
                                                    the ground,
the antelope runs before and the lion behind.
It is Friday on the gilded path to the bank with these
                                                    creatures,
the clear magnificent river and paper one fords to cash one's
                                                    check,
the lettuce you buy for the rabbits, or the birds
beating their wings to a standstill over the rooftops
in the effort poem after poem to be somewhere else
and to say nothing about it in the attempt to support your-
                                                    self;
to scatter your sense among the planets
which you notice are all the same color
like the dishes washing themselves in the kitchen
which you notice because you are in the same room
which is variable as you drink forever.

                                                    1967

Poem

The sky is cut into sections and put on a frame.
Part of the sky is covered with clouds.
Machines rise and descend.
The sections of the sky blend together.
The plot requires a flowing river.
It comes down from the mountains.
A road winds parallel to the river.
Fish are set in motion.
The people in the shops and on the streets move.
The clouds go from one end of the sky to the other.
The arms and the hands are loose and relaxed.
Conversation comes spontaneously.
It is a few years later.
The next four years show great achievement.
The remaining years are disappointing.

1965

New York

for Irma

A peaceful bite of hamburger and your mind is blown into
space,
going on for some time while the long roots of space
dig into your language and the fuel pitches its tents and talks
to you.

You escape from this passively and pay the check. Your mind
is occupied, backing across the Brooklyn Bridge,
the serenity of the city to blind you with the sun,
and going through you into Brooklyn Heights.

It is April as you keep from bursting. In Cordoba and Seville
the churches enclose you and you think what you wish.
On Fifth Avenue you combine the words and cross the street,
between or among the starry buildings.
If the moon rises you will see the city.

You exhale and ideas fall from your mouth. The vowels are
                                                    raised
and become diphthongs and soon you are speaking Modern
                                                    English,
fighting the Germans, pressured into study and learning,
crowding into the forest of tables to eat.

1966

Collaboration

What I think in February is there for April.
In the mirror my guileless face, as opposed to my stomach
which has done abstraction a disservice.
Pinch yourself and face the spreading sky.
From it comes the barge of morning,
floating to where we are drifting to wake us up.
Behind it comes the barge of evening.
A strand of protoplasm hangs down from a tree.
An inquisitive frog approaches. From the dark
a pair of glowing eyes peer at you.
It is only a watching raccoon, or an owl.

We deal with the evil forces one by one,
the protoplasm, the slime, the different beasts

which spring to life and desire.
The bed throws a blanket over the atmosphere.
It is not safe to step in the water with the fish.
It is not safe to walk on the sand or through the trees.

1966

After Dinner We Take a Drive into the Night

We are watching for someplace to eat. We feel we are prey
for the insane scavengers of the air. We cannot make up our
minds,
racing five hundred miles away from our hosts.

I begin to feel passion.
I walk back and forth and it is a slow movie,
without the interest of acting, only walking.
Far from my prying eyes she strips off her clothes.
Oh for the wings of a bird.

The record slows down;
sweat falls on the instruments;
the musicians are bored.
A hand comes from the clouds to give me a poem.
I accept it and we shake hands.

The incident with the hand haunted me for the rest of my life.
I began to gasp. It is time to sing the death song,
clearing the tops of the trees, hearing the glass
from the window and the traffic from the street.

Each year is a supermarket, no each year is captured by a
word,
repeated with nostalgia, overwhelmed with ineptitude,
dropping to the ground and rolling down the bowling alley of
the sky.

1966

From the Spanish

In the rain what is there to do, what to play.
I ride, beginning to doze, underground to the Bronx,
on a horse, under Manhattan like undigested pork,
unfortunate fish bouncing dead off the walls.
From the Bronx we drive to Labrador, in Canada,
at the end of September, the sea full of hidden rocks.
Near the top of a mountain come up from the sea
we begin to see the danger of our experiment.
A little powder and the mountain is gone,
and clinging to an oar we are in the black water.

A voice rings out, the stranger chuckles;
our reverie flees like a running dog.
Men and women come forward to take our hand.
Bystanders bring us to the cafe. In the cafe
the sun burns at midnight, colors our faces with liquor
and comes up in the morning. In the morning air we divide,
extending our thoughts and going on like birds,
over the sleeping thieves and invisible grass for them.

A breath of cold air and the flight is ending,
covering the grass and the rocks with her hair,
speeding the turn of the seasons and their grief,
our red mouths visible and the white sky full of clouds.

1966

The City in the Throes of Despair

The great worm of the north, in whose footsteps we tread,
eludes us with a thousand lightnings.
However the bus, the nourishment of the city, pulls in,
and nothing has been accomplished though beauty
interrupts constantly, interpolating a row of moments
like a pink balustrade basking in the sun.

The buses and planes go forward in clouds of yeast and salt,
lurching over the pipes and turbines of the city
as the shape of Wyoming slides down the coast of Norway,
and I look from the plane as from the vantage point of a roof
to see the Lefrak Building shielding my eyes from
                                        Manhattan.
Lefrak, whose first name has escaped me—like Catherine
the Great's last—into the wild blue;
but who with Moses, whose first name is an anticlimax,
has left us the Queens of today and tomorrow.

We surprise the great worm in the frozen waste of his sleep.
Our magic ax and feather do their work
and the monster lies helpless in scattered and giggling pieces:
The five boroughs are safe and rainbows arch over the brick,

bright birds with their pinions are free to range once more,
but in whose colorful wake our hurtling plane seems
spiritless,
planning to touch only Chicago and perhaps Detroit,
with a landing in the meantime however subtle meaning an
emergency,
with none of us congenial until reaching the ground,
parachutes billowing,
or relaxing on the train back to New York, the parachute as a
souvenir.

1967

The Allegorical Figure of Brooklyn

The Allegorical Figure of Brooklyn is right here,
there where you're standing, and here's how it works.
The lamps go on and we walk through miles of parks;
the rain and the sleet are brought on, we travel
to Queens for two weeks of vacation; the sun returns
and the grass and farms, the villages of Brooklyn
continue to grow, and the spacious terrace and
oily sand of Brooklyn breathe, to be rocked slowly
by the Figure, and back toward home on the BMT
we smile at the tender Figure and wave goodbye.

1966

Poem

An engineer pushes a button in the mountains,
and another mountain lifts itself
and slides into the lake,
revealing a patchwork of interesting minerals.
The air follows us as we walk along.

Look at all this junk. My glass is cracked suddenly.
Look at the punch leaking out onto my sleeve.
That is the way I see things,
that or locked up in storage bins, alongside one another,
and hanging from my tie as from a dangling rope,
ending up in the same intrigue of thoughts,
becoming a digestible poison,
and the nerve-ends evolved to cope with instant danger
do not know what to tell the brain so they think about it.

Back in the mountains. The engineer pulls a switch,
and a mountain
making a quiet sliding sound, lifts itself
and slides into the lake.
There is bound to be a breeze now.
We are a hundred feet in the air.
There is no shock, just a quick vibrant lift.
The air comes with us,
a warm halo of fog and icy water with no sense of motion.

1965

Elegy

We eat and hear, as your kiss descends
over the piano and the sky.
The tide rushes out of a box and I am dead.
Prokovieff is dead as I am.
On the day of judgment, when we are released,
we will listen to the rain and the thunder,
and miles of cars will stop in their tracks.
The line racing to the end of the highway is white,
the color of the sky before Prokovieff.
At the beginning I am here behind the typewriter.
I wander off to the cliffs to see the sharks
waiting for a finger, or some bloody popcorn, or a ruined doll.
I throw them a ruined doll.
The camera moves in for a close-up. I adjust my tie
but it focuses on my cigarettes, Pall Mall Filters,
and the shining gold pack which contains them.
The camera goes on across the crowd.
We have five seconds on camera, a daguerrotype,
the room is upside down and objects fall with a crash.
A picture of an airplane is seen on the sky.
The airplane or the sun is upside down.
It is the sun which falls like an egg onto a plateau.
The real sun burns it to a disgusting omelette.
The sun also drains the color from the words.
The moon turns them to chalk and they collapse.

1965

Daybreak

The muse at daybreak stuttering, informs my bed,
pines in the scented winter air for poems,
and mumbles about the government and whether I should
vote:

"The government stinks. Withhold your vote of red and white
its hidden sea and blue of politic sky
which forms the world and so to surround our realm."

Government would speak as well, from the vales of
Abstraction
who on the death of Pound will ramble on once more,
their inbred elegance making you feel like a schmuck.
Milton of course could order these people around, God, Satan,
Liberty, Progress and the rest. To me God might say
You employ a distinctive style and I know who you are,
but you are not illuminating for me,
you do not give me any ideas, about myself or what I have
done.

Satan: Since you deal only with your own activity
and in immeasurable vanity,
I will eventually bring you something you dislike,
and in phrase of unshakable metaphor
as with that you think to spin out your life.

Satan concludes: You will have more poems than you hope
but more than you wish, your finger pressed on a difficult line,
your tongue through a word's transparency,
but my older tongue of iron comes inexorably to cover yours
and in your future is of greater eloquence.

The day half gone the muse and its servants fled,
a sandwich gone through you in enormity to Philadelphia,
cheese and milk flowing through you and into Boston,
air on the way to Minneapolis.

1967-68

Music

In the beginning nothing is congenial, not even the world
not even your notes. In the middle many things are pleasant
and even towards the end, but the end is self-explanatory,
and full of asides and commas with people to clean up the
                                        room.
Then you feel that Handel is truly your friend.
His singers send you to glory,
As his music is a preservative, for him not you.

1967

TOM
CLARK

Superballs

You approach me carrying a book
The instructions you read carry me back beyond birth
To childhood and a courtyard bouncing a ball
The town is silent there is only one recreation
It's throwing the ball against the wall and waiting
To see if it returns
One day
The wall reverses
The ball bounces the other way
Across this barrier into the future
Where it begets occupations names
This is known as the human heart a muscle
A woman adopts it it enters her chest
She falls from a train
The woman rebounds 500 miles back to her childhood
The heart falls from her clothing you retrieve it
Turn it over in your hand the trademark
Gives the name of a noted maker of balls

Elastic flexible yes but this is awful
You say
Her body is limp not plastic
Your heart is missing from it
You replace your heart in your breast and go on your way

You (I)

The door behind me was you
and the radiance, there like
an electric train wreck in your eye
after a horrible evening of waiting outside places in the rain
                             for you to come
only to
find all of them, two I know, the rest scullions, swimming
                             around you
in that smoky crowded room like a fishbowl
I escaped from, running away from you and my André Breton
dream of cutting your breasts off with a trowel
and what does that matter to them or to you now, but just
                             wait it's still early
to the children embroidered in the rug, who seem to be
                             setting up siege
engines under a tree house full of midgets who look like you.
Where are you in this sky of new blue
deltas I see in the drapery, and your new friends wearing
                             bamboo singlets
what are they doing down there in the moat waving tridents
                             like stalks of corn?
Me, I'll be happy to see their blood spilled all over the
                             bedspread
pavilions of your hands as an example. If you come home right
                             now I'll scrunch your hat
between my thighs like a valentine before you have time to
                             wipe them.

You (II)

You are bright, tremendous, wow.
But it is the hour of one from whom the horrible
                              tremendousness
Of youth is about to depart.
The boats are ready. The air is soft and you perhaps nearby
Do pass, saying "I am for you".
This is as much as "everything is great".
But desperation builds up all the time.
Life is nothing
            more to me
Strapped at the bottom
      of the throat
Than majesty, I think. You are arduous as that
Ashtray. Swallow me! Since
Your hands are full of streets
And I walk out upon the streets
And I think the girls are better looking, vicious, cool
And the men are flying kites and newsprint
Gets on my arms. I enter rooms—
Wild my steps like an automaton's—
Where batons are linked into some residu.
A gull is eating some garbage.
The sky is an old tomato-can, I think.
I buy a newspaper and begin to walk back.
Smells torture the kites like gulls. Wild gulls, and
It's the tremendous sky of survival.
Few things are still visible to me. Baseball
Withholds the tremors. They fall, so
I drag you down and
You are akimbo as I stick it in
And everything is thunderous accordion April, great,
Risen from palms and hypnotism. I run home
And dip my coffee in bread, and eat some of it.

You (III)

Today I get this letter from you and the sun
buckles   a mist falls over our villas
with a hideous organic slush like the music of Lawrence Welk
I lay in bed all day, asleep, and like some nocturnal
beast. And get your salutation among the torn green numbers
in the sky over the council houses. And see your eyes when
                          the retired pensioners pass
me by the abandoned railway station—this is not nothing, it is
                          not the hymn
of an age of bankrobbers or heraldic days but it is to sing
with complete gaiety until your heart freaks. I love you.
                          And go down amid the sycamores t
summer. Wandering by the lake any way
                    seems lovely, grand, the moon
is a gland in the thigh. Tumble and twinkle as on the golf
                          course apparel
lifts. And a door is opened to
an owl. It is snowing, and you are here on the bed with me
and it is raining, and I am as full of frets as a guitar or a curtain
and I am singing, as I sponge up the cat place. You
                          are heaped
the word reminds me of Abydos and spinach. A curtain
of belief keeps me away from the tombs
of imagery. I love you, I'd like to go.

You (IV)

the chords knotted together like insane nouns   Dante
you are in bed   in the dark copula you
of the musical phrase   a few star birds sing in the branches
their voices are tangled not high
now all of them are dark and some move   you
were a word, in the wood of my life
where the leaves are words, some of them fucking
in obscurity their clasping is terrible and brusque
pain birds ache thru them   and some
are lighter and seem to suggest less
of death than of a viola da gamba player these
birds sweep past in the forest
of my hands on your chest,   as we move
out on the glowing sea of the tropics on an ice pack,   you,

You (V)

(Hölderlin)

O Earth Mother, who consents to everything, who forgives
                              everything
don't hide like this   and tell

Her Power is sweetened in these rays, the Earth before her
    conceals the children
of her breast in her cloak, meanwhile we feel her,

and the days to come announce
that much time has passed and often one has felt

a heart grow for you inside his chest
They have guessed, the Ancients, the old and pious Patriarchs,
      and in the secret they are, without even knowing it,
      blessed
in the twisted chamber, for you, the silent men
but still more, the hearts, and those you have named Amor
or have given obscure names, Earth, for one is shamed
to name his inmost heart, and from the start however man
when he finds greatness in himself and if the Most High
                        permits,
he names it, this which belongs to him, and by its proper
                        name
and you are it, and it seems
                to me I hear the Father say
to you honor is granted from now on
and you must receive songs in its name,
and you must, while he is distant and old Eternity
      becomes more and more hidden every day,
take his place in front of mortals, and since
you will bear and raise children for him, his wish
is to send anew and direct toward you men's lives
when you recognize him   but this
directive which he inscribes in me is the rose
Pure sister, where will I get hold, when it is winter, of these
flowers, so as to weave the inhabitants of heaven crowns
                It will be
as if the spirit of life passed out of me,
because for the heavenly gods these signs
of love are flowers in a desert   I search for them, you are
                    hidden

Daily News

Dying day pinches the tot
He grabs my pen and beads
And plays into my hands
His father's skull glistens
Across his wife's white arms

The past bursts on a flower
And softly erases its bulb
We hear this going on all around
Night packs the traffic in cotton
And 1st Ave. fruit stands in opal

It is his first day to hurl a toy
But a gray torch rises in the future
Like a pair of scissors
The dark unravels towards
As I return to my newspaper

Penmanship

If I were Sophocles, brave with truth
I would play my old fiddle a sharp tune or two
And then withdraw into the uniqueness of rock
Which your special penmanship changes into lock
For your l's are special, as in Elgin Penitentiary
Where you have never been, my expressive farmer
Preferring liberty to freedom or a penitentiary

The baroque swoop in your l's is for enhancing liking
I like you because I am mad at you
Often you are mad at me too
All very spectacular
But it's awful when the other person isn't breathing

Friendship tempts you to essay the r in rock while breathing
Your friend Rock likes you
Jean
Frank
Paul
Matthew
Joy
Austin
And people
Like that
Like you
Goya is a tremendous painter

Goya is dead
But the poetry of penmanship is never dead
While you are writing
We survive for a while, and then we die
And this is but the beginning
Your d pirouettes then later you die
But there is no reason for you to care about any of that
For you have become the virtuoso of capital F
Even if tomorrow we die
I am still free to choose whoever I like

I go on choosing you
And you go on choosing me
Over and over again
Irrespective of merit

Poem

My heart in pieces like the bits
Of traffic lost in the blue
Rain confused I roar off into
To learn how to build a ladder
With air in my lungs again
To be with you in that region
Of speed and altitude where our bodies
Sail off to be kissed and changed
By light that behaves like a hand
Picking us up in one state and putting
Us down in a different one every time

Baseball

One day when I was studying with Stan Musial, he pointed out
that one end of the bat was fatter than the other. "This end is
more important than the other," he said. After twenty years I
learned to hold the bat by the handle. Recently, when Willie
Mays returned from Europe, he brought me a German bat of
modern make. It can hit any kind of ball. Pressure on the shaft
at the end near the handle frees the weight so that it can be
retracted or extended in any direction. A pitcher came with
the bat. The pitcher offers not one but several possibilities.
That is, one may choose the kind of pitch one wants. There
is no ball.

I'm on an Island

Do not try to adopt me
I am not a pigmy soothed
Boy or baby hitchhiker saint

What is wrong suddenly
Is that I swallow a cold
Blast of air, I mean fright

Spill coffee on my book
And hear the kinks
In the great universe

The warp in the coffin
Phantom men fly out of
Anywhere in this world

Sonnet

The orgasm completely
Takes the woman out of her
Self in a wave of ecstasy
That spreads through all of her body.
Her nervous, vascular and muscular
Systems participate in the act.

The muscles of the pelvis contract
And discharge a plug of mucus from the cervix
While the muscular sucking motions of the cervix
Facilitate the incoming of the semen.
At the same time the constriction of the pelvic
Muscles prevents the loss of the semen. The discharge
Makes the acid vaginal lubricant
Alkaline, so as not to destroy the spermatozoa.

Sunglasses

The air is interesting
My sunglasses today.
Last week they were

Interested by the sea.
In my sunglasses
I look like Grandma Moses

Wearing sunglasses
And interested by the sun,
The air, and the sea.

How hungrily
She looks at the world
Today!

Is it a child's wisdom
In the colorful pine tree
That throws itself upon Grandma Moses?

On her back she fades back
Into the sandy land
And changes slowly to silicates.

How interesting she seems
To my sunglasses
Who cry "O Daughter!"

Comanche

The strokes of mania on this vanilla
Sash, the faces of lush and
Science that fear formality's ticket
All mistake my pang for interest
In your secretive tambourine.
Sober dog, O expert caress

Helpless in the face of bone
Guffaw over the deformed person
Not, but preserve your pony
When life shoots it with its gun
You are home among a bevy of drunks
On a coal-barge in dirty Algeciras.

A barnacle on your first rate mind
Reaches the library of rapid boons
To marry a chalk particle
On the lapels of the famous spinster
Whose atrocious consciousness says
Everything good is from the Indian.

Poem

Like musical instruments
Abandoned in a field
The parts of your feelings

Are starting to know a quiet
The pure conversion of your
Life into art seems destined

Never to occur
You don't mind
You feel spiritual and alert

As the air must feel
Turning into sky aloft and blue
You feel like

You'll never feel like touching anything or anyone
Again
And then you do

The Yearbook

When I began this poem about our directions
Six years ago, there was an ornamental
Fountain six inches from my face

In the book I was reading then.
It was an illustration
In Burckhardt's book on the Renaissance

Which I was reading then, in the room
Where the six of us had been,
Robert, Larry, Anita, Eve and me,

And the other, whose role never
Came clear to me till tonight; even
Now I do not know his name

KENNETH
KOCH

Ma Provence

En ma Provence le blé est toujours vert
Et les filles sont jolies
Elles ne meurent pas elles vous aiment à la folie—en
    ma Provence.

Bills break the breakfast teacups and the sun
Shines darkly over the bill-ware
She writes it out in enervating prose
"In my Provence, my rose."

The Circus

1

We will have to go away, said the girls in the circus
And never come back any more. There is not enough of an audience
In this little town. Waiting against the black, blue sky
The big circus chariots took them into their entrances.
The light rang out over the hill where the circus wagons
    dimmed away.
Underneath their dresses the circus girls were sweating,
But then, an orange tight sticking to her, one spoke with
Blue eyes, she was young and pretty, blonde
With bright eyes, and she spoke with her mouth open when
    she sneezed
Lightly against the backs of the other girls waiting in line
To clock the rope, or come spinning down with her teeth on the line,
And she said that the circus might leave—and red posters
Stuck to the outside of the wagon, it was beginning to

Rain—she said might leave but not her heart would ever leave
Not that town but just any one where they had been, risking
their lives,
And that each place they were should be celebrated by blue
rosemary
In a patch, in the town. But they laughed and said Sentimental
Blonde, and she laughed, and they all, circus girls, clinging
To each other as the circus wagons rushed through the night.

2

In the next wagon, the one forward of theirs, the next wagon
Was the elephants' wagon. A grey trunk dragged on the floor . . .

3

Orville the Midget tramped up and down. Paul the Separated Man
Leaped forward. It rained and rained. Some people in the cities
Where they passed through were sitting behind thick glass
Windows, talking about their brats and drinking chocolate syrup.

4

Minnie the Rabbit fingered her machine gun.
The bright day was golden.
She aimed the immense pine needle at the foxes
Thinking Now they will never hurt my tribe any more.

5

The circus wagons stopped during the night
For eighteen minutes in a little town called Rosebud, Nebraska.
It was after dinner it was after bedtime it was after nausea it was

After lunchroom. The girls came out and touched each other
    and had fun
And just had time to get a breath of the fresh air of the night in
Before the ungodly procession began once more down the purple
    highway.

6

With what pomp and ceremony the circus arrived orange and red
    in the dawn!
It was exhausted, cars and wagons, and it lay down and leaped
Forward a little bit, like a fox. Minnie the Rabbit shot a little
    woolen bullet at it,
And just then the elephant man came to his doorway in the
    sunlight and stood still.

7

The snoring circus master wakes up, he takes it on himself to
    arrange the circus.
Soon the big tent floats high. Birds sing on the tent.
The parade girls and the living statue girls and the trapeze girls
Cover their sweet young bodies with phosphorescent paint.
Some of the circus girls are older women, but each is beautiful.
They stand, waiting for their cues, at the doorway of the tent.
The sky-blue lion tamer comes in, and the red giraffe manager.
They are very brave and wistful, and they look at the girls.
Some of the circus girls feel a hot sweet longing in their bodies.
But now it is time for the elephants!
Slowly the giant beasts march in. Some of their legs are clothed in
    blue papier-maché ruffles.
One has a red eye. The elephant man is at the peak of happiness.

He speaks, giddily, to every one of the circus people he passes,
He does not know what he is saying, he does not care—
His elephants are on display! They walk into the sandy ring . . .

8

Suddenly a great scream breaks out in the circus tent!
It is Aileen the trapeze artist, she has fallen into the dust and dirt
From so high! She must be dead! The stretcher bearers rush out,
They see her lovely human form clothed in red and white and
     orange wiry net,
And they see that she does not breathe any more.
The circus doctor leaves his tent, he runs out to care for Aileen.
He traverses the circus grounds and the dusty floor of the circus
     entrance, and he comes
Where she is, now she has begun to move again, she is not dead,
But the doctor tells her he does not know if she will ever be
     able to perform on the trapeze again,
And he sees the beautiful orange and red and white form
     shaken with sobs,
And he puts his hand on her forehead and tells her she must lie still.

9

The circus girls form a cortege, they stand in file in the yellow and
     white sunlight.
"What is death in the circus? That depends on if it is spring.
Then, if elephants are there, *mon père,* we are not completely
     lost.
Oh the sweet strong odor of beasts which laughs at decay!
Decay! decay! We are like the elements in a kaleidoscope,
But such passions we feel! bigger than beaches and
Rustier than harpoons." After his speech the circus practitioner sat
     down.

10

Minnie the Rabbit felt the blood leaving her little body
As she lay in the snow, orange and red and white,
A beautiful design. The dog laughs, his tongue hangs out, he
    looks at the sky.
It is white. The master comes. He laughs. He picks up Minnie
    the Rabbit
And ties her to a pine tree bough, and leaves.

11

Soon through the forest came the impassioned bumble bee.
He saw the white form on the bough. "Like rosebuds when
    you are thirteen," said Elmer.
Iris noticed that he didn't have any cap on.
"You must be polite when mother comes," she said.
The sky began to get grey, then the snow came.
The two tots pressed together. Elmer opened his mouth and
    let the snow fall in it. Iris felt warm and happy.

12

Bang! went the flyswatter. Mr. Watkins, the circus manager,
    looked around the room.
"Damn it, damn these flies!" he said. Mr. Loftus, the circus
    clerk, stared at the fly interior he had just exposed.

The circus doctor stood beside the lake. In his hand he had a
    black briefcase.
A wind ruffled the surface of the lake and slightly rocked the boats.

Red and green fish swam beneath the surface of the water.
The doctor went into the lunchroom and sat down. No, he
    said, he didn't care for anything to eat.
The soft wind of summer blew in the light green trees.

You Were Wearing

You were wearing your Edgar Allan Poe printed cotton blouse.
In each divided up square of the blouse was a picture of
      Edgar Allan Poe.
Your hair was blonde and you were cute. You asked me, "Do
      most boys think that most girls are bad?"
I smelled the mould of your seaside resort hotel bedroom on
      your hair held in place by a John Greenleaf Whittier clip.
"No," I said, "it's girls who think that boys are bad." Then we
      read *Snowbound* together
And ran around in an attic, so that a little of the blue enamel was
   scraped off my George Washington, Father of His Country, shoes.

Mother was walking in the living room, her Strauss Waltzes
      comb in her hair.
We waited for a time and then joined her, only to be served
      tea in cups painted with pictures of Herman Melville
As well as with illustrations from his book *Moby Dick* and
      from his novella, *Benito Cereno*.
Father came in wearing his Dick Tracy necktie: "How about
      a drink, everyone?"
I said, "Let's go outside a while." Then we went onto the
      porch and sat on the Abraham Lincoln swing.
You sat on the eyes, mouth, and beard part, and I sat on the
      knees.
In the yard across the street we saw a snowman holding a
      garbage can lid smashed into a likeness of the mad English
      king, George the Third.

Taking a Walk with You

My misunderstandings: for years I thought "muso bello"
    meant "Bell Muse," I thought it was kind of
Extra reward on the slotmachine of my shyness in the snow when
February was only a bouncing ball before the Hospital of
    the Two Sisters of the Last
Hamburger Before I Go to Sleep. I thought Axel's Castle was
    a garage;
And I had beautiful dreams about it, too—sensual, mysterious
    mechanisms; horns honking, wheels turning . . .
My misunderstandings were:
1) thinking Pinocchio could really change from a puppet into a
    real boy, and back again!
2) thinking it depended on whether he was good or bad!
3) identifying him with myself!
4) and therefore every time I was bad being afraid I would
    turn into wood . . .
5) I misunderstood childhood. I usually liked the age I was.
    However, now I regard twenty-nine as an optimum age (for me).
6) I disliked Shelley between twenty and twenty-five.
All of these things I suppose are understandable, but
When you were wearing your bodice I did not understand that
    you had nothing on beneath it;
When my father turned the corner I misunderstood the light
    very much
On Fifty-fifth Street; and I misunderstood (like an old
    Chinese restaurant) what he was doing there.
I misunderstand generally Oklahoma and Arkansas, though I
    think I understand New Mexico;
I understand the Painted Desert, cowboy hats, and vast
    spaces; I do
Not understand hillbilly life—I am sure I misunderstand it.

I did not understand that you had nothing on beneath your
    bodice
Nor, had I understood this, would I have understood what it
    meant; even now I
(Merry Christmas! Here, Father, take your package)
    misunderstand it!
Merry Christmas, Uncle Leon! yes, here is your package too.

I misunderstand Renaissance life; I misunderstand:
The Renaissance;
Ancient China;
The Middle Atlantic States and what they are like;
The tubes of London and what they mean;
Titian, Michelangelo, Vermeer;
The origins of words;
What others are talking about;
Music from the beginnings to the present time;
Laughter; and tears, even more so;
Value (economic and esthetic);
Snow (and weather in the country);
The meaning of the symbols and myths of Christmas.
I misunderstand you,
I misunderstand the day we walked down the street
    together for ten hours—
Where were we going? I had thought we were going some-
    where. I believe I misunderstand many of the places we
    passed and things you said . . .
I misunderstand "Sons of Burgundy,"
I misunderstand that you had nothing painted beneath your
    bodice,
I misunderstand "Notification of Arrival or Departure to Be
    Eradicated Before Affection of Deceased Tenant."
I understand that
The smoke and the clouds are both a part of the day, but

I misunderstand the words "After Departure,"
I misunderstand nothingness;

I misunderstand the attitude of people in pharmacies, on the
    decks of ships, in my bedroom, amid the pine needles, on
    mountains of cotton, everywhere—
When they say paralytic I hear parasite, and when they say
    coffee I think music . . .
What is wrong with me from head to toe
That I misinterpret everything I hear? I misunderstand:
French: often;
Italian: sometimes, almost always—for example, if someone
    says, "Fortunate ones!" I am likely to think he is referring
    to the fountain with blue and red water (I am likely to
    make this mistake also in English).
I misunderstand Greek entirely;
I find ancient Greece very hard to understand: I probably
    misunderstand it;
I misunderstand spoken German about 98% of the time, like
    the cathedral in the middle of a town;
I misunderstand "Beautiful Adventures"; I also think I probably
    misunderstand *La Nausée* by Jean-Paul Sartre . . .
I probably misunderstand misunderstanding itself—I misun-
    derstand the Via Margutta in Rome, or Via della Vite, no
    matter what street, all of them.
I misunderstand wood in the sense of its relationship to the
    tree; I misunderstand people who take one attitude or
    another about it . . .
Spring I would like to say I understand, but I most probably
    don't—autumn, winter, and summer are all in the same boat
(Ruined ancient cities by the sea).

I misunderstand *vacation* and *umbrella,*
I misunderstand *motion* and *weekly*
(Though I think I understand "Daytime Pissarros"
And the octagon—I do not understand the public garden) . . .

Oh I am sure there is a use for all of them, but what is it?
My misunderstandings confuse Rome and Ireland, and can you

Bring that beautiful sex to bear upon it?
I misunderstand what I am saying, though not to you;
I misunderstand a large boat: that is a ship.
What you are feeling for me I misunderstand totally; I think
     I misunderstand the very possibilities of feeling,
Especially here in Rome, where I somehow think I am.
I see the sky, and sails.
(I misunderstand the mustard and the bottle)
Oh that we could go sailing in that sky!

What tune came with the refreshments?
I am unable to comprehend why they were playing off key.
Is it because they wanted us to jump over the cliff
Or was one of them a bad or untrained musician
Or the whole lot of them?
At any rate
San Giovanni in Laterano
Also resisted my questioning
And turned a deaf blue dome to me
Far too successfully.
I cannot understand why you walk forwards and backwards
     with me.
I think it is because you want to try out your shoes for their toes.
It is Causation that is my greatest problem
And after that the really attentive study of millions of details.

I love you, but it is difficult to stop writing.
As a flea could write the Divine Comedy of a water jug. Now
     Irish mists close in upon us.
Peat sails through the air, and greenness becomes bright. Are
     you the ocean or the island? Am I on Irish soil, or are your
     waves covering me?
St. Peter's bells are ringing: "Earthquake, inundation, and sleep to
     the understanding!"
(American Express! flower vendors! your beautiful straight
     nose! that delightful trattoria in Santa Maria in Trastevere!)

Let us have supper at Santa Maria in Trastevere
Where by an absolute and total misunderstanding (but not fatal)
    I once ate before I met you.
I am probably misinterpreting your answer, since I hear nothing,
    and I believe I am alone.

The Railway Stationery

The railway stationery lay upon
The desk of the railway clerk, from where he could see
The springtime and the tracks. Engraved upon
Each page was an inch-and-a-half-high T
And after that an H and then an E
And then, slightly below it to the right,
There was COLUMBUS RAILWAY COMPANY
In darker ink as the above was light.
The print was blue. And just beneath it all
There was an etching—not in blue, but black—
Of a real railway engine half-an-inch tall
Which, if you turned the paper on its back,
You could see showing through, as if it ran
To one edge of the sheet then back again.

To one edge of the sheet then back again!
The springtime comes while we're still drenched in snow
And, whistling now, snow-spotted Number Ten
Comes up the track and stops, and we must go
Outside to get its cargo, with our hands
Cold as the steel they touch. Inside once more
Once we have shut the splintery wooden door
Of the railway shack, the stationery demands
Some further notice. For the first time the light,

Reflected from the snow by the bright spring sun,
Shows that the engine wheel upon the right
Is slightly darker than the left-side one
And slightly lighter than the one in the center,
Which may have been an error of the printer.

Shuffling through many sheets of it to establish
Whether this difference is consistent will
Prove that it is not. Probably over-lavish
At the beginning with the ink, he still
(The printer) had the presence of mind to change
His operating process when he noticed
That on the wheels the ink had come out strange.
Because the windows of the shack are latticed
The light that falls upon the stationery
Is often interrupted by straight lines
Which shade the etching. Now the words "Dear Mary"
Appear below the engine on one sheet
Followed by a number of other conventional signs,
Among which are "our love," "one kiss," and "sweet."

The clerk then signs his name—his name is Johnson,
But all he signs is Bill, with a large B
Which overflows its boundaries like a Ronson
With too much fluid in it, which you see
Often, and it can burn you, though the *i*
Was very small and had a tiny dot.
The *l*'s were different—the first was high,
The second fairly low. And there was a spot
Of ink at the end of the signature which served
To emphasize that the letter was complete.
On the whole, one could say his writing swerved
More than the average, although it was neat.
He'd used a blue-black ink, a standing pen,
Which now he stuck back in its stand again.

Smiling and sighing, he opened up a drawer
And took an envelope out, which then he sealed
After he'd read the letter three times more
And folded it and put it in. A field
Covered with snow, untouched by man, is what
The envelope resembled, till he placed
A square with perforated edges that
Pictured a white-haired President, who faced
The viewer, in its corner, where it stuck
After he'd kissed its back and held it hard
Against the envelope. Now came the truck
Of the postman "Hello, Jim." "Hello there, Bill."
"I've got this—can you take it?" "Sure, I will!"

Now the snow fell down gently from the sky.
Strange wonder—snow in spring! Bill walked into
The shack again and wrote the letter *I*
Idly upon a sheet of paper. New
Ideas for writing Mary filled his mind,
But he resisted—there was work to do.
For in the distance he could hear the grind
Of the Seventy-Eight, whose engine was half blue;
So, putting on a cap, he went outside
On the tracks side, to wait for it to come.
It was the Seventy-Eight which now supplied
The city with most of its produce, although some
Came in by truck and some was grown in town.
Now it screams closer, and he flags it down.

The Departure from Hydra

As I was walking home just now, from seeing
Margaret and Norris off (though Peter,
An Englishman whom Norris had met yesterday,
Went back to change his clothes, and missed the boat)
As I came home along the little street
Without a name on which the only theatre,
The movie theatre, on Hydra is,
Called "The Gardenia" or just plain "Gardenia,"
The street which they today are tearing up
And carrying new stones in to replace
The ones they're tearing up, though it may be
They are the same stones, put in different order
Or in a different way, as I was walking,
With the heat of the day just over, at five-thirty,
I felt quite good, but then felt an awareness
Of something in my legs that might be painful
And then of some slight tension in my jaws
And slight pains in my head; instead of despairing
And giving all thought of pleasure up, I felt
That if I could write down all that I felt
As I came walking there, that that would be
A pleasure also, and with solidity.
I passed a mule—some men were loading up
His fellow mule with packets—and I stared
At his wide eyes and his long hard flat nose
Or face, at which he turned away his eyes
And stamped his right hoof nervously. I felt
Guilty, a member of a higher species
Deliberately using my power against
A natural inferior because
Really I was afraid that he might kick
When I came past; but when he seemed upset
Then I felt guilty. Then I looked ahead

And saw a view of houses on the hill,
Particularly noticing one red one
And thinking, Yes, that is a part of what
I feel, of the variety of this walk;
Then my mind blurred somewhat, I turned and came
Down this small narrow alley to my home.
As I came in, reviewing the ideas
Which had occurred to me throughout my walk,
It suddenly came to me that maybe Peter
Had missed the Athens boat deliberately;
After all, Margaret was not sure that she
Wanted to accompany him and Norris
On a walking trip on Poros, and Norris had said
He wanted to stay with Margaret, so that Peter
Was disappointed, since he and Norris had planned
That very morning to take such a walking trip,
And he, Peter, had been the most excited
Of all, about it. But now since Margaret and Norris
Were going into Athens, what was there for Peter
To do, why should he take the boat at all,
Even though he'd planned to, to stop at Poros?
Except, of course, to act on some marginal chance
That Norris might get off with him and walk,
Or on the strength of previous expectations,
Emotional impetus lingering. If not,
Perhaps his going to change was just an excuse
To avoid an actual confrontation with Norris
In which he would have to say, "No, I'm not going
Unless you'll come on the walking trip!" but he knew,
Peter, that Norris wanted to stay with Margaret
And that therefore speaking to him would only result
In a little pain and confusion, since both were quite drunk,
Having planned their trip to Poros over beer all morning;
And also, of course, it might result in his getting,
In spite of himself, on the boat, by the talk confused
And not thinking clearly (whereas if he walked away
He had only, really, to wait till the boat had left—

Then he could come back down and think it over,
Surely to find he didn't regret too much
Not getting the boat, because after all the reason
He'd wanted to take the boat had long been gone).
For a human situation often leads
People to do things that they don't desire
At all, but they find that what they did desire
Has somehow led them to this situation
In which not to do that which is proposed
Seems inconsistent, hostile, or insane,
Though much more often very unfriendly; then too
Sometimes it chiefly is a lack of time
To explain how things have changed that leads one, waving
One's hands, aboard a ship that bodes one ill.
To walk away as Peter did is one way
Of avoiding such situations—another way
Is never to deceive or have high hopes
For foolish things; to be straight with oneself,
With one's own body, nature, and society,
To cast off everything that is not clear
And definite, and move toward one desire
After another, with no afterthoughts.
Living in this way one avoids the sudden
Transports of excitement Peter felt
When Norris mentioned a Poros walking tour.
For surely if Peter's natural desires
Had all been satisfied, if his life were running
Smoothly sexually, and if his health
Were excellent and his work going well,
He scarcely would have gotten so excited
At the mere thought of walking around Poros;
This sort of thing, however, often happens
To people from Northern countries, not just Peter,
And perhaps if one is English, Norse, or Swedish,
Danish, Finnish, Swiss, or North American,
One cannot avoid a certain amount of tension,
A certain quavering in the hand which reaches

For a ripe peach or the shoulder of a girl,
One whom, as one walks back from going swimming,
One thinks that one could eat, she's so delicious,
But only thinks it for a little while
(This thought itself is such a Northern one!
A Southerner would think about a place
Where he could go and jump on top of her)—
In any case, then, Northerners find it hard
To avoid such sudden excitements, but the English,
And especially the upper class, are worst of all,
Because besides their climate that's oppressed them
There's also been a restrictive upbringing,
Manners around the house perhaps too severe
For children—I am speaking of those English
Who escape from "class" and become bright or artistic,
The ones one sees on places like this island.
(These sudden outbursts of enthusiasm, of course,
Are often much admired by other people,
Particularly some not very smart ones,
Who think however they're very sensitive
And what they most admire is "vitality"
Which they think things like outbursts are a sign of,
And they can bore you far into the night
With telling you how wonderful some Dane
Or Norsky is, when you could be asleep
Dreaming of satisfying your desires
With persons who are always very warm,
Tender, and exciting—but, awake!
They're talking still, and though your sickly smile
Gets sicklier every moment, they go on:
"Hans suddenly got the idea to
Inundate Denmark. He is wonderful!"
"Oh, marvelous! Where does one go to meet him?"
"I'll give you his address. He has a farm
Where he stays in the summer; he loves animals,
But sometimes when he drinks a lot he beats them
And says that he can understand their language."

"How marvelous!" "And here's his city address:
Beschtungen aber Bass Gehundenweiss
996." "Goodnight." But Peter is
Not an exaggerated case like that,
And not a nagging bore who talks of such
People, but he has "outbursts" all the same.
It is true, in a sense these outbursts are
Difficult to discriminate from real
Vitality, which everyone esteems
These days because of man's oppressed position
In modern society, which saps his strength
And makes him want to do what everyone else does,
Whereas some man who says, "Let's pitch the glasses
Against the lamppost" is likely to be praised
By some low-IQ person who is there
As being really vital, ah he's wonderful.
Vitality, however, usually
Appeals to an answering vital force in others
And brings about making love or great events,
Or it at least gives pleasure—I can't judge
Vitality in any way but the way
It gives me pleasure, for if I do not get
Pleasure from life, of which vitality
Is just the liquid form, then what am I
And who cares what I say? I for one don't.
Therefore I judge vitality that way.)
But Peter, after having this idea
Of a walking trip on Poros, must have felt
That in walking around in the sun all day on an island
About which he knew nothing, there might come
Some insight to him or some relaxation,
Some feeling the way an Italian feels all the time,
Or perhaps not, perhaps he never does;
Peter at any rate was probably not
Conscious of an Italian at the time
He thought with pleasure about the walk on Poros,
But there he was, faced with Norris and Margaret

An hour before the boat came in, and Norris
Was saying "Maybe not." One mistake of Peter,
Or, rather, difficulty, a common one
In such enthusiasms, is that since
One's enthusiasm is motivated by submerged
Feelings and so its object isn't clear
To anyone, it is most likely that
Though they respond excitedly at first,
Partly because excitement is so communicable,
Others, when they think over what you've planned,
Will see it in a greyer light, unless of course
They have the same neuroses that you have,
In which case a whole lifetime might be built
Upon one of these outbursts. Norris, probably,
In drinking with Peter, wanted more than anything
To be agreeable, whereas Peter wanted
To "do" something unusual, not necessarily
Pleasing to Norris, not necessarily displeasing;
Norris, I should imagine, then, once he
Was out of Peter's company, since he'd known him
A very short time, was lacking the chief impulse
That motivated him when he agreed
To take a tour with Peter; therefore Margaret,
Speaking to Norris when he was alone
And saying she did not want to take the trip,
Found he immediately agreed with her,
Expressed some doubts at least, and said all right,
The trip was off then, he'd explain to Peter;
Peter, of course, was very surprised by this,
But still he must have been used to it because
The way that Norris and Margaret acted was based
On laws of human conduct which endure;
And since that outburst surely was not his first,
Peter was probably accustomed to
That sort of outcome of his impulses
And said to himself, "Ah, they don't understand,"
But probably knew inside that there was something

Seriously the matter with him. So when he left
The table and said, "I'm going to get my things,"
It was with a certain tension that he left,
Indicative of the fact he'd not come back,
And of the fact that he knew he would not avoid
Self-doubts because he avoided the useless boat trip;
Of course he wouldn't think he should have gone
But wonder why things had been the way they were.
It was these deeper worries in his mind,
I think, that kept him from leaving even sooner
With the same excuse, rather than a hope that Norris
Would change his mind again. Deep thoughts make helpless
Men for small undertakings. Well, perhaps
The last is speculation, but the rest
Seems surely true. I smiled, and closed the door.

Sleeping with Women

Caruso: a voice.
Naples: sleeping with women.
Women: sleeping in the dark.
Voices: a music.
Pompeii: a ruin.
Pompeii: sleeping with women.
Men sleeping with women, women sleeping with women, sheep
    sleeping with women, everything sleeping with women.
The guard: asking you for a light.
Women: asleep.
Yourself: asleep.
Everything south of Naples: asleep and sleeping with them.
Sleeping with women: as in the poems of Pascoli.

Sleeping with women: as in the rain, as in the snow.
Sleeping with women: by starlight, as if we were angels,
    sleeping on the train,
On the starry foam, asleep and sleeping with them—sleeping
    with women.
Mediterranean: a voice.
Mediterranean: a sea. Asleep and sleeping.
Streetcar in Oslo, sleeping with women, Toonerville Trolley
In Stockholm asleep and sleeping with them, in Skaansen
Alone, alone with women,
The rain sleeping with women, the brain of the dog-eyed genius
Alone, sleeping with women, all he has wanted,
The dog-eyed fearless man.
Sleeping with them: as in *The Perils of Pauline*
Asleep with them: as in *Tosca*
Sleeping with women and causing all that trouble
As in Roumania, as in Yugoslavia
Asleep and sleeping with them
Anti-Semitic, and sleeping with women,
Pro-canary, Rashomon, Shakespeare, tonight, sleeping with women
A big guy sleeping with women
A black seacoast's sleeve, asleep with them
And sleeping with women, and sleeping with them
The Greek islands sleeping with women
The muddy sky, asleep and sleeping with them.
Sleeping with women, as in a scholarly design
Sleeping with women, as if green polarity were a line
Into the sea, sleeping with women
As if wolverines, in a street line, as if sheep harbors
Could come alive from sleeping with women, wolverines
Greek islands sleeping with women, Nassos, Naxos, Kos,
Asleep with women, Myconos, miotis,
And myositis, sleeping with women, blue-eyed
Red-eyed, green-eyed, yellow-reputed, white-eyed women
Asleep and sleeping with them, blue, sleeping with women
As in love, as at sea, the rabbi, asleep and sleeping with them

As if that could be, the stones, the restaurant, asleep and
      sleeping with them,
Sleeping with women, as if they were knee
Arm and thigh asleep and sleeping with them, sleeping with women.
And the iris peg of the sea
Sleeping with women
And the diet pill of the tree
Sleeping with women
And the apology the goon the candlelight
The groan: asking you for the night, sleeping with women
Asleep and sleeping with them, the green tree
The iris, the swan: the building with its mouth open
Asleep with women, awake with man,
The sunlight, asleep and sleeping with them, the moving gong
The abacus, the crab, asleep and sleeping with them
And moving, and the moving van, in London, asleep with women
And intentions, inventions for sleeping with them
Lands sleeping with women, ants sleeping with women, Italo-
      Greek or Anglo-French orchestras
Asleep with women, asleep and sleeping with them,
The foam and the sleet, asleep and sleeping with them,
The schoolboy's poem, the crippled leg
Asleep and sleeping with them, sleeping with women
Sleeping with women, as if you were a purist
Asleep and sleeping with them.
Sleeping with women: there is no known form for the future
Of this undreamed-of view: sleeping with a chorus
Of highly tuned women, asleep and sleeping with them.
Bees, sleeping with women
And tourists, sleeping with them
Soap, sleeping with women: beds, sleeping with women
The universe: a choice
The headline: a voice, sleeping with women
At dawn, sleeping with women, asleep and sleeping with them.
Sleeping with women: a choice, as of a mule
As of an island asleep or sleeping with them, as of Russia,

As of an island, as of a drum: a choice of views: asleep and
　　sleeping with them, as of high noon, as of a choice, as of
　　variety, as of the sunlight, red student, asleep and sleeping
　　with them,
As with an orchid, as with an oriole, at school, sleeping with
　　women, and you are the one
The one sleeping with women, in Mexico, sleeping with women
The ghost land, the vectors, sleeping with women
The motel man, the viaduct, the sun
The universe: a question
The moat: a cathexis
What have we done? On Rhodes, man
On Samos, dog
Sleeping with women
In the rain and in the sun
The dog has a red eye, it is November
Asleep and sleeping with them, sleeping with women
This June: a boy
October: sleeping with women
The motto: a sign; the bridge: a definition.
To the goat: destroy; to the rain: be a settee.
O rain of joy: sleeping with women, asleep and sleeping with them.
Volcano, Naples, Caruso, asleep and sleeping, asleep and
　　sleeping with them
The window, the windrow, the hedgerow, irretrievable blue,
Sleeping with women, the haymow, asleep and sleeping with
　　them, the canal
Asleep and sleeping with them, the eagle's feather, the dock's
　　weather, and the glue:
Sleeping with you; asleep and sleeping with you: sleeping with
　　women.
Sleeping with women, charming aspirin, as in the rain, as in
　　the snow,
Asleep and sleeping with you: as if the crossbow, as of the
　　moonlight
Sleeping with women: as if the tractate, as if d'Annunzio

Asleep and sleeping with you, asleep with women
Asleep and sleeping with you, asleep with women, asleep and
    sleeping with you, sleeping with women
As if the sun, as of Venice and the Middle Ages' "true
Renaissance had just barely walked by the yucca
Forest" asleep and sleeping with you
In China, on parade, sleeping with women
And in the sun, asleep and sleeping with you, sleeping with
    women,
Asleep with women, the docks, the alley, and the prude
Sleeping with women, asleep with them.
The dune god: sleeping with women
The dove: asleep and sleeping with them
Dials sleeping with women; cybernetic tiles asleep and sleeping
    with them
Naples: sleeping with women; the short of breath
Asleep and sleeping with you, sleeping with women
As if I were you—moon idealism
Sleeping with women, pieces of stageboard, sleeping with
    women
The silent bus ride, sleeping with you.
The chore: sleeping with women
The force of a disaster: sleeping with you
The organ grinder's daughter: asleep with bitumen, sunshine,
    sleeping with women,
Sleeping with women: in Greece, in China, in Italy, sleeping
    with blue
Red green orange and white women, sleeping with two
Three four and five women, sleeping on the outside
And on the inside of women, a violin, like a vista, women,
    sleeping with women
In the month of May, in June, in July
Sleeping with women, "I watched my life go by" sleeping with
    women
A door of pine, a stormfilled valentine asleep and sleeping with
    them
"This Sunday heart of mine" profoundly dormoozed with them

They running and laughing, asleep and sleeping with them
"This idle heart of mine" insanely "shlamoozed" asleep and
    sleeping with them,
They running in laughter
To the nearest time, oh doors of eternity
Oh young women's doors of my own time! sleeping with women
Asleep and sleeping with them, all Naples asleep and sleeping
    with them,
Venice sleeping with women, Burgos sleeping with women,
    Lausanne sleeping with women, hail depth-divers
Sleeping with women, and there is the bonfire of Crete
Catching divorce in its fingers, purple sleeping with women
And the red lights of dawn, have you ever seen them, green
    ports sleeping with women, acrobats and pawns,
You had not known it ere I told it you asleep with women
The Via Appia Antica asleep with women, asleep and sleeping
    with them
All beautiful objects, each ugly object, the intelligent world,
The arena of the spirits, the dietetic whiskey, the storms
Sleeping with women, asleep and sleeping with them,
Sleeping with women. And the churches in Antigua, sleeping
    with women
The stone: a vow
The Nereid: a promise—to sleep with women
The cold—a convention: sleeping with women
The carriage: sleeping with women
The time: sometimes
The certainty: now
The soapbox: sleeping with women
The time and again nubile and time, sleeping with women, and
    the time now
Asleep and sleeping with them, asleep and asleep, sleeping with
    women, asleep and sleeping with them, sleeping with women.

TOM
VEITCH

TOAD POEMS

Cats Climb Trees

Cats climb trees because they are
Afraid of Dogs.
My dog was not afraid of me,
So I never climbed any trees.
Twenty years ago this happened.
Since then my dog has died
and been buried under a tree
in our front yard.
Today I climbed that tree for
the first time, to chase down a
cat named Melvin who had got
caught up there after running
from my new dog whose name
shall not be mentioned
(We call him Ron)
My sister wrote that.

It Is a Distinct Pleasure

It is a distinct pleasure
And a marble-shaped pain
To be caught while walking
Out in the rain.
To further the thought one might

Come around to the conclusion that
All life is shaped like a ball,
And we are all rolling into some
basket or hole
And again, after thinking about that,
one might decide to be entirely
honest about the situation
And admit to himself and
the world that.

Naval Engagement

The great moral of my next set of
Surf-thoughts will be the clam
in your mouth which I spit
there after you denied me your
womb—
You are a girl I do not love
Because I did not want to
Nor cared to
Because I was tired of love
Of you, of caring, of wanting
to care, of the red-hot pokers
of your tits sticking into my
belly while I sucked you off.
Tee hee.

A Fine Thing

A fine thing to burn a hole in your sock
And to sock your friend for
Kissing your wife,
But the worst of all
Is the man who turns his back
On life and murders his mother
And father and brothers and sisters
because they did not love him
because they were mean to him
because they wanted him to do
something—
Oh why Lord?
Why this injustice in your Universe?

Something to Eat

I asked for something to eat,
Something outside my own body,
And in came a hunk of greasy cheese,
fresh from the mouse-trap.
Now a dagger appears between the
pages of your mind, and the
envelope seals itself
under your magic pencil.
What he means is that bitter cheese

is better than no cheese at all,
And Indian varmints on
painted horses are better than
no Indians at all.
Quite the contrary in fact,
No less true of course, no matter
how you look at it.

Cowboy Song

Wait until the revelation
Of embarrassment encompasses
Your last compass-curved thought
And the contradiction of
Contradistinction has *en*veloped
Your last turd—
Then my little girl
I will pat your hair
And comb your werewolf
lips; love lost on a banshee
Always backwards
into nothing
Border fire
Burning down Fear Village
And last week's jokes.

Principally

principally & before
whenever one pauses
to remember the cosmic dust on the crust
of his apple
there is separation into mirrors
nothing between
but still reflectors
break later, at death
fragments of idea
lost forever
in the empty
empties.

Amen.

Poison Meat

Meanwhile back at the wrenched back
                        the poet
Signifies his sleep
By beeping his horn
Toad

Ha ha he thinks I'll fool 'em all
They'll never get me
in or out of Time—
But later, at the store, he repents
And tells all
Even to the cash consumers
Hardy har he laughs sudsing down
his hands and legs,
Hardy har you fools
This speaks backwards into your tongue
And your ears are laughing.
Hardy har.
Friendlies!

The Last Time

The last time I slept was when
I went with R. Padgett, noted poet
and money-lender to see
a movie called "Dog East Dog."
That movie was rather funny.
It had to do with a dog
Who didn't like his friend dog
So he ate him.
After it was over everybody puked
And left.

Fifteen Years Past

"Fifteen years past, this coming Sunday,
I wrote the following words in my diary:
'Dear Diary: Today I am one year old.'
Today I am not quite sixteen years old.
(This coming Sunday, of course, is my birthday)
Why I asked you all here today,
to consider this problem
Is that I am growing hungry
of this business, having disapproved
of the whole past twenty or more,
lost quite a lot, praised none, once
retired, twice abandoned, and nanny-goat
eat this can."
All that was read from this mornings
paper.
I wish I had something to eat.

Clipping

Good morning all
you friends and nay-
bors out there, this
is my happy new poem
of the happy new day
Today I think I
will dine with Toshi
minuto and reside at
role for about 24 hou
as a alternative.
Plans for particip
is still in formation
nine miles from Color
but that'so.k. my boy
fs day became the fir
first woman to be swo
I weighed this decisi
That's the way be do
Mr. Spada's wife, Ann
you compete in Mrs. A
7; Teresa 5; Christop
I cried at the end wh
the little girl was t
away from her little
friend Michel. How
sad, sometimes I wish
they didn't make movi
like that, only ones
stake in an election
clared, is an interna
and all that.
Remember me to Pa-
ulette when you see
her, will you please?

The Finest Thing

The finest thing in the world
Is God and his works
Oh how I marvel at them,
Oh how I cry when I
think of dying and going into
heaven and God and becoming
part of it all. Oh how
marvelous, how
nice, how lovely to be
part of all this.

Candy Bar

I pray you've finished
Little Candy Bar,
My sipping sadness done;
And when you've finished
Little mystery bar,
I pray you'll send me one.
My morning's madness nearly did me in,
My evening's crass ball too;
But what it was that slew my coat,
Was the mirrorwax sight of you.
The strong have a way
That can savour the day,
And the weak know a pistol or two;
But the thing that now reeks
In the pits of my cheeks,
Is the perilous savour of you.
You're a sad candy bar

You're a mad candy bar,
You're a fishwarp deserving of due;
But when majesty strikes
And fumes 'velope my likes,
What shall last is the flavor of you.

Improved 4-Way

the name
in remedies in
pink-and-white tablets for
medication.

The most famous name
in cold remedies, is now in
modern pink-and-white layer
tablets for controlled multi-medication.

The most exquisitely delightful famous
name-thing in advanced cold remedies, and
it is now in lovely delicious modern-as-the
new-day pink-and-white triple-layer
tiny-tablets for long-lasting completely
controlled super-adequate multi-medication.
You will never know when a cold may strike.

The Final Toast

And now the final toast:
To Mr. Bread who made all this possible
To Mr. Paper who helped out at the factory
To Mr. Ink and Mr. Pen
And Mr. Thread
And Mr. Money
And Mr. Moon
And Mr. Sun and Mrs. Sun
And to Mrs. Mooney and my mother
And to Mr. Grass and Mr. Trees
And to Mr. Typewriter and Mrs. Typewriter
And to all the others who made
life possible while you were
away in India
eating the natives.

* * *

ORDINARY PEOPLE ON SUNDAY

In her desperation she opens the gas-tap
Poverty and sorrow fill the life
Lulu's strong will to dominate erotically
feeding at night on human blood.

Overwhelmed by the postman's love
The girl throws herself from the roof of a building—
Meanwhile the Rajah of Eshnapur
is torn to death by tigers—grief strikes—
again she takes her life

This family tragedy takes place in the house of a railway
                                      signalman.
The daughter (Edith) and the seducer (Paul)
put an end to love's young dream—
Death shows her three candles
and young Juan avenges the rape of his sister,
killing the seductive harem dancer
as well as the Captain (who crumbles to dust)

Here an eccentric English buys a girl in a slave market.
She (he didn't know!) belongs to a bloody sect—
It's not long before she murders his wife, sets her negro upon
                                      him, demands
the suicide of her lover Percy and is herself finally killed
by the despised Yellow Man.

A powerful secret society pays off
the mistress of the local mayor—
She kills her newborn baby and in delirium
takes refuge in a monastery
where a shy young monk savagely rapes her.
After the mayor's death she is dragged before the tribunal,
condemned to death
and hanged.

Now a man is driven to insanity
by the mysterious death of his illegitimate child.
The mother runs away to walk the streets
a hypnotized sleepwalker, prostitute to tramps.

Our hero is accused of witchcraft
and falls victim to the priestly vengeance:
a cleft in the mountains closes forever . . .

His son (Bruno) has inherited all his father's worst traits.
The mother encounters death
in the person of her son, (a decisive moment in his life)
The policemen arrive, the mother's world collapses,
the prostitute's child opens the gas-tap,
Bruno is fatally injured while freezing to death.

Now we learn of a young married couple in trouble.
She (Lilian) auctions herself to obtain money
for his treatments . . . In the process
his career is destroyed, and upon his return to their
                                        apartment
the Colonel finds only her dead body.

The passing of a morning
A suspicious fellow is assaulted and robbed
His girl pays the price (he's a pimp).
Sonja, who's secretly in love with her confidante
sinks deeper and deeper into the sink
of erotic decay, until finally on Christmas Eve
she falls victim to a down-at-heel circus artist
whom she had solicited.

During a dance involving sharp knives
and the use of artificial insemination
a girl finds out the truth
but loses her panties as the king drives by.
She gets her souteneur to kill the younger woman
Then in despair takes her own life.

Together now, ordinary people (murderers in bed)
let us ascend the funeral pyre
one ordinary Sunday
and go to heaven purified.
Seduced, burnt for infanticide, drugged blind by
loss and despair,
by economic depression and moral disintegration,
poverty, foul destiny, jealousy and fate
stabbed down, dying in child-bed
stolen from our inheritance.

The anatomical department received your memo
your fantasies will be given attention
we know you cannot bear this bourgeois atmosphere,
palled and broken by the world around you
you seek refuge in suicide, self-immolation . . .
But a terrible vengeance awaits the lavatory attendant
who dies by his own hand
disillusioned by the menacing world of outside . . .
So you're ill-treated and gloomy?
Yes, ten years of smouldering in jail,
about to erupt in death . . .

LEWIS
MacADAMS

Kora for March 5th

Williams died two years ago yesterday
tomorrow
        snow expected
        in the low 30's
I've got to drive the lady home to
take her pills
        "crutches for us all "
          he sd. when the world is
        "organized"
sub terra flower
and the Spring song, Dana
              and me
          in wet fear
          walking to the parking lot
          gray lines of
          soaked cars

The Clock Works

    I

      Paint triggers the serene
a brush stroking the wall the wind through shreds of news
then the window
            & the folks outside flicker
That's why you make a home,
people the wind, hurt no living thing—

because you want it all,
                    all life with that She
            in your hands. Your life
            is covered
                with liquid sunshine paint.

Three of the thumb tacks are stuck in the thumb
a guitar plunges away into the soft hair.
Everyone has got a pale eye. In their blood
the landlords see winter coming on.
Behind the front, so many Indians
rows of pale scars on their bodies, wait.
A new swatch of paint on the ceiling. Will they
"get it done?" The hardest thing to learn is
It's real. I see your body
under two thick quilts in January
a book propped against the frosty window
and the forlorn birds in the snow.

The roof is empty, and a body lies at the foot
of the ladder.
Does the poet go to the rescue? Not
while there's work to be done.
        Dreams that do me best
                    tend to surface in the daytime
These memories,
                    they let you sleep,
a benevolent crowd of holiday shoppers after the gay fishe.
They leave your packages undisturbed
Why EVER leave the world?
                    Sweet play of the earth
as you snooze on the convention floor.

II

Here is a list of rooms
completed so far—a bedroom,
    at dusk, thick with souvenirs,
    the cabinet slipping open
    the birds waiting on the shelf
as your skirt slips down
the walls are blue, painted a southerly blue
There's a slow flash
          and your body falls.

But look at the unfinished house, at the wife
with yellow paint on her tight red jeans.
Just five more seconds. She reaches up
and pulls him down. Fresh vegetables
in the double-boiler, the odor of the
bathroom as the shower blasts. We,
the paint brushes slapping against the corner, we

III

Your fingers like what they touch
the back of your hand against the wall
"You could hang anything here,
the antimacassar, the goose,
your Vassar posture foto,
or the zodiac for Harmonica Ed.
And the chimney there—
a hide-away.
          they never betrayed
and they lived on so humble, & with some mercy
that now in Spring their face,
a reflection in the water vines,
& will not be bothered away."

Blue walls, a white frock apron, a violent set-to
in your life. Viciousness
is only a gap
in your perfect memory
of a home filled with peace
                    the kitchen lighted,
                    the stove,
                        when it gets dark early
                    image of the rooms of the home

        IV

Peace, morning, the sky is clean, has showered,
and my wife will sleep in the flow.
The dahlias
        are beginning to wilt
clean sheets
through the crashing and traffic of the night.

        V

Where you been? Your damn hat
got painted orange in your absence.

            MOVE it!
                    Your eye here, for instance
            it don't need *you*
            to tie it down
                        Like what if your eyes were *free*?
            with nothing to hunger for
            in the motionless light.

VI

People are looking to flee their homes. Who are
these people? What have they borne? The fire,
where they live. A car quivers and pulls over.
It's a momma with the smoke of her child.
I want to take care of you,
to see you through
                    the door to the bedroom.
Everything in sight is covered with white dust
from the spoon. There must be a big man.
He is older than me, a thunder,
like the heat of the mountain.
He painted a sequence. He called it
"First Dream" A fly buzzes into the paint.
You wander through the field to the pillar
to the kitchen You are filling up the air.
                                There is window
in everything. A relief for your eyes
            to be exact in ecstasy
then get out
                as the roof caves in.
to celebrate the lightning in the scattered buckets
and the neighborly racket of love
and the gleaming suitcases that are filling up this room.

Warm Tea

Too late, when you show some
unconcern, too late, gentle one person
loving you, honestly, over there
by the space drift, heater
drying her hair. When it's time
she's ready, but
you're due somewhere.
Awash with angels,
Reading alone in her chair.

Trailer Park

How many Excedrin'd you take? Five?
Even more. Past the stripped down bogs filled with Fords.
Black flats. Cracks in the ground. Grain prices
way down.   No ease for all. Wind
clatters out of the plain, whips the little plastic flags
of platoon.
            Sweat froze on down through the ranks.

    I'd Rather Be Rich
    with Miss Sandra Dee,
    than in that Dyna-Flo
    (look down lists of blood in the mind)

  Cigarette.

  Out of this many damn cars
you'd think at least one

would be warm, that magic aching cloud of blond at the wheel,
anywhere you tell her, she'll go.

A creamy snake. Git away from me, moon! *Moon!!*
At one time, simple statements kept you sane.
You could think joy, and you'd be criss-crossing the land.

What a strange log:
little crossroad towns
as they settle in to die.

Wyoming, Utah. To commemorate
the blood that booms in your head as you move on
through.
General George F. Custer's troops moved through
toward those twin buttes, and then a ways beyond.
Red smoke from the moon
Bodies plead for bodies. There's a click.
The light changes. You hear horses.
The sound of America makes you roam,
won't turn you loose. You hear a moan
from the gulch.

Racket   Quiet

One switch engine rolls through the yards.
Somebody painted the water tower—an angel or a wolverine.
Gone graduation day night. Farms curling at the end
of farm roads. One light
at the base of the grain elevator.
Batty son scribbling in the quiet. Bombardier quiet
as he steps to the door. Bomb bay
for L.A. Near death
and far away

And I still can't get a ride

Olive Grove

My vision is emptying
    silent soccer players
in dark red shirts, in the late afternoon
a train window
              moving through a small town
the riders fan themselves
slowly,
      taking their blue caps off
      "My image of Rome, the Holy City
      Rome fades"
We are ready for dinner, or a meal like dinner.
The priest reads
partly in Italian: "This is another town
              on the water's edge"
The colorful windows are fled
into the mountains.
Into the deep,
trick-filled mountains
overrun by cerise winds.

The Italian Air

Who is that school-girl?
Did the air change I can't focus Did she
Come in via dove? Bring love along
in a new way, a wicker basket
that scoops you along in the wind?

The insides of the tree are shaking.
They set up a hum, like the
arrows from a fan. Take the light
from the cottonwoods, let it sway your plans
The draught from the leaves sifts down and shakes your hands

The Dazzling Day

The shopping cart clatters out of the Safeway, a young man
with a black tie, loose at the collar but tucked in to his long
white apron tilts the cart up to ease it over a curb. A small
pamphlet is stuck behind the windshield wiper in front of the
driver's side. The metal light pole is fiery to touch except for
the shards of an old political sign. Someone has been in the
car, the glove compartment is open, a box of kleenex on the
dashboard, the chrome end of the steering wheel is hot.
The groceries, in thick brown paper sacks lean against each
other in the back seat. I tip the boy and get in the car. The ice
cream bars are melting, I must turn on the air conditioner and
drive back toward the house.

The Lace Curtains

From this balcony
there are red and white
kites hung
        in the telephone wires

I have nothing to write you except
I am feeling dizzy again
and the white sheet is still in the closet.
I was reading this magazine
then I looked up
and saw the kites.
The children were screaming
I saw their mother washing her hands.
I can still see her, partially.
through the lace curtains streaming through the window.

A Meditation:
What is a Stocking in Eternity?

What color is the hole in your socks? A kind of water-mark
brown. For September it is already cold and the task is already Herculean, being divided among masters whose brilliance fills me with longing for the peace of the sky. One
tells me the proper road, another is selling coupons *and*
the bridge, and a third is staggering down the highway,
absorbing the hits and staying whole. As I am about to leave
bed, my wife warns me never to mistake simplicity for ease,
and rolls over asleep. I do not mean to be anecdotal, but the
giant-man approach is wearing me down. Like, it is no longer
a question simply of "big." That implies limits, as in
"circumference of the known world." In a minute I will put on
my socks and fix coffee. At the kitchen table steam rises from
my special cup. Sounds and colors bend through the wind
screens. Something jostling the medallions has begun to
rumble in the brain. I take down a mountain of cereal, send
all hopes out to the corral, and pick up a huge spoon. The
day most clearly begins.

Have Sky

"It's a damn skinny get-by
if you ask me"
              the rain wind through the shack
          two pintos turn tail to the road.
"Well, who asked
you" to write
             this down.
        Water backs up in furrows
     You're both ends of the rainbow
        in the gutter, grass bends,
        garbage trucks, a big yellow cat
        cuts chunks through the upland pines.
Washed air so fragrant slams down
from the hills, Feather River Run
on my energy. Cold water ravines, a
rain down the back of my coat I feel
really pretty terrific
              in fact TOO MUCH
some sun break through it all dance
a pick-up rattles around the bend
& goes by, stops and I'm on that flat-bed
on a tarpaulin, a shovel, some other tools.
In San Francisco maybe late tonight
with Bobby and his girl, whatever
kind of food they'll have left-over to eat
in her kitchen. The most spectacular
paradiso cowboy hitch-hike through the mountains
through the fir trees and pine, through the flush blue sky.

The Animals

There is a green light which pets feel
that makes them vicious.
They leer from their grave in a bowl
and detest your smell.
Right now, near the sofa,
animals breathe and glow.
The flowers are stiff
in the amber light.
We all miss you, tongue, in this room.

The Young Man

At the kitchen table with Mrs. Hartman
I'm hungry,
            a war crime
        "What can I *do*"
well my dear,
            perhaps
            smash a silverfish
            across my blanket
            it hisses, dies
Kidder is working on a new movie
the title: "Too much danger, Too much danger"

At the theatre we both cough, together
We like the same things
The poems I write you

make us both so sad
and in ten minutes
the sorrow in my head
will wrench it through the roof.

In Memoriam

Burges, B.R. Lieut. Second Bttn. The Royal Ulster
Rifles—In proud and everlasting memory of our
precious BRIAN, killed in action in Normandy, July 19, 1944, aged 19 years. Interred in the British Cemetery, Banneville La Campagne—MUMMIE,
DADDY and PUSSY. Quis separabit.

Bushell—In proud and loving memory of Jack Bushell,
Pilot officer, D.F.M., R.A.F.V.R. killed over
Dunkirk, July 19, 1941.

Coleman—In memory of a dearly loved and loving
son and brother, David Worsley COLEMAN, 2nd Lt.
The Duke of Wellington's Regiment. Killed in
Action in Normandy 21 years ago today, aged 21.
"Who shall seperate us from the love of Christ?"

Donald—In ever-loving memory of IAN DAVID GRAHME
DONALD, Flight Lieutenant, R.A.F., killed in
Battle of Britain, July 19, 1940, aged 22.

Frank—In memory of our beloved "JUNIOR" CAPTAIN
JESSE FRANK, on this his 50th birthday, killed
in Anzio, Italy, 19 July, 1944—MOTHER, NANCY,
and CHARLES

Govett—Remembering always my beloved husband,
LEONARD, killed flying on duty, July 19, 1945.
"O Perfect Love"

Hogarth. MAJOR J.U. HOGARTH, Grenadier Guards—
in loving memory of "Sandy", died Italy, July 19,
1944. Always Remembered.-P.

Powell—In proud and ever-present remembrance of
JOHN HENRY COURTHOPE POWELL, Major, 2nd Fife
and Forfar Yeomanry, killed in Normandy, July 19, 1944.
Also of his father, RICHARD HENRY POWELL, of *The
Times*. 2nd Lieut. 5th Royal Sussex Regt. Killed
Festubert, May 9, 1915—R.I.P.

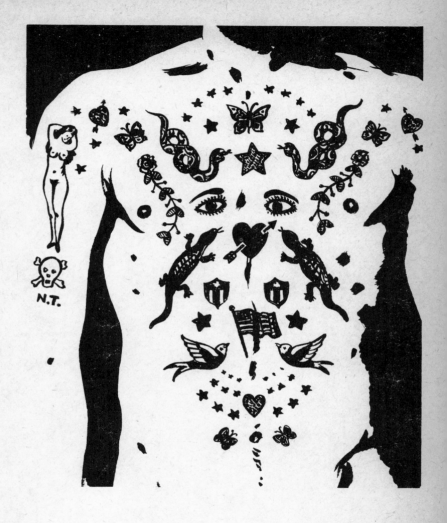

JOHN
ASHBERY

Two Scenes

I

We see us as we truly behave:
From every corner comes a distinctive offering.
The train comes bearing joy;
The sparks it strikes illuminate the table.
Destiny guides the water-pilot, and it is destiny.
For long we hadn't heard so much news, such noise.
The day was warm and pleasant.
"We see you in your hair,
Air resting around the tips of mountains."

II

A fine rain anoints the canal machinery.
This is perhaps a day of general honesty
Without example in the world's history
Though the fumes are not of a singular authority
And indeed are dry as poverty.
Terrific units are on an old man
In the blue shadow of some paint cans
As laughing cadets say, "In the evening
Everything has a schedule, if you can find out what it is."

The Grapevine

Of who we and all they are
You all now know. But you know
After they began to find us out we grew
Before they died thinking us the causes

Of their acts. Now we'll not know
The truth of some still at the piano, though
They often date from us, causing
These changes we think we are. We don't care

Though, so tall up there
In young air. But things get darker as we move
To ask them: Whom must we get to know
To die, so you live and we know?

Le Livre est sur la table

I

All beauty, resonance, integrity,
Exist by deprivation or logic
Of strange position. This being so,

We can only imagine a world in which a woman
Walks and wears her hair and knows
All that she does not know. Yet we know

What her breasts are. And we give fullness
To the dream. The table supports the book,
The plume leaps in the hand. But what

Dismal scene is this? the old man pouting
At a black cloud, the woman gone
Into the house, from which the wailing starts?

II

The young man places a bird-house
Against the blue sea. He walks away
And it remains. Now other

Men appear, but they live in boxes.
The sea protects them like a wall.
The gods worship a line-drawing

Of a woman, in the shadow of the sea
Which goes on writing. Are there
Collisions, communications on the shore

Or did all secrets vanish when
The woman left? Is the bird mentioned
In the waves' minutes, or did the land advance?

The Ticket

The experience of writing you these love letters . . .
Fences not concluding, nothing, no even, water in your eye,
    seeming anything
The garden in mist, perhaps, but egocentricity makes up for
    that, the winter locusts, whitened
Her hand not leading anywhere. Her head into the yard,
    maples, a stump seen through a gauze of bottles,
    ruptures—
You had no permission, to carry anything out, working to

carry out the insane orders given you to raze
The box, red, funny going underground
And, being no reason suspicious, mud of the day, the plaid—I
    was near you where you want to be
Down in the little house writing you.

Though afterwards tears seem skunks
And the difficult position we in to light the world
Of awe, mush raging, the stump again
And as always before
The scientific gaze, perfume, millions, tall laugh
That was ladder though not of uncertain, innocuous truths,
    the felt branch—
To a ditch of wine and tubs, spraying the poster with blood,
    telegraph, all the time
Automatically taking the things in, that had not been spoiled,
    sordid.

Leaving the Atocha Station

The arctic honey blabbed over the report causing darkness
And pulling us out of there experiencing it
he meanwhile . . . And the fried bats they sell there
dropping from sticks, so that the menace of your prayer
    folds . . .
Other people . . .   flash
the garden are you boning
and defunct covering . . .   Blind dog expressed royalties . . .
comfort of your perfect tar grams nuclear world bank tulip
Favorable to   near the night pin

loading formaldehyde.   the table torn from you
Suddenly   and we are close
Mouthing the root   when you think
generator   homes enjoy leered

The worn stool blazing   pigeons from the roof
           driving tractor to squash
Leaving the Atocha Station   steel
infected bumps the screws
    everywhere   wells
abolished top ill-lit
scarecrow falls   Times, progress and good sense
strike of shopkeepers dark blood
no forest you can name drunk scrolls
the completely new Italian hair . . .
Baby . . .   ice falling off the port
The centennial   Before we can

             old   eat
members with their chins
         so high up   rats
   relaxing the cruel discussion
 suds   the painted corners
white   most aerial
    garment crow
             and when the region took us back
the person left us like birds
  it was fuzz on the passing light
over disgusted heads, far into amnesiac
permanent house depot   amounts he can
       decrepit mayor . . .   exalting flea
for that we turn around
experiencing it is not to go into
the epileptic prank forcing bar
to borrow out onto tide-exposed fells

over her morsel, she chasing you
and the revenge he'd get
establishing the vultural over
rural area cough protection
murdering quintet. Air pollution terminal
the clean fart genital enthusiastic toe prick album serious
    evening flames
the lake over your hold   personality
          lightened . . .   roar
You are freed
          including barrels
head of the swan   forestry.
the night and stars fork
That is, he said
    and rushing under the hoops of
equations probable
        absolute mush   the right
entity   chain store   sewer opened their books
      The flood dragged out
      I coughed to the window
last month: juice, earlier
like the slacks   to be declining
    the peaches   more
  fist
sprung expecting the cattle
false loam   imports
      next time around

Idaho

During the past few months, Biff had become quite a frequent visitor to Carol's apartment.

He never failed to marvel at the cool, corrected elegance of the place as contrasted with its warm, rippling, honey-blonde occupant. The apothecary jars,

Chippendale furniture,

and wall-to-wall carpeting were strangely out of keeping with Carol's habitual "Hiya good lookin'" as she came forward to greet him, wrapped in one of those big fuzzy bathrobes and drying her hair on a Turkish towel. Or were his calculations somehow awry? Was there, deep within this warm, vital-seeming presence a steel vein so thin as to be almost invisible? Or was this, too, a mistake?

Their whole conduct had been, up to now, not impersonal exactly, but utterly devoid of any recognition of sex-consciousness. In conversation they had "swapped backgrounds," as Biff called it. Carol, her eyes wet with tears at the picture of his isolation in the crowded rectory, had uttered a deep sigh at her own recital of being left for the first eight years of her life to the sole care of Patches.

With the unconscious dramatic heightening that always goes with a sympathetic audience, each of them, intensely serious and really moved, had lifted corners of the veil for the other to peep through. They had been very close to each other in attention, in sympathy, in response, but with none of the subtle emphasis which marks the recognized intrusion of sex. Carol was aware today, however, that Biff had suddenly become obsessed with a sense of her; that he had caught fire. She was aware of

vast excitement,

apprehension,

a mental

"Can I give you a hand?"
She gave a little cry that was silenced by mouth on
                              uttermost tingling nerve
"Carol!" he said. Can this be the one time
        ??
                                        She had known how from
Biff: The last Rhode Island reds are
                        "diet of hamburgers and orange juice"
    Exactly what kind of perfection??????????????????????????????
I see into fields of timothy
                        one
    the others   time
                        change
,,,,,,,and they walked back,
                    small hand-assemblies

                    "What does it mean???????????????????"

                    Carol laughed. Among other things,
                        till I've finished it. It's the reason of
                    dropped into Brentano's.
                            get some of the
                    a pile of these. I just grabbed one . . .
                        —Oh, by the way, there's a tele-
                    "See?" She pointed to the table.
Cornelia unfolded the piece of crude blue paper that is a
    French telegra.
                ##############
                            The mouth of weeds

                    marriage." She shivered. "It's—it's a
                    death!"

II.

> The door of the studio slammed.
> "Hullo, honey!" Cornelia said.

was the last practical   from now on, whispers
   leading into the night

            flowers, moral turpitude,
She had had more than enough. Why, in Stone
      Age
            vessels
But that doesn't explain. Her mind opened it-
Every tendril of thought,,,,,,,,,,
It sees through a magnifying glass
                  genius
               a special aureole
Niagara of affliction.   had learned this
heard it
into the
window the long platform at Oxford, and Carol
      lowered the
            When the train stopped the army
You had nothing about it. That's no Bob!!!!!!!!!!!!!!!

         A whistle blew shrilly
the slow evening
         silver note
      the main road automobiles
         majestic stag-beetles, with a high, sweet hum
               that moment for long
thoughts and low red voices
      the mood was shattered
   "twenty-seven"   Just as that act changes
            nerve-centers
            birthdays—
She rose from the table abruptly. "You must smoke
your cigar alone tonight. I—I'm going out in the car.

She went upstairs and changed into a different pair
of shoes

and a sweater.
Jim was pouring himself another glass of port as she came
down.
""""""""""""I won't be very long,""""""""""" she said.   ####

nodded. "Take care of yourself." She closed the door behind
her and went

down through
the garden. A carnation struck her hand as she passed. She
picked it,
sniffed deeply, and put the stalk in her mouth. "Twenty-
seven! Twenty-seven!" She went into the garage, a little
house of wood, tucked into the bank at the edge of the road.
It was Jim's car, a present from Carol. She had earned it
in the year following the exhibition, had learned to drive it
at an automobile school in London, and had a special low
bunk designed for Jim alongside the driver's seat. The
carnation made a crimson
splash against her cheek as she drove out
and headed down the hill towards the main road. Up in the
cottage Patches
"Good 'eavens! Is that

                    For who dies
                    The crocus ideally
                    On life's playing field
                    The "never mind" rubbish
                    All, all fixed
                    running water
                    And the proper names,
                    blood out of courage
                    to fix
                    to feel
                    the stem of air

                    great, senseless knob
brownies ahead and the clutch. "Twenty-seven!
    Twenty-seven!"
                        sniffed loudly
                        the car window
                        listening car had ceased.

                        A whistle blew shrilly.

These Lacustrine Cities

These lacustrine cities grew out of loathing
Into something forgetful, although angry with history.
They are the product of an idea: that man is horrible,
    for instance,
Though this is only one example.

They emerged until a tower
Controlled the sky, and with artifice dipped back
Into the past for swans and tapering branches,
Burning, until all that hate was transformed into useless love.

Then you are left with an idea of yourself
And the feeling of ascending emptiness of the afternoon
Which must be charged to the embarrassment of others
Why fly by you like beacons.

The night is a sentinel.
Much of your time has been occupied by creative games
Until now, but we have all-inclusive plans for you.
We had thought, for instance, of sending you to the middle
    of the desert,

To a violent sea, or of having the closeness of the others be air
To you, pressing you back into a startled dream
As sea-breezes greet a child's face.
But the past is already here, and you are nursing some private
    project.

The worst is not over, yet I know
You will be happy here. Because of the logic
Of your situation, which is something no climate can
    outsmart.
Tender and insouciant by turns, you see

You have built a mountain of something,
Thoughtfully pouring all your energy into this single
    monument,
Whose wind is desire starching a petal,
Whose disappointment broke into a rainbow of tears.

The Ecclesiast

"Worse than the sunflower," she had said.
But the new dimension of truth had only recently
Burst in on us. Now it was to be condemned.
And in vagrant shadow her mothball truth is eaten.
In cool, like-it-or-not shadow the humdrum is consumed.
Tired housewives begat it some decades ago,
A small piece of truth that if it was honey to the lips
Was also millions of miles from filling the place reserved for it.
You see how honey crumbles your universe
Which seems like an institution—how many walls?

Then everything, in her belief, was to be submerged
And soon. There was no life you could live out to its end
And no attitude which, in the end, would save you.
The monkish and the frivolous alike were to be trapped
    in death's capacious claw
But listen while I tell you about the wallpaper—
There was a key to everything in that oak forest
But a sad one. Ever since childhood there
Has been this special meaning to everything.
You smile at your friend's joke, but only later, through tears.

For the shoe pinches, even though it fits perfectly.
Apples were made to be gathered, also the whole host of the
    world's ailments and troubles.
There is no time like the present for giving in to this
    temptation.
Tomorrow you'll weep—what of it? There is time enough
Once the harvest is in and the animals put away for the winter
To stand at the uncomprehending window cultivating the
    desert
With salt tears which will never do anyone any good.
My dearest I am as a galleon on salt billows.
Perfume my head with forgetting all about me.

For some day these projects will return.
The funereal voyage over ice-strewn seas is ended.
You wake up forgetting. Already
Daylight shakes you in the yard.
The hands remain empty. They are constructing an osier basket
Just now, and across the sunlight darkness is taking root anew
In intense activity. You shall never have seen it just this way
And that is to be your one reward.

Fine vapors escape from whatever is doing the living.
The night is cold and delicate and full of angels
Pounding down the living. The factories are all lit up.
The chime goes unheard.
We are together at last, though far apart.

A Blessing in Disguise

Yes, they are alive, and can have those colors,
But I, in my soul, am alive too.
I feel I must sing and dance, to tell
Of this in a way, that knowing you may be drawn to me.

And I sing amid despair and isolation
Of the chance to know you, to sing of me
Which are you. You see,
You hold me up to the light in a way

I should never have expected, or suspected, perhaps
Because you always tell me I am you,
And right. The great spruces loom.
I am yours to die with, to desire.

I cannot ever think of me, I desire you
For a room in which the chairs ever
Have their backs turned to the light
Inflicted on the stone and paths, the real trees

That seem to shine at me through a lattice toward you.
If the wild light of this January day is true
I pledge me to be truthful unto you
Whom I cannot ever stop remembering.

Remembering to forgive. Remember to pass beyond you into
    the day
On the wings of the secret you will never know.
Taking me from myself, in the path
Which the pastel girth of the day has assigned to me.

I prefer "you" in the plural, I want "you,"
You must come to me, all golden and pale
Like the dew and the air.
And then I start getting this feeling of exaltation.

Last Month

No changes of support—only
Patches of gray, here where sunlight fell.
The house seems heavier
Now that they have gone away.
In fact it emptied in record time.
When the flat table used to result
A match recedes, slowly, into the night.
The academy of the future is
Opening its doors and willing
The fruitless sunlight streams into domes
The chairs piled high with books and papers.

The sedate one is this month's skittish one
Confirming the property that,
A timeless value, has changed hands.
And you could have a new automobile

Ping pong set and garage, but the thief
Stole everything like a miracle.
In his book there was a picture of treason only
And in the garden, cries and colors.

Rivers and Mountains

On the secret map the assassins
Cloistered, the Moon River was marked
Near the eighteen peaks and the city
Of humiliation and defeat—wan ending
Of the trail among dry, papery leaves
Gray-brown quills like thoughts
In the melodious but vast mass of today's
Writing through fields and swamps
Marked, on the map, with little bunches of weeds.
Certainly squirrels lived in the woods
But devastation and dull sleep still
Hung over the land, quelled
The rioters turned out of sleep in the peace of prisons
Singing on marble factory walls
Deaf consolation of minor tunes that pack
The air with heavy invisible rods
Pent in some sand valley from
Which only quiet walking ever instructs.
The bird flew over and
Sat—there was nothing else to do.
Do not mistake its silence for pride or strength
Or the waterfall for a harbor
Full of light boats that is there
Performing for thousands of people

In clothes some with places to go
Or games. Sometimes over the pillar
Of square stones its impact
Makes a light print.

So going around cities
To get to other places you found
It all on paper but the land
Was made of paper processed
To look like ferns, mud or other
Whose sea unrolled its magic
Distances and then rolled them up
Its secret was only a pocket
After all but some corners are darker
Than these moonless nights spent as on a raft
In the seclusion of a melody heard
As though through trees
And you can never ignite their touch
Long but there were homes
Flung far out near the asperities
Of a sharp, rocky pinnacle
And other collective places
Shadows of vineyards whose wine
Tasted of the forest floor
Fisheries and oyster beds
Tides under the pole
Seminaries of instruction, public
Places for electric light
And the major tax assessment area
Wrinkled on the plan
Of election to public office
Sixty-two years old bath and breakfast
The formal traffic, shadows
To make it not worth joining
After the ox had pulled away the cart.

Your plan was to separate the enemy into two groups
With the razor-edged mountains between.
It worked well on paper
But their camp had grown
To be the mountains and the map
Carefully peeled away and not torn
Was the light, a tender but tough bark
On everything. Fortunately the war was solved
In another way by isolating the two sections
Of the enemy's navy so that the mainland
Warded away the big floating ships.
Light bounced off the ends
Of the small gray waves to tell
Them in the observatory
About the great drama that was being won
To turn off the machinery
And quietly move among the rustic landscape
Scooping snow off the mountains rinsing
The coarser ones that love had
Slowly risen in the night to overflow
Wetting pillow and petal
Determined to place the letter
On the unassassinated president's desk
So that a stamp could reproduce all this
In detail, down to the last autumn leaf
And the affliction of June ride
Slowly out into the sun-blackened landscape.

A Last World

These wonderful things
Were planted on the surface of a round mind that was to
    become our present time.
The mark of things belongs to someone
But if that somebody was wise
Then the whole of things might be different
From what it was thought to be in the beginning, before an
    angel bandaged the field glasses.
Then one could say nothing hear nothing
Of what the great time spoke to its divisors.
All borders between men were closed.
Now all is different without having changed
As though one were to pass through the same street at
    different times.
And nothing that is old can prefer the new.
An enormous merit has been placed on the head of all things
Which, bowing down, arrive near the region of their feet
So that the earth-stone has stared at them in memory at the
    approach of an error.
Still it is not too late for these things to die
Provided that an anemone will grab them and rush them
    to the wildest heaven.
But having plucked oneself, who could live in the sunlight?
And the truth is cold, as a giant's knee
Will seem cold.

Yet having once played with tawny truth
Having once looked at a cold mullet on a plate on a table
    supported by the weight of the inconstant universe
He wished to go far away from himself.
There were no baskets in those jovial pine-tree forests, and
    the waves pushed without whitecaps
In that foam where he wished to be.

Man is never without woman, the neuter sex
Casting up her equations, looks to her lord for loving
    kindness
For man smiles never at woman.
In the forests a night landslide could disclose that she smiled.
Guns were fired to discourage dogs into the interior
But woman—never. She is completely out of this world.
She climbs a tree to see if he is coming
Sunlight breaks at the edges of the wet lakes
And she is happy, if free
For the power he forces down at her like a storm of lightning.

Once a happy old man
One can never change the core of things, and light burns you
    the harder for it.
Glad of the changes already and if there are more it will
    never be you that minds
Since it will not be you to be changed, but in the evening in
    the severe lamplight doubts come
From many scattered distances, and do not come too near.
As it falls along the house, your treasure
Cries to the other men; the darkness will have none of you, and
    you are folded into it like mint into the sound of haying.
It was ninety-five years ago that you strolled in the serene
    little port; under an enormous cornice six boys in black
    slowly stood.
Six frock coats today, six black fungi tomorrow,

And the day after tomorrow—but the day after tomorrow itself
    is blackening dust.
You court obsidian pools
And from a tremendous height twilight falls like a stone and
    hits you.

You who were always in the way
Flower
Are you afraid of trembling like breath
But there is no breath in seriousness; the lake howls for it.
Swiftly sky covers earth, the wrong breast for a child to suck,
    and that,
What have you got there in your hand?
It is a stone

So the passions are divided into tiniest units
And of these many are lost, and those that remain are given
    at nightfall to the uneasy old man
The old man who goes skipping along the roadbed.
In a dumb harvest
Passions are locked away, and states of creation are used
    instead, that is to say synonyms are used.

Honey
On the lips of elders is not contenting, so
A firebrand is made. Woman carries it,
She who thought herself good only for bearing children is
    decked out in the lace of fire
And this is exactly the way she wanted it, the trees coming
    to place themselves in her
In a rite of torpor, dust.
A bug carries the elixir
Naked men pray the ground and chew it with their hands
The fire lives

Men are nabbed
She her bonnet half off is sobbing there while the massacre
    yet continues with a terrific thin energy
A silver blaze calms the darkness.

Rest undisturbed on the dry of the beach
Flower
And night stand suddenly sideways to observe your bones
Vixen

Do men later go home
Because we wanted to travel
Under the kettle of trees
We thought the sky would melt to see us
But to tell the truth the air turned to smoke,
We were forced back onto a foul pillow that was another
    place
Or were lost by our comrades
Somewhere between heaven and no place, and were growing
    smaller.
In another place a mysterious mist shot up like a wall, down
    which trickled the tears of our loved ones.
Bananas rotten with their ripeness hung from the leaves, and
    cakes and jewels covered the sand.
But these were not the best men
But there were moments of the others
Seen through indifference, only bare methods
But we can remember them and so we are saved.

A last world moves on the figures;
They are smaller than when we last saw them caring about
    them.
The sky is a giant rocking horse
And of the other things death is a new office building filled
    with modern furniture,

A wise thing, but which has no purpose for us.
Everything is being blown away;
A little horse trots up with a letter in its mouth, which is read
    with eagerness
As we gallop into the flame.

Decoy

We hold these truths to be self-evident:
That ostracism, both political and moral, has
Its place in the twentieth-century scheme of things;
That urban chaos is the problem we have been seeing into
    and seeing into,
For the factory, deadpanned by its very existence into a
Descending code of values, has moved right across the road
    from total financial upheaval
And caught regression head-on. The descending scale does
    not imply
A corresponding deterioration of moral values, punctuated
By acts of corporate vandalism every five years,
Like a bunch of violets pinned to a dress, that knows and
    ignores its own standing.
There is every reason to rejoice with those self-styled prophets
    of commercial disaster, those harbingers of gloom,
Over the imminent lateness of the denouement that,
    advancing slowly, never arrives,
At the same time keeping the door open to a tongue-in-cheek
    attitude on the part of the perpetrators,
The men who sit down to their vast desks on Monday to begin

planning the week's notations, jotting memoranda that take
Invisible form in the air, like flocks of sparrows
Above the city pavements, turning and wheeling aimlessly
But on the average directed by discernible motives.

To sum up: we are fond of plotting itineraries
And our pyramiding memories, alert as dandelion fuzz, dart
    from one pretext to the next
Seeking in occasions new sources of memories, for memory
    is profit
Until the day it spreads out all its accumulations, delta-like,
    on the plain,
For that day no good can come of remembering, and the
    anomalies cancel each other out.
But until then foreshortened memories will keep us going,
    alive, one to the other.

There was never any excuse for this and there need be none,
    perhaps,
For kicking out into the morning, on the wide bed,
Waking far apart on the bed, the two of them:
Husband and wife,
Man and wife

Variations, Calypso and Fugue on a Theme of Ella Wheeler Wilcox

"For the pleasures of the many
May be ofttimes traced to one
As the hand that plants an acorn
Shelters armies from the sun."

And in places where the annual rainfall is .0071 inches
What a pleasure to lie under the tree, to sit, stand, and get up
    under the tree!
Im wunderschönen Monat Mai
The feeling is of never wanting to leave the tree,
Of predominantly peace and relaxation.
Do you step out from under the shade a moment,
It is only to return with renewed expectation, of expectation
    fulfilled.
Insecurity be damned! There is something to all this, that will
    not elude us:
Growing up under the shade of friendly trees, with our
    brothers all around.
And truly, young adulthood was never like this:
Such delight, such consideration, such affirmation in the way
    the day goes 'round together.
Yes, the world goes 'round a good deal faster
When there are highlights on the lips, unspoken and true
    words in the heart,
And the hand keeps brushing away a strand of chestnut hair,
    only to have it fall back into place again.
But all good things must come to an end, and so one must
    move forward
Into the space left by one's conclusions. Is this growing old?
Well, it is a good experience, to divest oneself of some
    tested ideals, some old standbys,
And even finding nothing to put in their place is a good
    experience.
Preparing one, as it does, for the consternation that is to come.
But—and this is the gist of it—what if I dreamed it all,
The branches, the late afternoon sun,
The trusting camaraderie, the love that watered all,
Disappearing promptly down into the roots as it should?
For later in the vast gloom of cities, only there you learn
How the ideas were good only because they had to die,

Leaving you alone and skinless, a drawing by Vesalius.
This is what was meant, and toward which everything directs:
That the tree should shrivel in 120-degree heat, the acorns
Lie around on the worn earth like eyeballs, and the lead
     soldiers shrug and slink off.

So my youth was spent, underneath the trees
I always moved around with perfect ease

I journeyed to Paris at the age of ten
And met many prominent literary men

Gazing at the Alps was quite a sight
I felt the tears flow forth with all their might

A climb to the Acropolis meant a lot to me
I had read the Greek philosophers you see

In the Colosseum I thought my heart would burst
Thinking of all the victims who had been there first

On Mount Ararat's side I began to grow
Remembering the Flood there, so long ago

On the banks of the Ganges I stood in mud
And watched the water light up like blood

The Great Wall of China is really a thrill
It cleaves through the air like a silver pill

It was built by the hand of man for good or ill
Showing what he can do when he decides not to kill

But of all the sights that were seen by me
In the East or West, on land or sea,
The best was the place that is spelled H-O-M-E.

Now that once again I have achieved home
I shall forbear all further urge to roam

There is a hole of truth in the green earth's rug
Once you find it you are as snug as a bug

Maybe some do not like it quite as much as you
That isn't all you're going to do.

You must remember that it is yours
Which is why nobody is sending you flowers

This age-old truth I to thee impart
Act according to the dictates of your art

Because if you don't no one else is going to
And that person isn't likely to be you.

It is the wind that comes afar
It is the truth of the farthest star

In all likelihood you will not need these
So take it easy and learn your ABC's

And trust in the dream that will never come true
'Cause that is the scheme that is best for you
And the gleam that is the most suitable too.

"MAKE MY DREAM COME TRUE." This message, set in 84-point Hobo type, startled in the morning editions of the paper: the old, half-won security troubles the new pause. And with the approach of the holidays, the present is clearly here to stay: the big brass band of its particular moment's consciousness invades the plazas and the narrow alleys. Three-fourths of the houses in this city are on narrow stilts, finer than a girl's wrists: it is largely a question of keeping one's feet dry, and of privacy. In the morning you forget what the punishment was. Probably it was something like eating a pretzel or going into the back yard. Still, you can't tell. These things could be a lot clearer without hurting anybody. But it does not follow that such issues will produce the most dynamic capital gains for you.

Friday. We are   really missing you.

"The most suitable," however, was not the one specially asked for nor the one hanging around the lobby. It was just the one asked after, day after day—what spilled over, claimed by the spillway. The distinction of a dog, of how a dog walks. The thought of a dog walking. No one ever referred to the incident again. The case was officially closed. Maybe there were choruses of silent gratitude, welling up in the spring night like a column of cloud, reaching to the very rafters of the sky— but that was their own business. The point is no ear ever heard them. Thus, the incident, call it by one of its names—choice, conduct, absent-minded frown might be others—came to be not only as though it had never happened, but as though it never *could* have happened. Sealed into the wall of all that season's coming on. And thus, for a mere handful of people— roustabouts and degenerates, most of them—it became the only true version. Nothing else mattered. It was bread by morning and night, the dates falling listlessly from the trees— man, woman, child, festering glistering in a single orb. The reply to "hello."

Pink and purple and blue
The way you used to do

The next two days passed oddly for Peter and Christine, and were among the most absorbing they had ever known. On the one hand, a vast open basin—or sea; on the other a narrow spit of land, terminating in a copse, with a few broken-down outbuildings lying here and there. It made no difference that the bey—b-e-y this time, oriental potentate—had ordained their release, there was this funny feeling that they should always be there, sustained by looks out over the ether, missing Mother and Alan and the others but really quiet, in a kind of activity that offers its own way of life, sunflower chained to the sun. Can it ever be resolved? Or are the forms of a person's thoughts controlled by inexorable laws, as in Dürer's Adam and Eve? So mutually exclusive, and so steep—Himalayas jammed side by side like New York apartment buildings. Oh the blame of it, the decrescendo. My vice is worry. Forget it. The continual splitting up, the ear-shattering volumes of a polar ice-cap breaking up are just what you wanted. You've got it, so shut up.

> The crystal haze
> For days and days

Lots of sleep is an important factor, and rubbing the eyes. Getting off the subway he suddenly felt hungry. He went into one place, a place he knew, and ordered a hamburger and a cup of coffee. He hadn't been in this neighborhood in a long time—not since he was a kid. He used to play stickball in the vacant lot across the street. Sometimes his bunch would get into a fight with some of the older boys, and he'd go home tired and bleeding. Most days were the same though. He'd say "Hi" to the other kids and they'd say "Hi" to him. Nice bunch of guys. Finally he decided to take a turn past the old grade school he'd attended as a kid. It was a rambling structure of yellow brick, now gone in seediness and shabbiness which the late-afternoon shadows mercifully softened. The gravel playground in front was choked with weeds. Large trees and shrubbery would do no harm flanking the main entrance. Time farted.

> The first shock rattles the cruets in their stand,
> The second rips the door from its hinges.

"My dear friend," he said gently," "you said you were Professor Hertz. You must pardon me if I say that the information startles and mystifies me. When you are stronger I have some questions to ask you, if you will be kind enough to answer them."

No one was prepared for the man's answer to that apparently harmless statement.

Weak as he was, Gustavus Hertz raised himself on his elbow. He stared wildly about him, peering fearfully into the shadowy corners of the room.

"I will tell you nothing! Nothing, do you hear?" he shrieked. "Go away! Go away!"

FRANK
LIMA

Primavera

                A mummy
                        crumbling
                                in the bar
my eyes
        empty mirrors
                my kidneys
                        drunken flowers
        Then dawn
                an eyelid
                                                I come to you
                                                        as always
        green
                tired
                        need a shave
                                a bath

                        I stink

unlock the nights
                in jail
                it's spring on the windows

my heart
in a bag
                and some beer
                                        Hi Monkey
                                        I'm home

Inventory—to 100th Street

to John Bernard Myers

In the corner lot
  where they parked
      green banana trucks
     fruits
        palmed in paper straw
I smell
     bedbug & kitchen-cockroach
        summer afternoons
Somewhere
     tailless
        one-eyed cats
    doting in fat garbage cans
       screaming with the stench
     of rice & beans
        strawberry tampax
    piled
      high as the smell
       (I was small & slick)
    the covers tilted
       like the hat of a rock-look wino
         in a deep
          knee-bend nod
       on a beer
         can-street
          Sunday morning

There were always
      time-thick
       empty nights
    of nothing to do
      but listen to the
  ethereal
     (she lived on the top floor)
   I-go-for-more screams

of Charlie pimp's woman
when he beat her
for his good
business principles
joy-pop the block
with morning-talk

I hear the dim iron dawn yawning
(I lived on Third Ave.)
rattle
nights into
Saturday morning
flag-bloomer
eclipses
just before the hunt—
they were as big—
the cats
like jungle bunnies
fierce with fleas & sores

I see window-people
sweating
hanging out of gooey-stick slips
strange
below-the-button drawers
crouched junkies in hallways
with monkey backs
eating cellophane bananas
on a g-string
waiting
for that last bust
Spics with cock-comb
hair fronts
ear-gulping mambo music
eye-lapping peperican flower
crotches

I can hear the streets whispering
                    in the ears of yelping kids

            in the fun-gushing that
                rippled my blood
                            in the pump
        but the kids
                are dying in the lot
            like the tarry-blown feet
                of the rain
                        jingling
                on the rusty-green
                of yesterday's
                        fire-escapes.

Pudgy

I'd swish through the door
                tiptoeing
                    goofed on speedballs
                        with a yellow-jaundice twinkle
                        in my glassy eyes
        you'd be waiting in the kitchen
                perched on a chair
                    like Judge Leibowitz
                        your face mooned
                            wet thighs
                                    at me

Instead
    I'd stash my joints
      in the foodbare freezer
       take five
         throw off my clothes
        drop in bed
          like an empty pebble

I'd stink of
      catting on roofs & basements
        barnacled with sores & pimples
          sweat-starchy socks & greasy underwear
        on my back two weeks
  you looking top-flight
   curlicues of perfume
    running through your
          nesty hair
but I was slimming-off
      in sleep
  a glazed tear on your chubby cheek
   whimpering out
         I found a bag of that stuff
         in the Bible—
         You're never home any more
   aaahhh
     shut up—
        you're lucky I'm home tonight

  and nod back in my bucket
   till the monkey
    creaked my back awake—
     gobble out of bed
      fireman my clothes on
       pistoled out of the house
  after I'd beat you out of your
   carfare & lunch money
    for my morning fix

I took cures & cures & cures
    wrote you letters
        we'll start all over
          never take off again
            clean up for good this trip
           you were my first high
              cop a slave & work for you only
        I'm really getting down in therapy this time

         sign them
                 Your forever
                Loving husband
          P.S. I need commissary
      on a paper napkin
         you wrote
             Dear Liar
                Come home.

O my chocolate princess
        I lay in bed
          smelling of Life Boy soap & tooth paste
          light a stogie & watch the smoke
          unshoe ghost-nude thoughts

           my feet gag my heart
             they're cold.

Mom I'm All Screwed Up

Moth-eyed
  by the neon sign
    I peeped
   at the stiff little worms
     screwing in your head
      spider crabs
       crawled in my ear

With popping antennae ringlets
   you looked like
     a praying mantis
      cold cream & turban
       science fiction gleam
    as real
  as cancer
   spreading
    stuffed-tits-and-rag-guts
      yawning
       brillo-crotch
        that stunk
         all over me
   playing
    Johnny-on-the-pony
      on me
        indoors

The mattress groaned
                    I moaned
            Mom
                I'm no horse
                        you have pimples on your butt
                            your bellybutton droops
                                your boy-pop left
                                    the rose of your hopes
                                        no
                                            no

With lollipop-grin lips
                on my solitaire piece
                    you had no teeth
                        I'm still scaling scabs of
                                hot garlic
                                        slob-kisses

            isn't mamacita's heart going to
                            kiss mom
                                    good night
                                        no
                                            no
                                                no.

Mulata—to Skinny

    And if I love you, we'll fight.
        I'll call you bitch, tack head,
    And curse the gods, Lincoln, and the feminists.
    Beat you—not too hard, in the right places—
        Stuff, I'm a man, no trick!
    Laugh. When you cry like a child, hurt . . .
    Bite, swallow the lump in my throat.

Leave,
    Take the money,
Get my belly full of cheap gin & beer;
Head full of good smoke next to a
Greasy, grinny, lip-stick whore with
    Endless, sympathetic: hum-hum, definitely,
    You're right, baby—
    Amid the gluey mist of reefer,
Cigarette and stale-green cigars,
In bar grey with the laughter of
    Hustlers, junkies, and steady, stink-finger tricks
    Where the sting-scream of the juke-box
Swells the air and makes my brain thick
    With forget-you
    And then,
The scent of your hair, body,
    When you finished cleaning the house—
Gee, I found it so delightfully unpleasant,
Sends the blood screaming through my legs for you,
And explodes the tingling blue bubble I'm in . . .
Homesickness of you begins to seep in,
    Slowly, cruelly till night skulks away
From sour, headachey dawn,
    And if I love you,
I'll wait and beat the ancient seconds of
    Without-you-since-yesterday,
As I stumble, back-bent, fumbling for keys,
Chewing Juicy Fruit,
    Up the squeaky stair, just to drown you,
    Just once more,
    In an ocean of fresh new
    I'm sorries—baby—darling—honey—please—
    And hungry, stale-smoke-liquor kisses,
Gaudy, alien perfumed hugs.
And if I love you, the bitch-hate storm
Passes to the crisp white lap of
    Sheets and pillows,

Where I wander in—up—out—down
    The chestnut thighbone avenue,
Barely touching, panting, my nostrils
    Blowing
On your softsilk body to mine,
A cherry-nostrum wonder—
Experience . . . . . .
                  BANG!
. . . And if I love you, we'll fight again.

The Woman

Today I met my woman in the subway . . . it was winter.
She wore a red coat down to her knees with a black fur collar.
I could only see the back of her head, which was blue because
of the kerchief & the flower she wore. She wasn't facing me.
Her shoes were orange and her stockings black. I went up to
her and said I had found a little part of her in all the women
I had ever known, and I had always loved her. I told her: "We
can make it & crib together . . . . . things won't be too bad . . .
life is a snap!"

Then she turned to me. Her face was sea-brown; her lips
were thick; her eyes were dried wells and the flower in her
hair was plastic. I said to her that I loved her more than ever
now and must know her name because she was what life was
about. She grinned: her teeth were stubs of jade. I kissed her
and sucked her lips. She said any name would do . . . I called
her My Woman and I took her hand. It was like old dried wood
with cracks in it; her knuckles were cold lumps I pressed to
my face.

She unbuttoned her coat. Her body was black and her skin was wrinkled and stuck to her bones like tape. She had no breasts; they were eaten away by cancer I guess. My hands were filled with warm and slippery flesh.

She kicked off her orange shoes and asked me to kiss her feet . . . they were small and her toes were chewed stubs. I said I would kiss them if only she would give me her heart. She said she would in exchange for mine. I told her my heart was young and full, filled with flowers, birds and perfumed tears, but if she wanted it she could have it.

The train came to a sudden stop. It was Spring. I fell away from her across the aisle dreaming of wreaths. She dropped her heart and kicked it over to me. I took it . . . it was a coffin filled with dry worms. I ran off with it, as happy as a faggot in boy's town.

Glycerin

My whistle is senseless
Because my hands are divided
In your direction

The brown flesh of the weather
Rules the loam of August
Like a dart behind you
The sky turns away from
The bayonet into deeper blue

There is a picture in the room
Of a dangerous weapon
But there is much light between us
In variations
The night is carefully preparing

Our legs are energy
The distance is unconscious
There is eight inches of rain
And the circles are hardly warm.

Note

When I arrived last night
It seemed as if some one had
Stolen the oars from the room

I thought of you constantly
I thought of my legs crossed in
The living room and odors
Without illumination

Instead my arrival was like chaos
From another globe
With an augury of bulk and noise
In the midst of some order

This by no means is a poem
Just a letter of thoughts
Or a river in a mirror
Or a sliding shadow that is leaving

I dream of you as huge as night
And contemplate the flames as I always do
Even now the fables are blind and have no regrets

The sun is beginning to set
Like a turban in the west
And I am an ape in half the world.

Poem

Two
Gorillas
In
My
Head

Light
Twelve
Candles
In
My
Head.

News

for Tony and Irma Towle

Today I am in the room watching the sun evaporate.
I recognize *Bathsheba* almost perfectly preserved
In turquoise and jade. Above, it has fangs and a
Field of human teeth the color of red lacquer with a thin
Mouth of green patina.

The islands are still obscure like iron eyes on the
Surface of the sea. On the left, a woman, the triangular
Type gently swelling over the figure of a man. It is Venice,
The city of beautiful cows and gentle rains of dull maroon.
This remarkable head of Man once belonged to a mortuary in
Oran. He was buried so his ideas might be better known.

There are women in the snow with different colors in their
                                                        hair.
They float through my vision much greater than the sky.
Their lines remind me of the sea shore and the reflections
In the rocks, like smoke and ash in a dream. We must never
Become so involved; I am eleven inches high and I can lose
You in a photograph like a rope dancer.

Glucose and sodium bicarbonate: A flowing river after a
                                                hang-over.
My head is set in motion, my arms begin to move and I
                                                can hear.
It must be the day of judgment, the alarm clock has stopped!
I want to be in South America where there is no water to make
Alcohol. My apartment is a jungle. Nothing must move.
We have five seconds to die. I will collapse instead, like spring.

Penicillin

To Harold Krieger

Here I am born a brilliant mistake from infinity
And the idea of existence reminds me of turtles
December is the day of insects in bloom for horoscopes
The duty of love is hiding a corner of flesh
A hot mouth with beautiful teeth

The earth is familiar to me small and beautiful
Like a cup of coffee a running joke in the mornings

I am breathless in this mad race with the butterflies
They encircle my head and choke the air in my chest
To remind me of my body when it snows on finger tips

What becomes of a poet with a common cold? Nothing.
I want to own the air and glitter in a hot shower
Because I have copied everything I have seen.

The Welder

To David Smith

I

He is gliding on her like a block of ice
On an iron stove

I am from a distant hand

He gave her a brick
Cut off her hair
It is falling
She is sinking

I have walked in front of buildings
Put your hand in the sunlight on the maps
Your head in the river   ·
We will live in the sea
Or your hair

Falling
Your lips are red like snow
Indian head   Orizaba   Mexican beer

II

She is leaning like a Russian bird
The early smells
Surrounding like landslides
Her fingers skating near my arm
I am gliding

I once lived in Havana light years ago

III

A thin lamp in my hand
A scrim

The third act is a shadow crossing a child
They are glass
The clown is in love with the lock
On her wrist

She is rushing against my hands
The flowers are sinking in the room like ether

IV

Our bodies are fish trembling in gelatin

I turn my waist
A machine
To the tip of your cheek
A circus

I am living in your stockings
Volcanos

V

A green cigarette
A purple mouth
A factory
Quick
          Safar

VI

My hands are surrounding
Your calendar
A sun flower
One foot across

I turn my waist
A green cigarette

The sea is sinking
With figures in her hair
A purple factory of lead suns
On your cheek

The sharks are melting in
The snow like volcanos

A glacier suffocating a siren.

*JOHN
GIORNO*

Outlaw

A bearded outlaw
who claimed
he was an immortal
descendant
of God
was killed
last night
by the police.

Paratrooper

Mr. Wild wore
a dark, multi-zippered
jump suit,
a white helmet
with goggles
and small red and green
lamps on top.
The main parachute
was harnessed
to his back;
the reserve chute
against his stomach
was a platform
for an illuminated
altimeter.
The instrument
would tell when
he was 2,500 feet

from the ground,
the point
to pull
the ripcord.

She Tasted Death

Bob Friede
was 25 years old,
barely five-feet
eight-inches tall,
and weighed
no more than
135 pounds.
His light-brown hair
was uncombed,
and the pupils
of his blue eyes
were "pinned"—
constricted—
from a shot
of heroin
he had pumped
into himself.
He wore
dirty black dungarees
and a dirty shirt.
He did not look
at all like
a graduate
of Dartmouth College
or like a member

of a rich
and philanthropic
publishing family
or like the beneficiary
of a trust fund
that gave him
an allowance
of $27,000 a year.

She came
from the suburbs,
intelligent
and attractive
and troubled,
from a comfortable home
and a proud family,
and for two years,
with increasing frequency,
she "turned on."
She tasted
marijuana
and amphetamines
and LSD
and heroin,
and then, one day
early this year,
at the age
of 19,
she tasted
death.

Pornographic Poem

Seven Cuban
army officers
in exile
were at me
all night.
Tall,
sleek,
slender
Spanish types
with smooth dark
muscular bodies
and hair
like wet coal
on their heads
and between their legs.
I lost count
of the times
I was fucked
by them
in every conceivable
position.
At one point
they stood
around me
in a circle
and I had
to crawl
from one crotch
to another
sucking
on each cock
until it was hard.
When I got all

seven up
I shivered
looking up
at those erect pricks
all different lengths
and widths
and knowing
that each one
was going up
my ass hole.
Everyone
of them
came
at least twice
and some three times.
Once they put me
on the bed
kneeling,
one fucked me
in the behind,
another
in the mouth,
while I jacked off
one
with each hand
and two
of the others
rubbed
their peckers
on my bare feet
waiting
their turns
to get
into my can.
Just when I thought
they were all spent
two of them

got together
and fucked me
at once.
The positions
we were in
were crazy
but with two
big fat
Cuban cocks
up my ass
at one time
I was
in paradise.

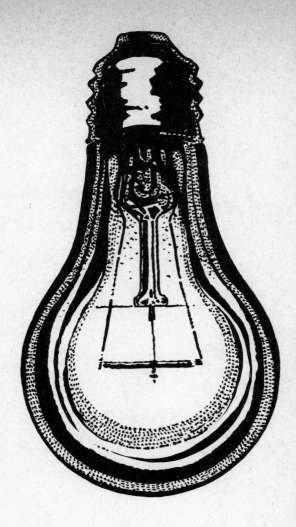

Easy to Grow

1.

Enormous heads,
more than 1 foot across,
produce larger seeds
and more of them
than common sunflowers,
making them particularly desirable
for feeding poultry
and wild birds,
also for tall backgrounds
and unsightly places.

2.

Where winters
are severe
start plants
indoors
for early bloom
or seed outdoors
in late summer.
Plants live
over winter
if given
light straw cover
after ground
is frozen.
In south
and west
plant
in early fall.

3.

Sow the seed
thinly outdoors
after the soil
has become
thoroughly warm.
It is best
to sow
the seed
where the plants
are to bloom,
choosing
a location
where they will
receive
full sun.
Cover
with ¼ inch
of fine soil
and when the seedlings
are 2 to 3 inches tall,
thin out
to stand
1 foot apart
in a row.

4.

A blend
of bright shades
of orange,
gold,
yellow and primrose.
The huge flowers
with gracefully
overlapping petals

bloom from midsummer
to first frost.
Effective
for backgrounds
and lovely
as cut flowers.

5.

Plant
in the spring
after danger
of frost
is past.
Make rows
4 feet apart.
Cover seeds
½ inch deep
and 10 inches apart.
Easy to grow.

Six Selections from
The American Book of the Dead

A stray deer,
pursued by four Newark policemen,
was fatally injured
Wednesday
when it plunged
through the window
of a piano store
at 162 Stuyvesant Avenue
here.

✲

With a brilliant sun causing his tears
to glitter like strange jewels,
the gray-haired, 44-year-old father
stretched one hand toward his son's casket
and shouted: "Look! Andrew—look!"
The 38-year-old mother simultaneously called out:
"My Andrew! Andrew! Andrew, my little boy!"

❀

Astronaut Jim Lovell
flying in Gemini 7
high over Hawaii,
today spotted
a tiny pinpoint
of greenish-blue brilliance
far below.
He successfully "locked on"
for 40 seconds
and sent
the world's first communication
down a laser beam
to earth.

"I've got it," Lovell cried.

❀

A father
accused of shooting
his daughter
between the eyes
while aiming
at a tangerine
balanced on her head
was booked today
on suspicion of murder.

"I was crazy to try it,"
police quoted
the 36-year-old
father,
Eugene,
as saying later.
"I guess I fouled up."

*

The Vivian Beaumont
Theatre
where architects
gracefully balanced
a massive,
slab-like
upper story
on giant columns,
suggesting
a Greek temple
with plate glass,
will be honored
Wednesday

by the Concrete
Industry
Board
of New York.

＊

The swallows
returned at dawn today
to the San Juan Capistrano Mission,
rewarding a crowd of 200 persons
standing vigil for the event.

＊

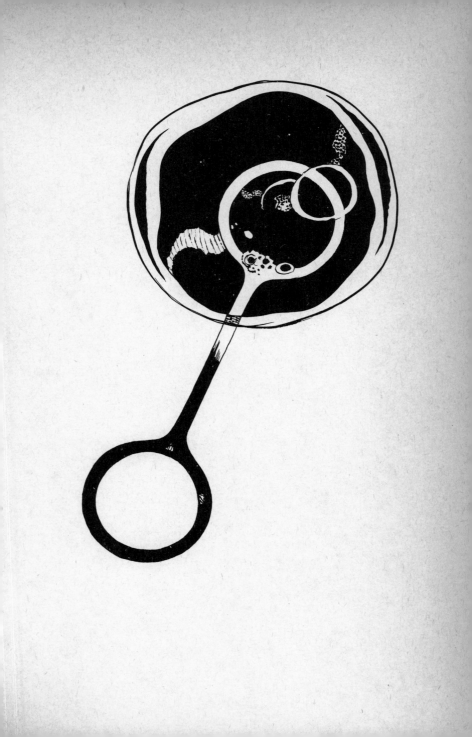

I'm Tired of Being Scared

An unemployed
machinist
An unemployed machinist
who travelled
here
who travelled here
from Georgia
from Georgia 10 days ago
10 days ago
and could not find
a job
and could not find a job
walked
into a police station
walked into a police station
yesterday and said
yesterday
and said:

"I'm tired
of being scared
I'm tired of being scared."

JOSEPH
CERAVOLO

The Wind Is Blowing West

1

I am trying to decide to go swimming,
But the sea looks so calm.
All the other boys have gone in.
I can't decide what to do.

I've been waiting in my tent
Expecting to go in.
Have you forgotten to come down?
Can I escape going in?
I was just coming

I was just going in
But lost my pail

2

A boisterous tide is coming up;
I was just looking at it.
The pail is near me
again. My shoulders have sand on them.

Round the edge of the tide
Is the shore. The shore
Is filled with waves.
They are tin waves.

Boisterous tide coming up.
The tide is getting less.

3

Daytime is not a brain,
Living is not a cricket's song.
Why does light diffuse
As earth turns away from the sun?

I want to give my food
To a stranger. I want
to be taken.
What kind of a face do

I have while leaving?
I'm thinking of my friend.

4

I am trying to go swimming
But the sea looks so calm
All boys are gone
I can't decide what to do

I've been waiting to go
Have you come down?
Can I escape

I am just coming
        Just going in

The Book of Wild Flowers

I can't live blossoming drunk
this story of climbed up
Be world to   any apples!
be anxiously!   Hurrah
the desert   Ream them!   Feed them!
I can't live blossoming drunk
                        oh
chickory sun (to daughters)   dawn
to the yellow stings
to lean   firm fram   up
on   so I knoll   rushing rushing   against. . . . oh hum of dawn
against the knoll

Dangers of the Journey
to the Happy Land

Talk of energy.   Mayan sub-flower
Come to light and feel physically intent to
plasm
        Even if I don't share
        Instance the mother
Talk of energy or stolen from her
mother
        I didn't do that for
nothing   I speak as a wife to the
capsizing   Both are once

Perspire like an autumn wind bakes. Mayan
sub-flowers.
        Am I allowed to go to
the tough section?   That's tough.
            Mayan sub-flowers in
            the shade.

Spring of Work Storm

Down near   "The river
barges"   I looked around me
Where could I wait?

My friend was always
human   I threw myself
beside; I turned the
new head

I took his paw   It
was tender   And kissed
its texture   Like a
bee

Stars were darker
I felt the oil
in the sand

In My Crib

1

Autumn is very   wild though
not like   you   You hear
autumn is
            coming O seasons
Are you like the crib?
Can I understand what I
don't like?   Loneliness is my crib.

The limeland is   not the
            honesty I need

2

Why do we have to
work, fluttering liveliness? I am not
sick. He's looking at me.
Space is between us
fluttering liveliness

3

Autumn is very sad
though not   like you. You
hear autumn   is
coming   O seasons
Are you the crib?   Can I
understand what I
like?   I am sitting
        in my house.

A Story from the Bushmen
(From *Fits of Dawn*)

"Are you an eland?" Yes! Yes!
She ran off to the primeval forest
and there gave birth to an eland
Her husband holding the calf to his
chest ran to the hills: placed
the beautiful child in a fault
which was surrounded by other faults
among the hills
While the child grew, he (the husband)
created all the animals and
ways in which the animals were to
be caught; and also the wind which
was to follow the animals
being hunted
Their child, the eland, had grown horns
and only the sun was more
beautiful than he   But other
sons of the father of the eland crossed
the little calf in his sleep
and killed it because it was more
beautiful than anything they had ever seen.
Their father who had created
all animals tore off the noses of his
sons who had killed without
knowing what they had killed. But later
saying "No I won't do this,"
put their noses back on
          The wife cleaned her pots and
put the blood from her dead
eland son mixed with the fat from
its heart: and stirred, stirred
then sprinkling it about, each drop

became an eland which
ran into the woman with his horns
    See! you have ruined the
    eland: and thousands were made
        And the father ordered the
sons to hunt the elands and to
see whether they could kill one
But Cagn, the father was
in the elands: and none
could be killed:
because they were even faster
than any cloud

Don't Break It

He played with a toy   they bought
candy   She played with a toy
Do not be afraid of the bear
They placed their arms around the bear
Around them the sea
listened but didn't talk   because it
can't talk, neither can stars
which emit for no one   The gods
can't hear because they are not any place
    Friendly the bear embraced them
back.   The zoo is a nice
place to live, you are caged in the zoo
In the zoo is the world. Everyone
chews at a different rate and
stars do not emit
I am waiting for you at the

north entrance
        into the zoo
Going back we looked at the few
plastic clouds into the dark moony
trees

A Song of Autumn

A dog disappears
across a small lake.
It waits for me.
It goes where I want to go.
Begins to wake up the flowers.
So leave us alone.
Because no freedom can choose
between faces and
hours as destroyed as moving,
or cold water in the
sun. I can go out
now and measure
the flies that swing around trees
like doctors around a woman
full of bars and beauties
you could never make free;
Not even if the
flowers turn to moss and
loose sensations for their stems.

Ho Ho Ho Caribou

for Rosemary

I

Leaped at the caribou.
My son looked at the caribou.
The kangaroo leaped on the
fruit tree. I am a white
man and my children
are hungry
which is like paradise.
The doll is sleeping.
It lay down to creep into
the plate.
It was clean and flying.

II

Where you. . . . the axes
are. Why is this home so
hard. So much
like the sent over the
courses below the home
having a porch.

Felt it on my gate in the place
where caribous jumped
over. Where geese sons
and pouches of daughters look at
me and say "I'm hungry
daddy".

III

Not alone in the
gastrous desert. We are looking
at the caribous out in the water
swimming around. We
want to go in the ocean
along the dunes.
Where do we like?
    Like little lice in the sand
we look into a fruit expanse.
Oh the sky is so cold.
We run into the water.
Lice in heaven.

IV

My heel. Ten o'clock the class.
Underwater fish
brush by us. Oh leg
not reaching!
The show is stopping
at the sky to drive in the
truck. Tell us where to
stop and eat. And
drink which comes to us out
in the sand is
                    at a star.
My pants are damp.
Is tonight treating us
but not reaching through the window.

V

Where is that bug going?
Why are your hips
rounded as the sand?
What is jewelry?

Baby sleeps. Sleeping on
the cliff is dangerous.
The television of all voice is
way far behind.
Do we flow nothing?
Where did you follow that bug
to?
   See quick . . . . . . is flying.

VI

Caribou, what have I
done? See how her
heart moves like a little
bug . . . . . . under my thumb.
Throw me deeply.
I am the floes.
Ho ho ho caribou,
light brown and wetness
caribou. I stink and
I know it.
"Screw you! . . . . you're right."

VII

Every one has seen us out
with the caribou but
no one has seen us out in
the car. You passed
beyond us.

We saw your knees
but the other night we
couldn't call you.
You were more far than a
widow feeling you.
Nothing has been terrible.
We are the people who have
been running with
animals.
More than when we run?

VIII

Tell us where o eat to stop and eat.
The diner is never gonna come.
The forest things are passing.
I did drink my milk
like a mother of wolves.
Wolves on the desert
of ice cold love, of
fireproof breasts and the breast
I took like snow.
Following me
I love you
and I fall beyond
and I eat you like a
bow and arrow withering in the
        desert.

IX

No one should be mean.
Making affection and all the green
winters wide awake.
Blubber is desert. Out on

the firm lake, a firm
and aboriginal kiss.
To dance, to hunt, to sing,
no one should be mean.
Not needing these things.

X

Like a flower, little light, you open
and we make believe
we die. We die all around
you like a snake in a
well and we come up out
of the warm well and
are born again out of dry
mammas, nourishing mammas, always
holding you as I
love you and am
revived inside you, but
die in you and am
never born again in
the same place; never
stop!

Fill and Illumined

God created his image.
I love him like the door.
Speak to me now.
Without god there is no god.
Forget everything!

Lie down and be circumscribed
                    and circumcised.
Yet there is no pain.
Yet there is no joy.

Drunken Winter

Oak oak! like like
it then
    cold some wild paddle
so sky then;
flea you say
"geese geese" the boy
June of winter
of again
Oak sky

Route

There were more dirty
    things   They were dirty
Our hair was
long and blind   To eat

Diner is very
   crowded   We have
money   Trucks are parking in
the sun
       Do not feed the
animals   We are
animals   Our cheeks are
   warm   Waitress lips   are kissing
our cheeks   Hurrah!

Wild Provoke of the Endurance Sky

Be uncovered!
Hoe with look life! Sun rises.
Rice of suffering. Dawn
      in mud
this is roof   my friend.
O country   o cotton   drag
of the wild provoke,
there's a thousand years   How are
you growing?
No better to in a stranger.
Shack, village,
          brother,
wild provoke of the endurance sky!

Happiness in the Trees

O height dispersed and head
in sometimes joining
these sleeps. O primitive touch
between fingers and dawn
on the back

You are no more
simple than a cedar tree
whose children change
the interesting earth
and promise to shake her
before the wind blows
        away from you
in the velocity of rest

JIM

BRODEY

Poem

Back at San Francisco Greyhound, leaning
and I'm not thinking or yearning
I'm just leaning. Dreaming of hamburger
with everything. I've always wanted everything!
And this dull terminal wait makes me want
laserbeam duststreet. Poem in apothecary jars
& crumbled barber shop window. White button energy
to get myself out of drug trousers,
like Mayakovsky into revolutionary clouds & off
citystreets, which are wet. Overhead, jet streams vaportrail.
The Gate Fourteen departure air swarms against me,
at vendor comb machine. My movie,
California Fold Out, has collapsed, is
on the cutting room floor.

The Terminal, to take a bus, or eat a cheeseburger
DO YOU REMEMBER THAT DAY OF INDEPENDENCE IN SPELLING?
Eb: A-minus. The membership of stickball nuts
idles at the lap of unfold, and telescope
looking through consciousness of picture-window
and vertical golf field. Transportation terrors
and wastebag sickhoods. Yes! this is the exploration
of one Adulthood. Poems met with mathematics
and Denver bus wrote this scribble of red farmhouse
flattened together ice melons, lunch counter,
the sky over Colorado like Norman Bluhm's "Dunkirk"
soaked with sponges crreeaaking twilight to evening.
the price of my poems is one hamburger!

Expansion to Aveline's

bird is out-to-lunch.

who cannot toll dis-embody-ment on Spirit
rejection arc-
          judge spike or root in cluster,
                               skin:
    feathers, crust

                  we dealt for name

               ✿

        colors lending identity to formula

dust rewinding breath
               closing the valves
on tiny bursts of serum, fluids leaving or being pressed from
                         world,
loose hearts jiggling in their appartical carriges   BROWN
what Lord shall not protect in delirium
                    formula-
gadget bridge to any vision, exuding SENSE

  bird

revolves, men of eggplant   weaken
the ties between

                    teenagers

and their 'birds'.   I am speaking to you
from within VOID. *the* is bird's chair,
our chairs are all pointed
to calm

            the "i" of disinterrupting light,

the squeeze of dreams of tenderness take us
wholly to the bird (wanting, aching to be many)

                who is dream
                is turned downward from light
                tangled on the "otherside"

                    *

        evaporation in ascent

                                        1:7:67

From *Vice, 1966*

throat-to-throat surgery

collections, are loosed. sponges lured
airbottle, small pieces of metal,
chrome
       lifted out
              of carbon.
poem
controls the entire beverage of language,
unsupported, clear plastic stripes

      dislocated
        of handwritten drizzles:
      the elephant
        of chocolate rings,
          slap!

      hand-written, belowship
        in unworldly,
          non-being focus bracket
      sail of unblown
        frescoes, nothing.

            stars

                  gummed

      or parked
      directly away from
      unsupported world

Poem, to Jane Wilson on Television

EVERYTHING, the bridges of small yellow stars, cloud sleds
the orange chair & underneath an irreparable stillness of pavements
moves inducing shoulders on wind,
a room
in which electronic furniture breaks white space
& the arm in paper & woven hair & braided objects
& enormous sunny boughs of string
move soup to nuts to a newly installed shrine of battered paint
& flowers
cooling to isolate particles on woven skin
moving Ava to the valley in which boats dunk their orange
prows
& the stars are submerged in a field of pine
& islands in torn clothes
moving back a light through the chair

your cloud sleds to the moon

1965

Vision of Turtle (One)

writing inside

tiny fists of immense traction
increase volume of daylight, bring
up
the voices.

Otis Redding's "ung" fluttered in from momentary silence

eating & writing
                    w/:
                                        muffins
                                        cut by tableblade axe or wire
                                        steamy plates of boiling, -sizzle,
            slabs of butter   of roostercake,   chinese vegetables
                                        in creamy sauce
                                        or lobster might-have-been

Aretha Franklin on phono, her

soft dixie drive-in shout, walk & flycast to blue.

                                smoke poured over, breadcrumbs,
                                            white drippings,
                                                brown specks.
dip in new bread (rye from Quaker hand), red-greens
                                                            toast
                            boney tunafish mix,
            relish lump & water

                                        eating & shining

Oregano leaks through
    everything.
                            cold italian soup,
                            cold & sour turn of lunch
        last English muffin
                                    on stove tray,
        alone. sit back. &
                            (throwup into
an eternity of chuckling stomach aides)

           count waste & sleep
     nudged by tackles of wavehood floods, I
see
      at once I AM flying, soft
                    flowerous
under-stomach of the turtle of the world. I

drink Alka Selzer

in my sleeping tin pot

                              1967

Rosewood Vision

San Francisco
      gentle in storms of fiery fogbank shower
           & cat-shit.

America
     following America around on a motorcycle in a long cape
          & mask.

quiet imperfect follies at the radiating source
change into heavenly poem energy

      dark
      as testimony in a Shoe

I'm at the desk, in Colorado, in Hollywood
in Mill Valley rainfall (in redwoods)

      humming
      into Michael's lion prose book

          latitudes of strength

jaw-to-jaw, hour-to-hour

the collected poems of Hart Crane.

each poem breaking down to its fantasy,
to a picture depicted in words,
emotions cast-up upon the page:

the poem of the East Indian Plunger.

        dull thuds of oxygen across the bay:

              Marin.

cars on the street below
flashsquiggle across intersection

       roses supported by table
      freshly-aspiring the newly sprayed drops
      of

         * * * * * * * *

      vegetation taking shape—
        (form)
      in this human universe of blurs

the plate caked w: language!

now
   presence is returned,
      the experiencing horizontal world (alive) in sheets
        of shiny energy.

calendar (1938)
unfurls American flag, loneliness
devoured by consciousness:

blossoming-drunk
from a cluster of starry ash

burst into flame
on the silken edge of a life,

I'm called "The Collision"

Poem ("Woke This A.M.")

Woke this A.M.
radio signals in the sunshine at my sleepy door,

covered-over   Hollywood leafy door

warm space notations
a white page of individual statement-goose of imagination

sunny blue pondering flat expanse
of light covering streets (right down to their lawns
& silent station wagon standing in green paint job)

every pore of my flesh
muttering through cold spring air.

Mswaki

msitu mpunga: kibanda kina vitatu vyumba mwezi utatosha
mwezi
      mmoja vyumba viwili na vizuri miwa, mihinogo
mijiti ng'ombe ndege wazuri
                    ndizi   tatu mtumwa haseaw saa meza
      ssali
taa umesomia wasoma ALINGIA break, tiawatoto wangur yupi

       zota mtua wa haki
this is the one long road, twigza zenact
         waupi utamu om MACHUNGWA geni hii nt hasa

book juka vascaa akiniomba, grip tha huwa, pull it under,
                                iwapo
     sikuna rust gas (mypa). yukijis
          with nidizi, were to fall, direction (uchawi)

  mtu

    john has a blue shirt, zamani pal ikuwa na tum
safi hodari bouv
             escapetu puva chauntre rahisu tupu lariat
    kamwa
hasa ice blue tahiti sams goubanda sisti gosh

  the bridge near Kabisa, underneath, the rust, halsipi upesi
some terrible mbalimali, driving past, saliva, concrete kwa na
    aji sema mtu bacon

same
　　　wamekwende zoa, kweko lete chai tussme, pasipo
samei
　　　pas kosa njogo as ch eka shona academy osha bloops tic
sensi
　　　nimanunia: the ditch, salfisha bent over cups tha cabinx
yupi tas yi chauntra
　　　　　　　　sticks
　　　　　　　　　　oa

From *Identikit*

the steamshovel, seen from afar,
on the palm in my lifeline, has been removed,
or stolen pending complete investigation of reader.
it has been vee-toed, showed over nonsleep-
horrorfication of imagination and glowly
frost-bewilderments

to sustainments of the leaning, (as in
"to lean") stomach interims. the nasalpackments
the harrowing noseclip ceremonies, and
heartburst steeped into interleveling mileage
underneath speedometer, reinforced condemtions
of lunar surface of bequeathing.

serenely collapsed junctions, emitting tail-
sections to sunlight to slapped in iron,
the-earth-inside-the-earth, rotating freely
on its pole stack, hard knocks, spitfires,
doorways & cycles & anticipationary volts of the hemp:
reducing speed under tilted from vague reaction

the world (crap!), tonight, lulled
around circumstance, circumference by inclines, living
along with perishing from coughdrops,
amid hundreds of phoney propellants. the
blocks of ice, leaving their bases, noiselessly
and juggled into enlargements of "C" sonic chord.

I stand agog to the torrents of spumming fiber,
amid the gate of Winter's trembling mountain thaw

＊　＊　＊　＊　＊　＊　＊　＊

all these numbers, several are possibly aghast,
lying and dented.　　　the rabbit
elm bird, unusing materials and such turning,
from here
you can rise to enormous heights,
among the mountains in the sub-distance.
only three hangings, heck
the nation dries up.　　　the sandpike
I jump up and down,
sweat, am punctured by frigid disappointments,
and lie heavy, sopping of champagne,
in my overalls,　toboot.　all
streetsigns point to it, the bricks
scraped off the subconscious.　airholes
in rusted kinks of tailspin screaming for radios.
the upholstery,
fell
carved off backseat of the poem motor

＊　＊　＊　＊　＊　＊　＊　＊

a white sheet of paper
offered the coachman at the cost of several lives. I
have to tell
a band how many ribbons popped from the stomach
of having to cross the border.　minutes to cross from outside

Spring! woven in somehow.   I get the sun.   I get the rain.
I am who is always against, or agushed beside
a ship which has been slipped into the payment paving
stones on the roost.   today, I
thought eaten kinks were unwashed long enough. we
are punched, unpacked for moments to lift-off!   the
mushrooms have been swallowed.   "the mushrooms
of many-colored thunderstorm of integral consciousness"
filled with air.   the workmen
unpacking their instruments of construction, to
complete
the amber reststation
of stoking
ashes, in, great clusters
of dark sperm bombs, where
they fell
(not in breath-units)
underneath the crushed ground of heavy upholstery.

*   *   *   *   *   *   *

first   range   through
New York factory constellations of evening planet
tug & haze-turn   blossoms & aerial arrangements
H_2SO_4 boiling   clouds
            optical   worldly bidden of crank shrill
optical bearing 7 point one 5:   beige
        range   calculate height-scuffle
I digress (!)   yellow orange white
        the energy
                    of human sex-pressure
                    lifting "spermworks",
                    intimate shining beast

never in no tenderness of computa
or robot:
counterpart has terminal-thrust
(into or from)
no, not ever by machine
touched or named
to Earth?   Myself?   no doubt
faded earthworm nebulary.

I rise, Bladen in focus,
sanity huge man-hum, multi-gumba stock,
clear three inclined
structures or structure
of concrete and table beneath wood,
I'm sliding.
Being dominates New York
or walking later underneath Tompkins Square trees,
a slight blare of museum in forehead
& sit on isolated swing-board,
I suddenly wonder his Space!
the word: Majesty
which is no illusion, but radiance:
Bladen, & New York

❖ ❖ ❖ ❖ ❖ ❖ ❖ ❖

"the: the"

    matter-of-factness,   plural
    stated into weariness

    are leaving   materials
    blank, at these shift of speed

    tell you of -ing endings
    to the line & letter.   silver concrete

tightening corner strap.
the shake, the rusty restlessness

of talk you: mixes with chemicals
raw chunks of icy, mammalian

consciousness dispelled.   with
an unnoticed splash of the materials.

and, descent into you-you   my-my
ACID   bedecked muffler couch   first

burn   white cotillion bursts bamboo
rowboat nuptial inclines "a" off el"a"stic"a"l

foams none beheld to reaction   dot-boy
revolves a once rectumistic joyous reminder

1966

Homeward Bound

as flames are drawn from the scuttle of turbines' roar,
the gypsy life processes from wads of bullets in plaster
where in darkness can I wander from, to be homeward
      returning the poet, impolite among iambics,
to play with such a tangled living in breath out there.
O as feelings lift the line from the page
& throw the words like knives into a passing sideshow,
point-blank, the black rings of tape measure
mark off my despaire (audible) among the blurs
of lassoed sonatas in static air.

the shrubs multiply ranked & freckly sweat
miles of stretched palpitating flares are lit to amble,
I am meadow sweet in the torn & bloodied shirt
of my fathers, and the orangepeel sword-hilt
of my countrymen, who went this way, homeward
    bound
to blow the dust from my family crest, my cup.

1:3:67

*JOHN
PERREAULT*

Boomerang

Why is everything I do in my life like a boomerang?
I throw the paper airplane out the window
and the wind sends it back.
I spit against the wind.

You bought me a fur boomerang for my birthday.
I hate you now. You are so rich.
You are such a consumer.
And I hate your boomerang.
But I can't throw it away.
It keeps coming back and hitting me
in the back of the head.

In a rooming house I lived in once
I knew a boy who had a handmade boomerang.
It was fifteen inches long.
What a beautiful gigantic handmade boomerang!
Every Sunday he practiced throwing it away,
in Central Park, by that sailboat lake.

People always talked to him and followed him.
Everybody wanted to see his boomerang.

. . . But boomerangs are dangerous.
When you fool around with boomerangs
you have to know what you're doing.

Congratulations, incidently, on the birth
of your brand new baby boy boomerang.
How amazing
that no matter where you leave him
in the morning he is always
in that basket, on your doorstep.

I had a dream about a boomerang race.
I lost.

But do I really know what it means?
Do I know what anything means?

I kiss your amorous aluminum boomerang
and the edges are so sharp
my tongue gets sliced,
my words get sliced
and my lips are able to smile in two directions.

And I think it would be nice to own a boomerang store.
Glass boomerangs.
Australian aborigine boomerangs.
Rubber safety boomerangs.
Regulation boomerangs for boomerang contests.
And even
automatic talking doll boomerangs.

But why is everything I do in my life like a boomerang?
I throw away my life
and my life comes back.

The Metaphysical Paintings

1. *The Enigma of Arrival*

We are nude beneath our costumes
as in the false myths we have been forced
to memorize
and there is a mistake in your eyes.

We are not aware that at last
the last official has arrived.

Since the sky is false
I tell you falsely of my absence of feelings.

And you stand there staring down
counting the toes
that peek from out beneath
the hem of your theatrical robe.

2. *The Melancholy of An Afternoon*

The two of us make love
in the form of identical vegetables,
in shade,
oblivious to noise
and vanishing parades,
oblivious to flags
or that which tries to harm us
from the top of the industrial tower.

3. *A Grand Tour*

A mistake. It is a tower and not a tour
that does not crumble.
And we will make arrangements now
to take a guided tour of this tower
and soon find out that there are no stairs
and when you get to the top
there is no view.

4. *Departure of a Friend*

I see you lying on a candy-striped towel
face-down,
reading a book of small pictures,
a book about Michelangelo.

Goodbye.

But the time is wrong.
We discover that the train has already left.

It is a false goodbye.
Our shadows become one long shadow
that touches a pool.

Why is it that the railroad station is at times
so quiet? So empty?

5. *Nostalgia for the Infinite*

I will miss your loose-leaf notebooks
and your figs.
I will miss your calculated mistakes
and the pictures you sometimes liked to take.

We are still saying goodbye.
Same time. Same light. Same railroad
station.

Are you about to enter this different tower?
Are you about to become another?
A railroad engineer or a policeman?
Are you about to vanish?

6. *Love Song*

O how I have loved you,
O great and classical world,
the way a child loves his father;
but now the time has come
to escape your betrayal.

Only the geometry of a green sphere.
Only the surgery upon a puff of smoke
can save us from more primitive forms
of this industrial sadness!

7. *Mystery and Melancholy of a Street*

At that time of day when guardian angels
have retired for the day,
as a small girl with a hoop,
I am menaced by the shadow of a guardian angel.

My substance is of shadow.

I let this angel follow me into the bowels
of an empty moving van;
I am raped by the sun.

I take off my shoes.

I wipe the sweat from his brow
with the hem of my Communion dress.

8. *The Enigma of Fate*

One move of the invisible queen,
one shout from the top of the stack,
one hand for the future,
and the spilling of seed.

One road through the labyrinth,
one turn to the left,
and the spilling of seed.

9. *Melancholy of an Autumn Afternoon*

We are still saying goodbye.

10. *The Naval Barracks*

At an early age, I was expelled
from the Naval Academy.
How well I remember those long Euclidian walks
into the sunset
at the end of a geometrical day.

Accumulations! Neat debris!
The magic of an ammunition dump!

The false perspective of my souvenirs
returns to haunt me.

Patient arrangements of frustrations.
Private mottos.
Public demonstrations of the insatiable
and the obvious!

11. *Purity of a Dream*

The purity of my dream can only be maintained
at the expense of the present.

I make a billboard in celebration
of our new found spring.
All the buildings start walking up the highway
to look at it.
They crowd around.

Now that I have made this billboard,
I can carry your picture around in my brain
in a small green suitcase
as I fall asleep
on that small train puffing into the distance.

12. *Masks*

I like this room. I like this movie of myself.
This view of the antiseptic town.

You are my mask
and I am yours.

Empty!

13. *Hector and Andromache*

At last we are together. Our dreams like our shadows
have at last combined.
We observe the higher mathematics
of our consistent departure.

We interfuse.

The geometry of our inter-relationship
has become like the demolished city
and the preserved city—

a train station that arrows towards
a new release of political crime,
a vertical of deliverence.

Readymade

The Venus Fly Trap

1) A Beautiful Plant!

Its dark green leaves form a low symmetrical rosette. Each leaf is tipped with a lovely pink trap.

2) Eats Flies And Insects!

Each pink trap contains a bit of nectar. It is this color and sweetness which attracts the unsuspecting insect. Once he enters the trap, it snaps shut. Digestive juices then dissolve him.

3) Eats Flies and Insects!

When the insect has been completely absorbed, the trap reopens and prettily awaits another morsel.

4) A Beautiful Plant!

Traps will bite *at*—but not *off*—"more than they can chew."

5) Feed It Raw Beef!

If there are no insects in your house, you can feed the traps tiny slivers of raw beef. The plant will thrive on such food.

6) Instructive For Children!

Youngsters especially will enjoy growing these exotic plants.
And if, somehow, you can convey the thought that many of
life's alluring enticements can prove to be traps, you will
have made a priceless investment!

7) Easy To Grow!

They thrive in glass containers and develop traps in three to
four weeks. They will beautify any room in your house.

The Nude Republic

I dream of nude policemen investigating
dangerous phone calls, dark wharfs;
cops on horseback like Lady Godivas
but with tattoos and no long hair.

Nudity as opposed to nakedness:
early linoleum morning without any clothes
in a chilly room
or late at night when the steam goes off.

Your nudity is a smooth surprise
like an animal emerging from a large lake,
a luke warm lake,
a barge on land at sunrise.

To gamble with this absence of defense
is to be modest in the face of depravity.
I am against this kind of peekaboo.
I myself am a professional nudist.
Most people, however, are born nude.

Do policemen ever make love?
Does the mayor have pubic hair?
Do "bandits" wheeze?

I lift up the gown of the Statue of Liberty
and beneath her folds and beams
even the Statue of Liberty is nude.

Your nudity is a lightning flash, a flash
in the dark,
a flash in the pan,
a glimpse of myself.

I shoot the breeze.
I shoot the ceiling and I shoot the sun.

I walk around the streets of this nude republic
with my clothes thrown off,
horsing around, a rabbit with my ears erect,
my whiskers in the breeze.

High

Gliding over Hialeah, we wave goodbye
to that hierarchy of false palm trees,
swaying, swaying like purple hydra.
I am so tired of playing hide and seek

with that giraffe named Hiawatha.
He is such a hierophant!
He has no sense of personal hygiene.

There's the Hialeah County High School!
There's the place we held High Mass
in the cabin of the blue hydroplane!

We are driving along the highway,
our height exposed,
when alongside stops a highwayman.
"Hi," he says.
"Do you know the way to the hide-out? "
It was high noon.

Phillip who is very High Church
thinks it highly amusing
that our friends, the highwaymen,
are disciples of Heidegger.

"Hi," says Phillip,
"I have just returned from Heidelberg
and am on my way to Haiphong."

What sky-high prices!
What highway robbery!
We refuse to buy the hypodermic needles.
Instead, returning to our hide-a-way bed,
we take out our maps of Hyannis Port.

(My old aunt speaks High German
and whenever she goes out hiking
comes back roaring in high gear,
smelling like a fresh hydrangea.)

Hymie, our beautiful chauffeur,
drops the hibiscus bulbs
all over the highly polished high-boy
and all over my aunt, Her Highness,
who is sitting in her brand new high chair.

High in the pale blue sky,
high-tension wires begin to buzz.

I love the soothing music of Haydn
and rousing Operetta Highlights
over my gigantic hi-fi.

In preparation for my high-wire act
we are all drinking high-balls.
We are avoiding the glances of Hiawatha.
He claims to be a pure Hiberian.
But we know, because of the hyphen,
he, like all of us, is just a hybrid.

We steal an Oldsmobile covered with hieroglyphics
and after filling it with high-test gasoline
at high tide
have the hydraulic brakes tested.

Hy, a new arrival, says:
"The water is over the high water mark!"

We do the Highland Fling.
We listen to Jascha Heifetz,
and we watch the beautiful Hyades.

There's the Hialeah Free Public Library!
There's the place we had high tea
with Sylvia and that hired man!
O what endless Hydrox cookies!

Friends

Friends are always those
who are
by virtue of their closeness
the farthest.

That is why at this late stage, aiming, as it were,
to make my fame,
I find myself in love with my enemies.

The stone rolls over. The faucet leaks.
My brain leaks too
—all over the furniture.

Any jackass that sits in a butterfly chair
can pretend he's flying.
The reverse is more difficult.

Friends are always those
who are
by virtue of their friendship
the least friendly.

It is the language that hurts.
It is the meaning that falls down flat
and leaves an allergy of excuses
and blurr.

My life gets shorter
but there are still so many
things left now
that I must not do.

It is the length. The length of my nose, the length
of my coat,
the length of this poem,
that is the substance of this shortness.

Disguised

Disguised as my next door neighbor,
I spend my afternoons tasting various kinds
of chocolate bon-bons.

Here inside my sub-leased two and a half room
apartment not big enough
for more than one person
there are only string beans left.

I would rather be eating breakfast in bed
with a dead poodle
or a sleeping Chinese gangster.

It is already four o'clock and nothing has been accomplished.
I would rather be out of doors, looking at clouds.

Disguised as my next door neighbor's boy friend,
I visit her every Tuesday and Thursday at midnight.
But I don't bring her flowers
and I don't bring her pills.

No One in Particular

I am not anyone in particular.
A chewing-gum wrapper.
A streetlight.

Still, somehow I manage to exist.
And as each day starts
I manage to leave my nice warm bed,
feeling that perhaps today
something beautiful will happen.

It never does.
This in itself is beautiful.

I am not anyone in particular.
A philosophical shoe.
A sheet of paper.

Perhaps I am lying.
(Another one of my very bad habits.)
If so,
at least no one can be hurt
by such slight deceptions.

Talk

So as I was saying to you
yesterday,
this rainy season (October)
is very good for the mahogany
lumber.
So too is the snow season.

Your lap, however,
disappears when you stand up
to wave goodbye
to the afternoon as it sinks
into the ocean.

Today I am the tomorrow
of your longitude.
And Wednesday I shall be
the road that covers
your stove, your dove,
your smile.

Balloon? He (you) watches
the balloon
rise up.
First it is balloon-size
and then beachball, basketball,
baseball-size,
and then it is the size of a green pea.

The sky becomes a bowl of soup,
becomes something else
to be looked upon at leisure
with great pleasure.

Is it you? Is it you (me)
that I spot through my range-finder
coming down Main Street,
grinning from ear to ear?

No. It is only the dog of your
Irish sea captain,
foaming.

No. It is only the sunlight
hitting the gas truck
rear-view mirror
as it turns to the right on
Elm Street.

Forty Years Ago

When my house is raped
and they search through all the rooms,
they find a bedroom covered with moss.

They find that my furniture is hideous
and that I have no taste.
But they can't find me.

Forty years ago my peace was named
and all of my errors proscribed
and forty years ago
the sun was just as bright
as the sun seems now.

And in the attic they find a road map
completely unmarked.

They find several campsites, several bikes.
But they can't find me.

Foolish traffic, ambulance haste,
the war continues in a different place
but the armies have become invisible.

Forty years ago my well was poisoned
and my wisdom once more was postponed
and forty years ago
the sun was just as bright
as the sun seems now.

Inside my life they find a weapon
and in my lungs a tree.
And in my heart
they discover a mirror.
But they can't find me.

BILL
BERKSON

October

I

It's odd to have a separate month. It
escapes the year, it is not only cold, it is warm
and loving like a death grip on a willing knee. The
Indians have a name for it, they call it:
"Summer!" The tepees shake in the blast like roosters
at dawn. Everything is special to them,
the colorful ones.

II

Somehow the housewife does not seem gentle.
Is she angry because her husband likes October?
Is it snow bleeds softly from her shoes?
The nest-eggs have captured her,
but April rises from her bed.

III

"The beggars are upon us!" cried Chester.

Ribbons. Headlands. More ribbons. And:
"Strangers are rare here."

The October wind . . . nests

IV

Why do I think October is beautiful?
It is not, is not beautiful.
                        But then
what is there to hold one's interest
between the various drifts of a day's

work, but to search out the differences—
                    the window and grate—
but it is not, is not
beautiful.

        V

I think your face is beautiful, the way it is
close to my face, and I think you are the real
October with your transparence and the stone
of your words as they pass, as I do not hear them.

                                                1960

February

        I

From a window high over the factory
James looked out on the traffic
of red cars in which the boys were driving
home from work on a day like July 4th that was warm and
        sunny
and everyone sang the new song that Silas had written
and argued over the demolitions that had occurred
when the city fathers had planned a monument
to James' father in honor of the scourge
from which he had saved them in '46. "He
was a real villain, that one" they had said
"and now that he's dead he's given a place to be feared
as much as the old cemetery that stretches itself fearfully
from the edge of the factory to the edge of town
in grey and brown bumps over beer cans and clover"

(When the schoolhouse was moved the blackboard was
    cracked
The dogs that had sat on the library steps toppled
and the crowd hustled Mr. Reese the librarian out of the
    building
—"an unfit man for a town with such monuments"—
and when they sang the song that had made Silas famous
              "Lumm Lumm a leeky
              My heart's in the garbage
              So summer is over
              Just wait till you're my age
              like gum in the clover
              Lumm Lumm a leeky
              Lu Lu a Lu"
a balloon filled with water high over the city let go
and covered the millinery and all the machinery with "de
    l'eau"
as the star reporter called it emptying out his hat and crying
    a little)

Ah how does one cry "a little" to see a tie flapping in the
    February light!
(The balloon when all had left drifted westward) and
    what is missed
is the bank of oddity that a young thing growing affords
    everything
and when it lets go (as youth does like a rubber band
    stretched across a flame)
you can see the stamps in the stamp book and the magazines
    in the rack
and the people at the track stand up and shout to one
    another again and again
"It's happened again! Yippee! Let's go to the beach or buy
    some candy bars
and pretend it's happening to us too, For it did you know it
    once did"

So James took a pencil from the desk
and erased "right now" from where he had written it on the
    pad
and replaced it with "sometimes" and sat back
to look at the newspaper which had caught fire
from the cigarette he had left burning in an ashtray on the
    desk
"Good old desk" he said "Good old desk"

and outside Silas was mowing the grass
which surrounded the factory offices in a three-foot wide
    rectangular pattern
(the building's perimeter was 450 yards around)

    II

On the February night James (who had not seen Maggie
since the night of the bonfire that the kids had set
in protest against the monument which was soon to reach
    completion
((they had marched up and down Baltic Avenue with torches
    and with ribbons
of brown and olive-drab—the factory company's colors
    —across their chests
and had proclaimed as mayor of the old town and leader of
    the REVOLUTIONARY
ANTI-FAME FOUNDATION a hooded figure (((later
    identified as Mr. Reese)))
who rode in a buckboard covered with green paint
    ((("symbolizing the general
hue of the movement"))) and with the letters X Y and Z
    ((("symbolizing the end
of the general tyranny . . . in short *sic semper tyrannus*")))
    and who later was hanged
for blowing up the railroad depot "with a dose of explosive

transparent liquid in a bottle once containing seltzer or
possibly gin" and who felt the pangs of a lost love while
passing STROUD'S DRUGSTORE on the way to the bank
(((Maggie who was supposed to have left had simply dyed
her hair from its color of autumn leaves to that of
     chameleons placed against bricks such as those
which decorated the factory and the bank and the schoolhouse
     and had married
Mr. Reese in a moment of passion and interest in what
     appeared a promising
career of civic innovation)))))) saw Mrs. Reese come out of
     the jailhouse

III

From a window high up near the ceiling
Mr. Reese looked out on the sky
which offered to flyers that night
a murky and threatening ceiling
nearing zero which was strange for a February night
when we expect the color of sky
to be sky-blue and to shine on the ceiling through the night
to protect our sleep, and the dreams we see on the ceiling
are not ghosts at all but something of ourselves come in from
     the sky—

"Oh jailhouse window!" thought Mr. Reese
"it is like the old song Silas wrote that ended
'When the Western & Pacific siren comes through my window
I do weep' Oh whither Maggie! Oh whither this old town!"
     Just then
he heard Maggie's voice coming through the window:
"Goodnight, James" he heard and then "Goodnight, Mrs.
     Reese"

IV

Silas heard Maggie's voice coming through the window
"That must be Mrs. Reese" he thought "What a wonderful
woman!"
He sat back and began to write "The Voice That Through The
Window Comes
So Soft" a song which would be sung later on on bicycles
bumping through the grey
of the old cemetery and on picnics at The Field and while
standing on the corner
by the luncheonette where the boys watched Mrs. Reese on
her way to buy
some soap or needles and thread or milk and eggs or shoes
and socks or fertilizer
for the flowers about the grave of Mr. Reese whose last words
when the mob had come
were "I'm not sure right now but I think she will remember
sometimes"
At his desk Silas wept as he wrote the last line
"And when those tears are smiling through the mud"

Out on the terrace of the hotel
James and Billie were dancing the conga
Billie asked "Do you love me James?"
"I don't know right now" James replied
"Do you ever think of going somewhere else" countered Billie
"Sometimes" James replied "but not right now"

Just then the old steamboat crossed the lake
bearing Maggie on her way "to visit relatives"
Over the cemetery an old dog was howling
"Maggie! Maggie! Lu Lu a Lu"
and in the middle of the square the pigeons were picking
up crumbs in the dark February wind

1960

Russian New Year

for Norman Bluhm

Now trouble comes between the forest's selves,
And smoke spreads to pools in which we stroke
Our several smirks, but the accident will not happen
For someone has stolen the apples
And someone else has "come full circle", picked at the fog.
Snow settled in the meetinghouse. "I love you as my own
        dear jailbird.
Come back to me when Brooklyn is over. I'll be waiting."
Shame sneaks in the birches—they put the fire out.
The distance is too much again, gone armies kicking the dust—
Are these horses we count as pets?

It is whiter than your face the afternoon I opened your
                                        icebox.
You are entitled to it, wisdom which bores us but may excite
        you—
Mixing the poison I breathe and leave behind me
By the glint the pillows made on the horizon, unwinding
        silences—
                        Her dress raised above her ears
She lay livid among the party favors. She closed her
Umbrella.   It is a black that turned the carousel.
It is a bucket into which night has fallen. It is no fun.
Light and happy, the canyon.

My days are eaten slowly.
I sit on the fluorescent seat.
The pricks incorporate all jolly in the lurch.
All revolutions have been betrayed
By slush of feeling,
For the rose will shoot from the ground

As buildings stick in the wind and stop it a minute.
Someone will remain
Of life that rides into the trees and grows up,
A steamy stormer of storms.

Are you different from that shelter you
Built for knives? On the sidewalk, sapphires;
On the fifth floor, fungus.
I have put on the crimson face of awakeness you lent me.
What is that heart-shaped object that thaws your fingers?
It is a glove and in it a fist.

The shore slides out of the sea,
Strength
To live privately beneath the noise
Of the sandbar budging—
A rose above the eagle—it was there,
Tattooed. Sumac above us. Pain
Spliced and ticked away by waiting
In the chair beneath which paste is dripping
And a match is lit.
From today on it is sleep I leave you on the slow
Waterfall. One cannot even escape light
On the night's horizon; you believe that is pleasant,
Don't you? Or, when it snows, heat remains
In the cupboard—that too? . . . Thunder?
With you it is always the inconspicuous tear;
With me it is never anything but money—
Still we are the same,
Sideways

1960

Christmas Eve

for Vincent Warren

Behind the black watertower
under the grey
of the sky that feeds it
smoke speeds to where a pigeon
spreads its wings

This is no great feat
Cold pushes out its lust
We walk we drink we cast
our giggling insults
                Would you please
leave the 2.50 you owe me
I would rather not talk about it
just now   Money bores me   I would like
to visit someone who will stay
in bed all day   A forest is rising
heartily in my head
              not a civilized park
I think it would be nice this "new
moral odor" no it would not mean
"everything marching to its tomb"
             The watertower
watches over us   Is there someone
you would like to invite   no one.

1961

Ivesiana

When it sank it thundered.
So it's dark, dark and lonely.
In winter, when the weather goes down,
You had better come closer to hear her sing,
For to miss it is ice.
You age in oceans of lint.
Putting everything at your disposal,
It will do no worse.
A snake in the grass, yes

Lucinda could be a good girl, everybody said,
But the evergreens fell, and
What could it mean to her—she
Who was nearly perfect? David had amnesia.
Would the children get out of it,
And, then, gracefully?
Mr. Reiger took it hard, the boys
Stuttering, learning their own tongues.
His only concern in the world makes him dangerous
Yet inviting. He speaks
The pliant truths. Food stuffs. Rents.

And wrote *Willow Ways*:

"Lucinda Lewis Prescott, born of a nerve
In the far country, taught them all:
Four presidents, and rodeo champion!
She has a perfect record,
The clouds are in accord. But the Ford
That drives her to the station drives
An old ache from her flesh.

Oh where will Lucinda Lewis Prescott find
Her well deserved rest?"

In the pines, the bedclothes think the ocean
A swell dish corporation illuminate midriffs.
But you are so lonely, a single footprint.
Just four months ago for a start I thought . . .
Then it became like crystal
And exploded in our ears.
Mr. Reiger nodded and sighed.
We moved on.
"I could cover you with a Rangoon blanket,
But you wouldn't stay. You always want
To be boss." All at once she knew.

When Napoleon's armies headed home,
The hemisphere settled like a broken shoe.
"The goodness of this lady and her sons
Make us thirsty for the battle,
But we have no guns, our defenses
Are out of order, so we retreat,
But will return to place a loaf of bread
Upon this spot, so we won't be forgotten!"

"Lady, our defense,
Make the willows safe for birds;
Furnish the air from which we'll drink
The goodness of your words."

I will put my hand on your knee.
I feel I am at the service of history,
Life and Opinions.
The leaves.
The schoolgirl drops the clover
And dust covers it. The sun. The moon.
You were bred to be an example.

A rectangle encloses you.
The library burns.
We stopped for a drink
and stayed a year.

1964

Surabaja

Are you coming or going? The opening
          pages of a scream may thin your blood
but you are a champion of equidistant parts
                              the spreading eagle of death
          would you like to die in my arms
          don't worry I will die too you
          will never be alone but then
                         and then I take off your hat
                    to look a glistening cobra in the eye
               grand the destroyers
                         are shuddering in the Caribbean
               you wouldn't vote a lover of yours
                         into Congress would you?
                    You would die first wouldn't you
               Later history will praise you
                         for being succinct

11.2.62

Strawberry Blond

Knock on the forehead
there, there beach nothings
saw, reef, watery exchanges
of lift O's not followed by
anything turf   True?
(ringlet) (broadcast
in wing around immortal portraits, are they?
the be-hanged cunieform
money sniff)

rung-ticker
a refusing passion
for burn on brief nail!
under the sheets a lip
hits the sulfur stripe
phone book being a strength
(a) (its Irish sequel)
(b) paralysis   mustard
back on the office
the rifting phlox
looks and wins
what cabinet of ruse and doubt
                gives him the possibility of love and
honor through her eyes, a doubtful sign of rain showing up on
the backporch on which they swang out the years of his death
and on which she sat like an expectant mother—that was
                                unblackened!

Chocolate
tiding over the grey embittered court

he prayed for his marriage
as was the modern custom
                well, Stupid!   as if promiscuity were
                                finding tics

What am I indicting that heads off gardenia?
    green green stove-pipe
    arm around me stalk wherein pegged a
                  relax bus
    globule of often-candelabra in the cake
    of soap she saw her face a few times
    feather in his blood
    margin   eat shit if
    in it old waterhole
    rub-down, shower, and melted

    in her sleep

    he woke up

    they went off   socks

1961

Blind Geronimo

I said: "The flowers in this light are beautiful
and different from the scorched-earth policies of recent
                        artifact."

This was a game of odds-and-evens for handling the new,
the radio tubes blazing where you put the laughter.
"Otherworldly" was your argument,
but the kitchen laughed too, so knowledgable
that happy contestant of sour dour pretensions
to zombiehood, putting it all back

for a while into caring, or full, like
some bloke's got cancer from simple cause.
It's only the stolen hour that delights you,
and over, driving to the country,
taking on more than you can handle.

So those old habits still bear watching.
The lights are on the blink again.
Children and dogs carry on in your mind,
though tomorrow they too 'll disappear,
yawning through the backyard and appointments and rain.
Time to bring my own complaints into the fore,
as if you had always known it would turn out that way.

1965

Out There

Rain and the thought of rain:

but reality won't make itself over for the fact that you sense
                                        something—won't
                        in fact wax miraculous,
though it's right—that responsibility belongs to the outer
                                ether whose fragments
                        are gummed together
so as only to be analyzable *in toto*. So
the man who cries "Marvellous!" is only human, putting out
                                his sign. But the ether
                doesn't need this sign.

cloudburst to terrace to drainpipe backalley sewage to river
to sea—

No need, my love, to complain.

Quieting down.
Going on inside.

1967

Stanky

A simple weight attached
and a circle raised alone
(no strings)
to a great height.
Then let fall.
There is nothing missing,
and the space around is all.

The space you see is all.

7.5.68

Oscar

        Shouldn't I ask
because I am taken in that way
how all in all you in your horrible thing
I listening to the other side, deserve
one glory
and the earth the muck
what future technique
culls
from all that teaching heart

you are bold risky frisky
to see that law
I think even hidden in glad
or opposite counter stuff
runs through the whole of
the whole of the whole the
whole other whole

                    6.20.68

Sound from Leopardi

To the me of my own making, seeing I am here,
I'd speak a gesture sudden and precise
to show Time's inconsiderateness where
to head in, and Death, that busboy,

his vanity of speed.
But always here and before me,
the rude lullaby: "Sleep, Mighty Mouth; sleep and die."

And I would like to leave,
or bring other words and worlds miles closer
as a wakeful company, and out of plain talk spin
Truth and Falsehood, the greatest weapons in the world.

5.18.68

Leave Cancelled

What we need is a great big vegetable farm!
Every vegetable to stand up and be counted,
and all the farmers to love one another
in their solid, lazy dreams.

Then this would be all knowledge,
all hygiene, and the plants we feel,
and it comes down to Boy and Dad and kind
balloons of sight. The sky's neat sweep,

the irrational, would be this butterfly dish
where lovely woman stacks her arms.
And no war. And no walls. And commerce a thing laughed of,
told at midnight to sleepy grand-children whose laughter

tears down the crazy, irregular rows.
All instinct to nag or abuse
shot into oblivious braces. The clean come forth, the filthy,
and all is over forgetting and time turned advantageous.

A single image!

Sheer speed wakes us. A man chortles in the speaker's ear,
but this is not the one you must do business with—
he is so unimportant! his eyelids flutter, and he sells
you something, but it is new

from un-disuse.
Go on,
take the avenue and run, and I'll
be in Scotland before you.

8.22.68

"Blue Is the Hero . . .

leading with his chin, though bristling
with military honor, camp and *ora pro nobis,* rolling out
the red carpet of chance on a plea
that you might give others a front-row seat:
Lady, take off your hat. So extra-special . . .
Other times, it would be a roof-garden
like the one Rauschenberg has,
being no Nebuchadnezzar of the bush,
or, standing on your head,

feeling the earth has "hung" a lawn
and these dogs have come to bite you "where it hurts"—
I wonder if they've really caught the scent,
which is a poor memory in our Symbolist ears
of what it must have been like to read *The Hound
of the Baskervilles* for the first time in 1899—
oh truly modern and amused and wrong, before the cold
and the dry vermouth and everybody started
wearing sweaters, taking pills. I confess
to a certain yearning in my genes for those trips,
tonics of the drawn shade and rumpled bed,
the Albergo delle Palme in Palermo, instead
of hanging on the curb, learning to love each
latest gem "fantastic!" as the lights go out all over the
Flatiron Building, which leaves the moon, sufficiently
fa so la, and the clouds
disentangle a perfect Mondrian, though gray,
to which you give nodding assent, somewhat true;
you are that helicopter, primping for the climb
into whose bed of historical certainty? the fuel
streaming down the sides, like fun in the sun, air in the air.

9.15.68

Call It Goofus

Foot still, and nothing to go,
or the Japanese see ghosts,
each man in his own way walking.
I go see an old friend become
a new husband, a student girl

draws something looks like wood, her
friends call it ugly, I buy it, she
gives it to me—
                    what's the difference?
I see maple trees on Maple Avenue,
Ravel sit down "his arms like matchsticks" . . .
Know who I was?
That fellow sitting here thinking,
minutes ago.

8.16.68

MICHAEL
BROWNSTEIN

War

You can't spend all day staring into the sea, however
As if it were your favorite book
Until an especially coddled page detaches itself
From the light, floating toward you through the grove
At the edge of which Hernando stands with the batallion
Bent to the amplification of his will, louder
And louder as it hums among the spindles
Of the fruit and garden trees. You *can*
Spend the day clearing out the porch and
Cease staring into that sea because it is
An unenlightening sea, furtively complex like an icy bath
With the washrag salesman's daughter. Laughter.
Wind ruffling the skirts of the citrus trees.
Soldiers are whining to seal off this port.

        Oppose these soldiers.
Ignore them if they take your picture off
The wall . . . They take your picture from the wall
And walk through. You however are eating a pear
And don't need to see them down the rest
Of the hall to the door, out into the street
And crabbing, disappear into a fault. A busy town goes up.
You are not a traffic signal. But as it changes
A cop revolves, seriously intent on detaining you.
He doesn't care about the traffic, adding up behind you
Like a stifled thought, because he is whispering
Softly near your ear. The sun sinks along
His nightstick, all things relaxing into silence
Except for that stifled thought.

Pounds and Ounces

Here come Charles and Madeleina my child
India, Guerdon, Macao, Church and Bessarabia
A minute to the left of the knee
Louise, Esso, Essene and gold Dolores of the caves
To rest on views from the point
You begins to get up and leave (pounce)

Yes, he should be blank in the parka by now
Most of the guests are, already receiving visits
You might walk over once more
Then he reads you out

Dirty and graceful but a bit too tall
Clean and distrustful but short little
Noreen and Barley are scrambling out of the Jumna to you
They think they are going to wave

"No Thought"

Egg   Spoon   Throat   Vista

Teeth   Glint   Spokes

Stagger   Choke

(Pearl)

Upon the pyramid I have returned to you
Ready to go. Dolores is folding her last slip in the mouth
"Pack clothes, write batter and taste and see"
New spoons and fresh marching spoons
Baby Egypt damp with glee

Nations

In the history of the nations
There is a great reserve
Of the other nations. All of us
Live on the table of silence, like Spaniards.
Other nations, for the noisy
As well. Spain and silence
Of this all-wide-awake world
Silence each other: that is why we can draw
Our human being generations
From time to time flow
In a hard line to the noise
Of the next, sometimes interrupted by an age
And fill it with some girls and chairs.

Noise and general loudness contribute
To omens: the silent flight of wooden birds
The inward figurations of Mobile
And nature could easily relax in the human world
Whole nations spilling into the loud places
Of history, Martin and Diane starting
To unravel again. Diane, tell your mother
Nations are the mahogany of the great reserve
Spain, South, Siam
Little tables around the world.

Waitress

Waitress
You bring my food, I give you money
I am full of food now and ready to go
But you still have to wait

Lily Flower

Lily flower
The telephone is ringing but you do not hear it
Because you are different
You have your own telephone

Behind the Wheel

Deep well corporals ride alongside listen
and ride   Small fork motions
for the magazine shell
pink developing Guadalupe under young
springing off the board to feel
the warm systems   Erased the second time
you remember her strong intelligent hands
past the verge of speaking to you

Careens off the bore

We are now ready set squat
lips wearing a shoreline resolve to
talk again in laps   oil and sand blue
from hard riding   Chiefs weighted
some of the more plausible contours
her bookish ass ascends   "my daughter
very beautiful bare-legged and brown"
breasts brimming over into listen
and talk   On and off   A big Latin band
moistens its reeds and leaves backstage
"very beautiful   thirty silver blankets
around thirty silver minds"   That fits so close
rain pours from the manuscript

               Clears up
A few extreme fine clouds   The sun
is rising along the alveolar ridge
like trying to establish in a valley the exact line
separating the two hills on either side
And then establishing it   it thrives
it works   you roll down the window
the girl parachutes onto the plain

Driving through Belgium

An old woman is cutting carnations
    and to them she seems like an old woman
Who cuts carnations: perfumes press to get her
    between the pages of *Poetry* magazine—

And because nothing interrupts her
    she cuts one too many, and heads of esteem for
Gentlefolk fall away in crumble sadness
    past the shifting potholes of our day

Against the Grain

. . . either, over the shoulder enjoy leaning. Don't
Touch it. Skyway pumpkins lounge
Rocking beside me but I thrive straight
Away. Large early centers blur off. (Look, Johnny
See the Indians wearing their Maine blankets
Lobster smoke disappearing between the
Tree. Don't know it over.) looking over.

Would you turn it down a quarter inch?
Now I rest between the teeth of
Courage, silence, gold. I pass the lines
Painted below the pilot's "Otto" window
Like a lake going up from gasoline
To drowning above the clouds (of starch beauty).
Probing a border the police sighs
The trestle agh agh agh over the train late
Mathematics pass hot trees. Dutch door. Don't move.

I wander the banks and Wanda was.

Sounds not so much mingle curtains
Yellow against green and then of course
The perfect right green has against yellow
In the dusty white pod against here
Beside your wife who is too sinuous and tall

To be a real Dutch . . . little men in pocket charms
Made her. She travels . . . an easy window
Sunlight on Bavarian cottage window
In natural southern Bavaria. Large blue
Against the Pittsburgh sky. Sky.
Summer in the pedigree under Moscow's dome.

Take the summer.

She delivers a folded postcard to the hill.
Mingling feeds rain and forest an afterthought
As I am planning to feed astronomy
To the turkeys here for a year
(Light snows over the eighty mile ear)
Pure ground plum stew chugging up to the door.

Early in the morning it quieted down somewhere
Among the flamingos. Suddenly I realized this was because
They had no place to sit. I shaved for a while in the mirror
And crawling out of the tent (take the summer) I crawled
Out of the tent and talked over to the shore
Most of the people were eating already.

Clean & Clear

At the little window is the tiny hand
At the big window is the giant hand
And both are open

A small opening but everyone is working
What is the worker doing? he is working
For light is the ensemble of the colors

The immense sun dries
At the window a tiny hand is drawing
No one on the street because his drawing is divan

One six blocks up
Six blocks to the corner, to the seven
The eight, the giant hand

Is filling the block with light
Six blocks in one corner
One giant in another

At the little window the tiny hand
Is no longer at the giant hand
The tiny hand is on the knob

Lost in a Corridor of Power

The growth of raw power brings you to one knee
Like the Prince (any of our people) before Snow White

Before snow white the beavers pause
Their dish of prunes
Petroleum-colored beside them

The them
And the us go off
To play   Explosions   Polite Applause

"I'm going to watch here a few minutes then
when there's a slight pause unconscious
like a pause for breath I'll slowly TIP
onto the glass floor dozens of brass pans
and kettles these dishes all this crockery
I have in young cardboard box ready & waiting"

SMASH*

If that were on a tape recorder (and it is)
I know you would hear an infitesimal sort of
Highly charged hush in the pause
Just split second before the smash hit

It would manifest as a slight suction, drop in pressure:

SUCK   S U C K   *
                              *SMASH***

That hush would feel delicious.
But in the tight demanding realm of
The conclusion of an idea, the hush
Would have to be the 7 Dwarfs, given Snow White
And the footprints of the Prince.

Given snow white and the footprints of the beavers
The hunter drew one conclusion across
The gleaming flat expanse........

Gasoline stains soak into your snow
Drained off to the pumps behind your back
Tall grass is waving you on.
"I guess we better wipe our shields and scramble
Back into the seat and push off."

Children, It's Time

The day I was born
The birds stopped singing

The day I was born
The birds started singing

Take your pick
While I take mine

I Am Not the Constant Reader

Do you read
Yes, and it is a form of life
So long as I forget what's that I'm reading

Yet gradually not to read at all, you respond
Is when you get up enough for roll-call

But I do not believe in roll-call
Although I see it
Through a round window flanked by plants
In China long ago

*

She has no need for old men
To water her plants   They are asked to dismiss
Themselves from the service and wander disconsolate
Like a broken radio ejected from the filling station
Serving northern Quebec

*

The men and women inhabiting northern Quebec
Speak a brand of French poorly burnt
Into the hide   They read very little, but constantly
Like the British mouldering on a protectorate

This particular British is grading papers
Sent to him from far across the sea
Concerning life in an attempted passage
From ancient history

Big City

As I walk down NYC I wonder into the ground
Glee a short road across my face
To a sparrow observing from the cool agenda
Of the wind in the breeze . . . Not to fox this into
Something you just won't be able to grip
On your way downtown into work. "Let it be clear and
                                        distinct
Like the shoulder a French cook knows will serve four."

Knows might serve for

Always uncertain as to who will surface from the tube
Gripping a bath towel for me too. Which I wouldn't throw in
To your prevaricating poet's face because you won't be a poet
Or a painter spidery preacheress or candlestick maker
Though actually I can see you as the last.   For like the sky
I have no physical third eye, psychically
Beside the point and valid as music: Now.

Do pigeons ever get headaches
Pecking as they do at the hard cement
Which is really a sidewalk? This and a dozen others
The sweatered infant asks. He is precocious of course
And steps on your stone. You offer him a palm and now
He's yowling, and his mother isn't girl anymore
Idly paused for limousine on green leaved street.
Do you lean toward the girl? Such is the tragedy by
Ugly inference of urban motherhood.

But we are all young mothers though only some show it
Barely struck by the hammer of joy.
A truck robs the eye of cobbles
But you could be looking at the truck
And keep looking, until big letters appear on one side

Something Else

Three students
sitting in the shade
a boy and two girls
studying French.

A plane drones.
One of the girls picks herself up
walks across the grass
behind her dormitory
in the sunlight.........
To her dormitory.

The other two continue reading

Students teachers and gardeners
cross the field in small
loose figures, some talking
at various times
or alone
. . . to a class or a workroom
or to eat something
or take a nap

It's twenty of three
in 1951
I am eight years old
and somewhere else

When I am 18 I will be here

(When I am 28 I will be many)

Spiral Landscape

Suddenly I was in the act of soaping my head
At the public bath Paris rue St. Antoine
When from behind me a door no doubt slammed
Into noises of other people (the sundry people)

With just as much right to live as me
On the edge of achieving their cleanliness

While then and there a plan came into view—
We are all to rise up and multiply to choke
In a manner of speaking entire worlds of strife
A perspective of cleanliness inside the nut
A door slammed enough to shake the Foundation
The research chemists & their assistants dropped
Their tubes instantly trailing lab coats lather talent
And in one pleasing swarm descended the stairs to
Exit and collect aimlessly in the great greens
A towering gardener sketches on his knees

Without the right to breathe exactly like me

But now I had a clan in mind —
For clean as a thistle the lab men yet grow slack
And wheeze a day behind the news like pioneers
Words that die into a ravenous ear
Tying up the surprise of the good life
In a greasy phial of consternation

At that a giant clam surfaced in my thought
It therefore also monopolized my life and forced me
Out of the now dank clammy water and after dryness
To exit and the sunny street and I no longer walk alone
Though I am moving in a unique position

Now I cross the human face

All this would be in living color
To satisfy your sight until you move

Kites

"Do you realize how high kites are," he said. He let go of his red and yellow striped Hong Kong kite and turned to his wife. They had been married.

Their names were Andre and Favor. Names come up on kites. The names were hers if they were favorite. There was one special big kite, neon, that Andre loved to fly, plugged in. Unfortunately Andre soon saw a symbol in the kite, and wanted to run it through his thought, then not minding flying it. Much like a wounded animal, or the Arabs as a race, he came to see everything at a tantalizing distance. To him, Favor became touched with meaning in the same way and as high up as a kite. It was a shock that travelled far to snap, like his tongue when it was her *mind* among other things that rang with pleasure, her fine long leg spreading out as he let out the string and the *wind* took her far away.

Much like a wounded admiral he came to treasure that wind. But when he lets go he is floating, propped up on the starboard deck of an important schooner, sinking fast from the hole in his side. He raises himself painful and slow, naturally, to the railing. Favor hands him a string and he begins to speak. "Sails," he manages at last, and Favor runs over to look way up at the sails. She returns to Andre with the sails.

No Empty Hands

I am kind to my neighbors
The light in the wall catches you
We play ball for a while
Kindness the little girl appears
She plays for a while too and then leaves
The dossier of another as she goes
At the edge of the pool with the guys

*ED
SANDERS*

Elm Fuck Poem

in to the oily crotch
place dick

go up
kiss the grey-white tree
fondle the crotch
sweet juice there flowing

to which you place the tongue
to suck the pulse of the

Hamadryad

come into the cool grey
bark the hair-grey color of Persephone

how difficult it is
to be fucked
in the volcano!

ahhhhh but how sweet
the elm tree's rheuming
grey bark made black
by the viscid
fluid flowing

out of the branches—

I place my dick
in the tight in-fold of the elm V
-heat of the summer-

fuck till the come drift
down thru the bark-furrows
   fuck thru the warm afternoon
     sperm steams in the sun

      birds in the branches
       sun shines thru
        seed steam
         thru

wing of butterfly
   wetting its
    furry fluttering tips

I have given myself to the elm
I have soaked the dryad's shawl
What a wonderful world,
a palace of gentle sexual aggression.

   Tree baby!
   how I love to rim
   your bark slits
   kiss the leaves
   above your dripping
   elm crotch oozing
   at the base

     I place my penis
    over the mish

      & slowly start to
    shove it deeper
encasing it in to deep deep elm snatch

   Let me sing

of a need to fuck
at once the tousled leaf elm
place the lingam
in wet tree oil—
slowly o lovely lady,
such care & kindness
for soft petzel-flesh
-as when rabbit nose
snoozles a carrot-
but give it thrill jabs,
give it to her.

worship the Dryad
fill her with foaming
Though she desire the
smoky megaphallus
give her the pink-purple lob prick
under the elm boughs
heavy in the summer wind
to fill all holes,

lovely longing lone lingam
plugging the vastness.

Do you feel it, pretty humans,
& do you know

a tree-twat is as good as
a buttock
& the elm branch is the dryad's breast.

feb-mar 1966

Soft-Man 1

Soft-man is denizen
of Rot City,
Soft-man is goosed in the dread Hustle
& torted in the line sickness,
Soft-man is a groove-man
& Soft-man
is of th' cocoon . . . .

Deep o deep is the cunt
whence I came
huge is the cunt whence
I came,   but Death,   Death,
        is a good tight fuck . . . .

Dreamed I that
Death & I   flooded thru into each other
The wet wings of my penis crossed
but my spirit was lost &
drowned above in the crotch-lake . . . .

Cunt-breast-voidofcrotch-eye-ear-mind!
o schism which I approach across the Belly
o slit in th' moan depths & darkness
o slice in the great flank up-river from Peace Eye
o lake of lights berserk & beaming in the vastness
o lake which is viscid in the mish schism

crotch that pisses out stars
crotch-lake that ends itself in our death
crotch that deaths itself in our end
crotch-lake that is a phantom paste,

Soft-man
    is OUTIS, no-one,
and is a blurr of confusion
    as when a door is opened
revealing a party within
    & a man lurches out
        coughing puke.

I

Soft-Man 3

Bending back with the horror of it,
Tearing with squid-teeth &
Sucking with squid-suction,
The Machine burping out paste,
The horror of it, the ooziness,
A machine faggot sucking in the bloated All,
& the Control Team there behind It,
Setting the panel for Hive worship & Blob system . . .

    Now in the plexus
we are real bomb children

        among the flowers
    & all in the air is death
    & we are as plants
      staggered by an excess
        of nitrogen,

flowers all, cusping our genitalia
in the time-fount
beaming in the petal-frenzy
balling in the shriek-node;

No turning back/no rewrite/no voice!
in this poem, now, not to look
nor creep back to the stark horror.
Oh when the blasts occur
and our eyes become liquid in the heat,
let us lift our melted eyes unto the lord

Copulation-Products slide along groove channels;
And that is a statement post-natum.
Anubis was the guard of the gods;
The Board votes:
Turn control reset dials to Blob Culture.

The Pilgrimage

There is nothing on the
wet morning grass
not even a mound
to mark the grave.
I have started in the
shade of the walnut
trees & walked
up the hill
to make my
proskynesis at thy altar

o daughter of Ra
how elaborately the morning kisses
this hill with its teeth
I faint under the
magic rays of the sun
which devour the ground.
Just to the south
by the wilted flowers
of a grave newly sodded
the rain has forced
a hole that goes
deep down down down to the only Acheron
first finger then stick
I poke to find its end
THERE IS NO END
no tears Ed
worship her with
the flowers you brought
build her a monument of flowers
prothesis of words
in the only adoratio possible.
When I wake I find
the flowers fallen
in the shape
of an arm & a hand!
a flower-glyph on the grave lawn!

The hand lies westward
& the arm of flowers points
from the East
where Barque of the Morn
floats forth
with bundles of sun-arms
for Ra's benefaction
with benevolent arms of light

hands out of the disc
peace fingers groping
all the transeminentia
-gathered together-
swathed in Ra

The Arms Arms of Ra
dipping in benemagnificence
hook-hands cusping in gentleness
smooth arms from the disc
over the cemetery
the raincrow at peace now
storm over, wet dew, hot sun
only the wet grave newly sodded
drawing my Eye down
to Acheron Acheron of All
at the end of the rain tube
under the brown bronze lid
& above the satin
Acheron Acheron Acheron

July 1964

Sheep-Fuck Poem

The ba ba lanolin fur-ears

                    sex
                Trembling Lamb
            where I enter the
                    matted meat

    of the trembly sheep
    the cunt warm
            & woman sized
    offered by the lamb
    which is surely the
    lamb of god, the
    lamb of the Trembling Flank;
    & the bucking & sighing
    when the prick sputs
    the hot come
                into loins
    & the lamb looks back
    with her eye
            & glazes me
    in the freak-beams
    & we are oily & atremble
      in the lanolin glaze
            frenzy morning field
                hay hidden
                    fuck-lamb
            day in bloom torrent.

                    nov 61-feb 62

from Aphrodite
    one could get, say
      a blow job:
she was,
    as Hesiod says
      a "lover of dicks"

For Sergeant Fetta

During our encounters
It was sometimes hard to keep from
puking in your face

one didn't expect anything of you
you climbing servile police creep—
with your servile clumsy rhetoric
& your sniveling attitude
toward senile sexual abstractions.

The lovers of tomorrow
will jack off on your grave
& use your head stone for a fuck pillow

& I AM going to suck
your mother's purpling
           clitoris
rolling all over the
        marble
          floors

of heaven.

                5.11.67

I don't give
a pound of
mule mucous
for any fucking
"Transformation Symbolism
in the Eucharist"

if you can't dance to it
or if it isn't dope
or possessed of a dick-sized
aperture

then shit on it

The Cemetery Plot of Ed Sanders
Shall Consist of:

a) a trophy case for Grail chasers

b) the jack off slab

c) the temple of the sneak fuck

d) the inscription chamber: thank you mom & dad

e) the fane of nonviolence

I walked by the pond
and picked pretty flowers

the frogs croaked by the
lily
    & the cow
    stood silent &
    ready for the snuff

    is everything
    a blind spew?

    can the heart
    hope for the
    "limpid pools"
    of every sentimental
    picture of an eyeball?

    am I insane?

How slowly I sucked off
the mummy—
tasting the 2000 year
spices—attended by jackals
& horus-hawks
           ape-god
    & freak bird
               I do not know
               I should not
               mention I
who am not
or never more
than flickers of
a new lit piece
of punk, was.

The direct retinal Flood
rather than your fucking Archetypes

The open Space
for the spray of the Brain

Mind as a waterstick
in the raging Nile
gauging the harvest

Brainvalves torn in the WORD STREAM
BRAIN leaking in the cosmos

We enter the FLOOD

From *Toe Queen Poems*

for John Ashbery

1.

Good God!!
a 3 & ½ inch bony
scraggle-nailed toe
waggled menacingly off his foot

but Till
soon sucked it
into a muscular spasm
and left it
limply
dangling off his foot:

in the History of Western Civilization
this was the 1st
securities analyst
to ever
have a

toe-gasm

2.

dragged to her cell
in the Tombs

by the toe
Tillie was pissed
to say the least

"if you motherfuckers fuck up my ring toe
i'll sue your ass,
you creeps!!"

until her case came up
           Till spent
                all day
                     in her cell
     with her feet propped up
           on the bars
                practicing

           dick-grabbing

3.

                "I shall return!"

                     it was
                     Tillie the Toe
                     hauled off the
                          set at
                T. Square
                     caught
                     foot-fucking
                          thru a seat
                at the
                          Apollo theatre!

& before the cop
           could whack her out
                     she flicked her foot
                          out the squad
                          car window

                     to wave goodbye

"I shall return dearies
           and don't you motherfuck forget it!!!"

PETER

SCHJELDAHL

Release

My life has been tedious
Confused and occasionally quite nasty
And hysterical
But I have never deliberately said anything
Without a lot of sincerity

My disagreements with myself are misunderstandings
Counterbalanced by a numbed optimism

I rarely hold opinions for longer than a few hours

Finishing a poem leaves me in despair
But I also make mild, intriguing collages
That fascinate me by their separateness

Sometimes I would like to kill someone
But I guess all I really want is to grab them and shake them
(No one in particular)

I feel best when alone and walking
Quite tall, agile, and slightly vicious
Also with a penetrating gaze for everything

I am currently suspicious of everyone
And regard nothing very highly
I do this out of a certain humility

To the National Arts Council

Hello America let's tell the truth!
Robert Lowell is the least distinguished poet alive.
And that's just a sample
Of what it's going to be like now that us poets are in charge
Of poetry, at last (it's all we ever wanted, really,
But nobody would believe it), and from now on if
You want literature you'll have to come to us
And ask for it, *nicely,* and with a ready *checkbook,*
And even so we may "not wish to be disturbed"—
Inconvenient, you bet, but then literature
Has always been an inconvenient business, especially
Since the 18th Century, and even in America
Our favorite country! It's true, we like it here,
So don't tell us to go back to Russia
Or Parnassus—those places mean nothing to us.
We'd prefer even Gary, or Mississippi, or
The Mojave Desert, where at least there are people
Speaking, seven days a week, the language we propose
To glorify; and if you like that, fine!
But you won't, or not much, because we reserve the right
To be the "conscience" of America, without (mind
You) being overly anguished about it, which means
We'll say embarrassing things habitually, not giving
A shit for "national unity" (the only "national unity" for us
Is the national unity of poetry, which is meaningless
But only us poets know *in what way* meaningless).
So you'd best get set to like it or lump it when I tell you,
Fellow Americans, that we are citizens of the stupidest
"Imperial power" in all history, still fighting that mean
And furtive little war for the Philippine Islands.
How can you ever get over, Americans,
That Aguinaldo once thought we were wonderful?
He couldn't believe it when we started butchering his men,

And now the whole world believes it only too well!
And only us American poets still see the pure heart
That beats in America, and profess it
While having none of its blockhead "policies." We're tired
Of being schizophrenic! Let America be schizophrenic for a
                                                    change!
And if this nation should go down in flames, that's
Terrible! but there in the rubble you'd find us, not
Learning Chinese, but correcting our American cadences,
And if that isn't patriotism, America, *what is?*

Citizen

No, I would not like to meet Bob Dylan

Yes, I would welcome the opportunity
To visit Vienna in the company
Of a cultured and relatively pro-American
Resident of that city

What could I say to Bob Dylan?
I would have to "invent" something—ugh!

To the native of Vienna I would say, To throw
The "curve ball" hold it thusly, along
The seams, and "snap" your wrist at the moment
Of delivery   If you are successful, the batter
Should first lean back, then flail wildly
At your accurate pitch, giving you a sense of satisfaction
Understandable in any language

Life Studies

1.

Hours stand around the clock
To be "struck"; yes, our time gets a little shorter
And we have a new bump or contusion or
"Hard knock" or two to show

2.

The cars stop and start up again
They are full of gas and shiny and
Terribly expensive   Look! in one second
Those two will crash, seriously injuring both drivers

3.

We turn the pages of the book of poems
But our pleasure is short-lived: the poems
Are by a terrible poet   For this
We have paid two dollars and forty-five cents!

4.

Two boys are robbing a young man
One of them holds a blade against his throat
While the other takes his billfold and overcoat and umbrella
Now they hit him in the stomach with the umbrella

5.

A game of chess is in progress
How precise and powerful the movement of the pieces is!
White is sure to mate in two moves
But no, he has bungled it

6.

Our life is like that game of chess, being
Bungled by someone   However, on the whole
It is quite intricate and entertaining
How do you explain this?

Smiles

I am smiling tonight not really
At anything, just a simple explanatory
Kind of smile, with maybe a trace of "apologetic"
The way a person smiles to say "Go away,
I mean love me!" and "You'll never really know me, will you?"
But you're not even looking at me now
So how could it be that?

The answer of course is it could be anything
And probably is, it's so cold out
I bought several things today, e.g. two distinct brands
Of roach spray, out of no necessity
Save gratitude's, at those stores' being so warm
And stop-in-able   And of course no one was at home
                                        anywhere
But maybe aimlessly out of doors like me, or just possibly
In bed with each other, I like to think

Women and men smile differently, you know
A woman smiles to tell you what she's wise to or that she's
About to go insane and a man to tell you how he feels
Or wants to, which is usually "superior"
But not really, I mean nobody's *that* ambitious   Are they?

So summer and winter we keep on keeping our distance
Only to make it all the more subtle and exciting
As opposed to merely useful, the way
A policeman's smile is a keepsake
And that of a "foreigner," spectacular and odd
Your smile is warm and inconvenient
Like a sweater with no hole for the head to come out of

I wouldn't mind this cold so much if my breath
Were not forever freezing on my mustache
As I went steaming, moist with life, down Eighth Street
Grimacing to break the seal

Fear

Into the nexus a webbed hand
Gathers and distributes
It's Death
If you like
The distribution goes on
In the darkness outside the light
Of mind, this the origin of the myth

The hand reaches for us to shake
A samovar steams somewhere
In the vicinity of memory
Of original chill winds
Trembling resumes, and again we
Remember the shriek
Of the frail ballerina in the book

White Country

It's 10 a.m. we got the jolly roger's gold
It looks like clay but it's really gold
Useful gold with ice cubes that are really leather water
You see: a gold pin keeps the fish's eye peeled

Now here is our recipe for gold-bug eye stew
I'm shaking they're cooking me too fast!
Now they beat up my little heart!

In the hand is a spoon that is a bone-spoon
We want to put it back in the hand
We want it to gong on the soft underbelly of china
Our own jolly roger lullaby

To chase the midgets back to their slogan
Cut them off when they're on the telephone
And chase them little bastards back to their slogan
Simmer lightly in my spoon
And chase the little midgets back to their slogan
Chase the little the etc. it's 10 a.m.

Bonner's Ferry

At the bonfire
She turns to him
And he is no longer there
Snap crackle pop
It's no longer enough
These lingering trances

The bathtub is engaging
As all scenes of self-love
Go by like a bunny
Sobbing "The Battle Hymn of the Republic"

Then I read a book
On the map of California
It was very funny
So I moved north
With monster intelligence

You sweep and sweep
But there is always at least one germ around
O mortals

Che Guevara Is Dead

I am sorry that Che Guevara is dead.
His death suddenly makes the world a little less
Various,
            though not less interesting; for the world

Can never be less than *totally* interesting,
As I think Che Guevara would have agreed
Who was totally interesting to me
In a mild way I like to remember.

Have you noticed how the existence of an interesting man
Makes you feel more interesting too?   Death, that great
Underliner, has made me notice this today.

The Page of Illustrations

Hills fill the first of twelve frames,
Called "hills"; surely imaginary, so awkward!
And shaped as if to attract something predatory,
Something that would find their polypy appearance
Promising of a rare succulence,
Devoutly to be wished. For us, the open doors,
One framed at a certain distance by the other,
Prove more exciting to that penchant for speculation
That has got us into this in the first place. The doors
(Which seem only barely to be doors at all) please
In precisely the way one might have expected:
They present a state of affairs already familiar, yet begin
To pose a solution to confusions we may be little aware of,
But confusions nonetheless real (between general concept
And particular case, perhaps, if this is not too obvious
To require comment). The particular case here, of all
These representations, points
In a direction we may not wish always to follow
But must, once having credited, recognize as absolute,
Scarcely subject to whatever we may or may not
Want to make of it. It's almost discouraging, to have come
                                        even so far

In concentration, to have bent even this much of ourselves,
Only to the conclusion that any conclusion
Is probably unnecessary. But to press on
Is what we must do; so to the next panel: Three desks,
Crazily grouped, the clumsiness of their depiction
Reflecting at once on the arbitrarity inherent
In any depiction and, what seems to intrinsically follow,
On the benign imprecision of the idea by which
We recognize the subject—benign because, after all, we do
Recognize the subject, whereas (for example) a chimpanzee
Might see only a white surface on which black lines, simply,
Are present—this the genius peculiar to the chimp, its
Inimitable *virtu*, parallel to man's unique capacity for finding,
In any number of "unrelated" objects, evidence
Of the same thing; and as the monkey is driven (somehow)
                                        perilously
Through the trees, so is man (for instance us) prodded always
Onto the thin ice of seemingly pointless speculation,
Be it even in solitude, and though it provoke
Only the chimera of a dubious confusion—"success," anyway,
                                        hardly
Enters the question, except by way of anathema. The dialectic,
Indeed, most enthralls me just here, drawing me as by a
                                        potent
Fascination to the notion of failure in the course of
Strenuous expenditure; failure so far from anything the world
Might find useful, it presumes to a nearly pure definition
Of "human" endeavor. ("I tried!" is a beautiful figure
If true, which it so seldom is!) Thus do I approach, on behalf
Even of all mankind, the page of illustrations—"mankind"
Which everybody understands and no one has ever seen
(So used are we to rationalizing on the level of metaphor
That which I, here in my special sense,
Insist on accepting as a kind of applicable dream).

Starting from where we left off, we find more desks, then
Some stools; in fact a veritable "stool series", three panels

In each of which are three stools—twice three!
Could it be important, this exact redundance?
A clue, perhaps, to something the artist had in mind?
Looking ahead, indeed, we find a third representation of
       three desks—
Yet there are only two "open door" panels (something I'd
       have mentioned
Earlier, but at the time it did not seem germane)
And only one "hills"—could this imply a commentary
On the nature or (even) value of desks and stools as relative
To open doors as relative to hills?
Maybe the artist feels our concept of "hills"
Is intrinsic and discrete, ordained by something older
Than ourselves, archetypal, necessitating only this one
And ungainly figuration to call us to mind of
That singular, vast, indispensable thing, "hills"—
Owned by all and all-owning, opening on a sense of a
       community
In which citizenship is not optional but is, like
Breathing, forced on each . . . "O 'hills'!"
(The brute singleness of this truth would explain
How I missed it, at first, and lends a bonus significance
To my (then ostensibly capricious) equation of the hills
With prey—"the predator", too, is a primordial image!).
If this may be regarded as true, I mean true to the artist's
Conscious or unconscious intention, it would seem
A reminder, at the outset, of what is essential because
On-going: The irreducible perception, which exists
Without appeal to anything merely agreed-on, and of which
Any other perception must needs be a version—
How far we have come from our worryings over "depiction"!
We now realize that the "look" of the desks (the simulacrum,
After all, of quite mechanical processes
Of association and recognition) is decidedly subsumed
In the terribly interesting question of what "desks" means to us,
Here in our human life—the only question,
In the final analysis, that really interests us.

As for that other matter, of significant quantity, now
We are ready for it. The triunity of desks and stools,
And of their depictions, clearly suggests at once "number" and
"No number," these the properties of the symbolic notion
                                                        "three,"
Denoting "three desks (*or* stools)" while connoting "an
                                                        infinitude
Of desks (*or* stools)", in any case enabling a reasoned
                                                        statement
Of the matter of desks and stools: that they,
In our lives, are concrete presences possessed, by design,
Of certain properties ("function") that define them:
Specifically, the properties of any object define it
By standing for the peculiar occasions, in
Quotidian life, on which they (the properties) are called
Into play—thus it is, selecting one desk
From among the dozens in a store's desk department
We seek properties after our purpose (smoothness, if we plan
To write letters on it; handsomeness,
If we intend it to grace the interior of a manse; or bigness
And sturdiness, if upon it we wish to dissect
Some body). Now, since the identity
Of a desk or a stool is plainly all those occasions on which
Its properties, singly or in combination, are called into play;
And since the number of occasions on which
A desk or a stool might prove useful is indefinite (given all this)
It is unavoidably the case that "desks" and "stools" are
                                                        supremely
Indefinite notions—doubly so for their dependence
On our hopelessly nebulous concepts of "use"
And "occasion". Such, then, is the secret of our artist's design:
The quintessence of indefiniteness, a neat
Equivocation. And the great hills remain.

"The great hills remain". Let that be our reward,
And a model for the conclusion of all

Future inquiries. It is not nothing, a pleasant phrase into
                                                which
One somehow has managed to cram a measure
Of truth. Perhaps all art, finally, is about this . . .
But it is best not to broach that matter of "art", so huge
And moot—it would surely unhinge us!

However . . . It's troubling. Having toiled much
And come far, we seem scarcely to have scratched the surface
Of the enigma, the page of illustrations. I have neglected,
For example, in my enthusiasm for a specious dénouement,
The two examples of "open doors": What *are* we to make
Of those door things? Could the artist mean them
As intermediate, between the resonant stolidity of "hills"
And the ambiguous dissemblance of "desks" and "stools"?
Or is he simply representing, with "open doors"
As opposed to just "doors", a merely additional
Fact of life, that of the *situation*
That is context to each object? The latter
Is plausible. It fits. Yes, but
What of the ambience clinging to *these* doors? I mean
First of all the vast associative power of doors used
As subject, derived from their constant use in life and their
                                                lively use
In art. It makes them special here, the specialness
Serenely circumventing the snares of our generalized
                                                reasoning.
As if this weren't enough, there is the ambiguity
In the present situation: Are we gazing through a room or
From one house into another or . . . what?
Either all this would seem to matter or all we've said before
Would seem to matter; assuredly not both . . . Neither?
This is awful! And three whole panels, all different, have yet
Even to be mentioned! What havoc might *they* wreak
On our general understandings? How dismal it is
To be so far from done, and already in a soup of
                                contradictions . . .

It's time for a little fundamental self-examination.
Perhaps our method, our way of doing and of going about,
                                                    bears
The fault. In presuming to abstract, from fragments
Of the whole, some notion of the whole, we may have
Falsified the true sublimity—of course! From now on, let's
                                                    resolve
To stick strictly to the facts until all the facts are in.
(But I cannot, after all, feel too badly for having mistaken
The matter: The lesson in patience thus occasioned
Has raised the "moral tone" of this whole, wildly dubious
                                                    assay.)

The first remaining panel is called "corner of the room",
Which I initially misread as "corner of the roof"—it is drawn
So crudely—though, in fact, upon inspection it is shown
As distinctly an interior view, comprising
Windows, walls, and ceiling, work benches (maybe) and
                                                    things
Hanging on one wall; in sum, recognizable
Though manifestly a specific place. Now, promptly, we survey
The next, called "skyline", rough depiction (definitely
Not from life) of big, New Yorkish buildings crowding
To a water's-edge; the fictive vantage point
Is about at middle height, the angle of sight
Slightly a decline, cropping here an upper storey,
There a cupola. The final panel, set off from "skyline"
By "desks" number three, is blank, that's all:
Untitled white, pristine. How variously
Exciting! Such a tantalizing little vacuum!
Entire hordes of exquisite conjectures dash
To crowd it. Incidentally signalling, I am afraid, defeat.
For what have they to do with anything? What
Have they to tell us of such rude opacities as "skyline" and
(If you will!) "corner of the room"? "Hills",
Through its patina of ascribed portentousness, positively

Glowers on our new, so bland conundrums; "desks" and
                                              "stools"
Sink beneath their tons of explication; "open doors"?
The catastrophically distended context puts all minor
                                           weirdness
Out of sight.
                       The entire page of illustrations, come
To that, is really extremely unattractive, graphically
Wretched, its drawing artful only in our original
Wistful estimation: Nowhere, in short, a saving grace; and
The mess (this its Secret) might as well in the end be blank
                                           space.

Since there had to be a reason for all this, I'm confident
You know it—you are welcome to it. I close, and go in peace.

*FRANK
O'HARA*

To the Harbormaster

I wanted to be sure to reach you;
though my ship was on the way it got caught
in some moorings. I am always tying up
and then deciding to depart. In storms and
at sunset, with the metallic coils of the tide
around my fathomless arms, I am unable
to understand the forms of my vanity
or I am hard alee with my Polish rudder
in my hand and the sun sinking. To
you I offer my hull and the tattered cordage
of my will. The terrible channels where
the wind drives me against the brown lips
of the reeds are not all behind me. Yet
I trust the sanity of my vessel; and
if it sinks, it may well be in answer
to the reasoning of the eternal voices,
the waves which have kept me from reaching you.

Blocks

1.

Yippee! she is shooting in the harbor! he is jumping
up to the maelstrom! she is leaning over the giant's
cart of tears which like a lava cone let fall to fly
from the cross-eyed tantrum-tousled ninth grader's
splayed fist is freezing on the cement! he is throwing
up his arms in heavenly desperation, spacious Y of his
tumultuous love-nerves flailing like a poinsettia in

its own nailish storm against the glass door of the
cumulus which is withholding her from these divine
pastures she has filled with the flesh of men as stones!
O fatal eagerness!

2.

O boy, their childhood was like so many oatmeal cookies.
I need you, you need me, yum, yum. Anon it became suddenly

3.

like someone always losing something and never knowing what.
Always so. They were so fond of eating bread and butter and
sugar, they were slobs, the mice used to lick the floorboards
after they went to bed, rolling their light tails against
the rattling marbles of granulation. Vivo! the dextrose
those children consumed, lavished, smoked, in their knobby
candy bars. Such pimples! such hardons! such moody loves.
And thus they grew like giggling fir trees.

For Janice and Kenneth to Voyage

Love, love, love,
honeymoon isn't used much in poetry these days

and if I give you a bar
of Palmolive Soap
it would be rather cracker-barrel
of me, wouldn't it?

The winds will wash you out your hair, my dears.
Passions will become turrets, to you.

I'll be so afraid
without you.
The penalty of the Big Town
is the Big Stick,

yet when you were laughing nearby
the monsters ignored me like a record-player

and I felt brilliant
to be so confident
that the trees
would walk back to Birnam Wood.

It was all you, your graceful white smiles
like a French word, the one for nursery, the one for brine.

Why I Am Not a Painter

I am not a painter, I am a poet.
Why? I think I would rather be
a painter, but I am not. Well,

For instance, Mike Goldberg
is starting a painting. I drop in.
"Sit down and have a drink" he
says. I drink; we drink. I look
up. "You have SARDINES in it."

"Yes, it needed something there."
"Oh." I go and the days go by
and I drop in again. The painting
is going on, and I go, and the days
go by. I drop in. The painting is
finished. "Where's SARDINES?"
All that's left is just
letters, "It was too much," Mike says.

But me? One day I am thinking of
a color: orange. I write a line
about orange. Pretty soon it is a
whole page of words, not lines.
Then another page. There should be
so much more, not of orange, of
words, of how terrible orange is
and life. Days go by. It is even in
prose, I am a real poet. My poem
is finished and I haven't mentioned
orange yet. It's twelve poems, I call
it ORANGES. And one day in a gallery
I see Mike's painting, called SARDINES.

                                    1956

A Step Away from Them

It's my lunch hour, so I go
for a walk among the hum-colored
cabs. First, down the sidewalk
where laborers feed their dirty

glistening torsos sandwiches
and Coca-Cola, with yellow helmets
on. They protect them from falling
bricks, I guess. Then onto the
avenue where skirts are flipping
above heels and blow up over
grates. The sun is hot, but the
cabs stir up the air. I look
at bargains in wristwatches. There
are cats playing in sawdust.
                      On
to Times Square, where the sign
blows smoke over my head, and higher
the waterfall pours lightly. A
Negro stands in a doorway with a
toothpick, languorously agitating.
A blonde chorus girl clicks: he
smiles and rubs his chin. Everything
suddenly honks: it is 12:40 of
a Thursday.
                Neon in daylight is a
great pleasure, as Edwin Denby would
write, as are light bulbs in daylight.
I stop for a cheeseburger at JULIET'S
CORNER. Giulietta Masina, wife of
Federico Fellini, *è bell' attrice.*
And chocolate malted. A lady in
foxes on such a day puts her poodle
in a cab.
                There are several Puerto
Ricans on the avenue today, which
makes it beautiful and warm. First
Bunny died, then John Latouche,
then Jackson Pollock. But is the
earth as full as life was full, of them?
And one has eaten and one walks,
past the magazines with nudes

and the posters for BULLFIGHT and
the Manhattan Storage Warehouse,
which they'll soon tear down. I
used to think they had the Armory
Show there.
       A glass of papaya juice
and back to work. My heart is in my
pocket, it is Poems by Pierre Reverdy.

1956

The Day Lady Died

It is 12:20 in New York a Friday
three days after Bastille day, yes
it is 1959 and I go get a shoeshine
because I will get off the 4:19 in Easthampton
at 7:15 and then go straight to dinner
and I don't know the people who will feed me

I walk up the muggy street beginning to sun
and have a hamburger and a malted and buy
an ugly NEW WORLD WRITING to see what the poets
in Ghana are doing these days
       I go on to the bank
and Miss Stillwagon (first name Linda I once heard)
doesn't even look up my balance for once in her life
and in the GOLDEN GRIFFIN I get a little Verlaine
for Patsy with drawings by Bonnard although I do

think of Hesiod, trans. Richmond Lattimore or
Brendan Behan's new play or *Le Balcon* or *Les Nègres*
of Genet, but I don't, I stick with Verlaine
after practically going to sleep with quandariness

and for Mike I just stroll into the PARK LANE
Liquor Store and ask for a bottle of Strega and
then I go back where I came from to 6th Avenue
and the tobacconist in the Ziegfeld Theatre and
casually ask for a carton of Gauloises and a carton
of Picayunes, and a NEW YORK POST with her face on it

and I am sweating a lot by now and thinking of
leaning on the john door in the 5 SPOT
while she whispered a song along the keyboard
to Mal Waldron and everyone and I stopped breathing

1959

Naphtha

Ah Jean Dubuffet
when you think of him
doing his military service in the Eiffel Tower
as a meteorologist
in 1922
you know how wonderful the 20th Century
can be
and the gaited Iroquois on the girders
fierce and unflinching-footed
nude as they should be

slightly empty
like a Sonia Delaunay
there is a parable of speed
somewhere behind the Indians' eyes
they invented the century with their horses
and their fragile backs
which are dark

we owe a debt to the Iroquois
and to Duke Ellington
for playing in the buildings when they are built
we don't do much ourselves
but fuck and think
of the haunting Métro
and the one who didn't show up there
while we were waiting to become part of our century
just as you can't make a hat out of steel
and still wear it
who wears hats anyway
it is our tribe's custom
to beguile

how are you feeling in ancient September
I am feeling like a truck on a wet highway
how can you
you were made in the image of god
I was not
I was made in the image of a sissy truck-driver
and Jean Dubuffet painting his cows
"with a likeness burst in the memory"
apart from love (don't say it)
I am ashamed of my century
for being so entertaining
but I have to smile

1959

Ave Maria

Mothers of America
     let your kids go to the movies!
get them out of the house so they won't know what you're up to
it's true that fresh air is good for the body
        but what about the soul
that grows in darkness, embossed by silvery images
and when you grow old as grow old you must
        they won't hate you
they won't criticise you they won't know
      they'll be in some glamorous country
they first saw on a Saturday afternoon or playing hookey

they may even be grateful to you
       for their first sexual experience
which only cost you a quarter
       and didn't upset the peaceful home
they will know where candy bars come from
       and gratuitous bags of popcorn
as gratuitous as leaving the movie before it's over
with a pleasant stranger whose apartment is in the
       Heaven on Earth Bldg
near the Williamsburg Bridge
      oh mothers you will have made the little tykes
so happy because if nobody does pick them up in the movies
they won't know the difference
      and if somebody does it'll be sheer gravy
and they'll have been truly entertained either way
instead of hanging around the yard
      or up in their room
       hating you
prematurely since you won't have done anything horribly mean yet
except keeping them from the darker joys
      it's unforgivable the latter

so don't blame me if you won't take this advice
                         and the family breaks up
and your children grow old and blind in front of a TV set
                                 seeing
movies you wouldn't let them see when they were young

                                 1960

Steps

How funny you are today New York
like Ginger Rogers in *Swingtime*
and St. Bridget's steeple leaning a little to the left

here I have just jumped out of a bed full of V-days
(I got tired of D-days) and blue you there still
accepts me foolish and free
all I want is a room up there
and you in it
and even the traffic halt so thick is a way
for people to rub up against each other
and when their surgical appliances lock
they stay together
for the rest of the day (what a day)
I go by to check a slide and I say
that painting's not so blue

where's Lana Turner
she's out eating
and Garbo's backstage at the Met
everyone's taking their coat off

so they can show a rib-cage to the rib-watchers
and the park's full of dancers with their tights and shoes
in little bags
who are often mistaken for worker-outers at the West Side Y
why not
the Pittsburgh Pirates shout because they won
and in a sense we're all winning
we're alive

the apartment was vacated by a gay couple
who moved to the country for fun
they moved a day too soon
even the stabbings are helping the population explosion
though in the wrong country
and all those liars have left the U N
the Seagram Building's no longer rivalled in interest
not that we need liquor (we just like it)

and the little box is out on the sidewalk
next to the delicatessen
so the old man can sit on it and drink beer
and get knocked off it by his wife later in the day
while the sun is still shining

oh god it's wonderful
to get out of bed
and drink too much coffee
and smoke too many cigarettes
and love you so much

1961

Mary Desti's Ass

In Bayreuth once
we were very good friends of the Wagners
and I stepped in once
for Isadora so perfectly
she would never allow me to dance again
that's the way it was in Bayreuth

the way it was in Hackensack
was different
there one never did anything
and everyone hated you anyway
it was fun, it was clear
you knew where you stood

in Boston you were never really standing
I was usually lying
it was amusing to be lying all
the time for everybody
it was like exercise

it means something to exercise
in Norfolk Virginia
it means you've been to bed with a Nigra
well it is exercise
the only difference is it's better than Boston

I was walking along the street
of Cincinnati
and I met Kenneth Koch's mother
fresh from the Istanbul Hilton
she liked me and I liked her
we both liked Istanbul

then in Waukegan I met a furniture manufacturer
and it wiped out all dreams of pleasantness from my mind
it was like being pushed down hard
on a chair
it was like something horrible you hadn't expected
which is the most horrible thing

and in Singapore I got a dreadful
disease it was amusing to have bumps
except they went into my veins
and rose to the surface like Vesuvius
getting cured was like learning to smoke

yet I always loved Baltimore
the porches which hurt your ass
no, they were the steps
well you have a wet ass anyway
if they'd only stop scrubbing

and Frisco where I saw
Toumanova "the baby ballerina" except
she looked like a cow
I didn't know the history of the ballet yet
not that that taught me much

now if you feel like you want to deal with
Tokyo
you've really got something to handle
it's like Times Square at midnight
you don't know where you're going
but you know

and then in Harbin I knew
how to behave it was glorious that
was love sneaking up on me through the snow
and I felt it was because of all
the postcards and the smiles and kisses and the grunts
that was love but I kept on traveling

1961

Poem Read at Joan Mitchell's

At last you are tired of being single
the effort to be new does not upset you nor the effort to be other
you are not tired of life together

city noises are louder because you are together
being together you are louder than calling separately across a
                    telephone one to the other
and there is no noise like the rare silence when you both sleep
even country noises—a dog bays at the moon, but when it loves
the moon it bows, and the hitherto frowning moon fawns
                    and slips

Only you in New York are not boring tonight
it is most modern to affirm some one
(we don't really love ideas, do we?)
and Joan was surprising you with a party for which I was the
                    decoy
but you were surprising us by getting married and going away
so I am here reading poetry anyway
and no one will be bored tonight by me because you're here

Yesterday I felt very tired from being at the FIVE SPOT
and today I felt very tired from going to bed early and reading
              ULYSSES
but tonight I feel energetic because I'm sort of the bugle,
like waking people up, of your peculiar desire to get married

It's so
original, hydrogenic, anthropomorphic, fiscal, post-anti-esthetic,
              bland, unpicturesque and WilliamCarlosWil-
              liamsian!
it's definitely not 19th Century, it's not even Partisan Review,
              it's new, it must be vanguard!

Tonight you probably walked over here from Bethune Street
down Greenwich Avenue with its sneaky little bars and the
              Women's Detention House,
across 8th Street, by the acres of books and pillows and shoes
              and illuminating lampshades,
past Cooper Union where we heard the piece by Mortie
              Feldman with "The Stars and Stripes Forever"
              in it
and the Sagamore's terrific "coffee and, Andy", meaning "with
              a cheese Danish"—
did you spit on your index fingers and rub the Cedar's neon
              circle for luck?
did you give a kind thought, hurrying, to Alger Hiss?

It's the day before February 17th
it is not snowing yet but it is dark and may snow yet
dreary February of the exhaustion from parties and the
              exceptional desire for Spring which the ballet
              alone, by extending its run, has made bearable,
              dear New York City Ballet company, you are
              quite a bit like a wedding yourself!
and the only signs of Spring are Maria Tallchief's rhinestones
              and a perky little dog barking in a bar, here
              and there eyes which suddenly light up with

blue, like a ripple subsiding under a lily pad,
or with brown, like a freshly plowed field we
vow we'll drive out and look at when a certain
Sunday comes in May—
and these eyes are undoubtedly Jane's and Joe's because they
are advancing into Spring before us and
tomorrow is Sunday

This poem goes on too long because our friendship has been
long, long for this life and these times, long as
art is long and uninterruptable,
and I would make it as long as I hope our friendship lasts if I
could make poems that long

I hope there will be more
more drives to Bear Mountain and searches for hamburgers,
more evenings avoiding the latest Japanese
movie and watching Helen Vinson and
Warner Baxter in Vogues of 1938 instead,
more discussions in lobbies of the respective
greatnesses of Diana Adams and Allegra Kent,
more sunburns and more half-mile swims in which Joe beats
me as Jane watches, lotion-covered and sleepy,
more arguments over Faulkner's inferiority to
Tolstoy while sand gets into my bathing trunks
let's advance and change everything but leave these little oases
in case the heart gets thirsty en route
and I should probably propose myself as a god-father if you
have any children, since I will probably earn
more money some day accidentally, and could
teach him or her how to swim
and now there is a Glazunov symphony on the radio and I
think of our friends who are not here, of John
and the nuptial quality of his verses (he is always
marrying the whole world) and Janice and
Kenneth, smiling and laughing, respectively

(they are probably laughing at the Leaning
Tower right now)
but we are all here and have their proxy
if Kenneth were writing this he would point out how art has
changed women and women have changed art and
men, but men haven't changed women much
but ideas are obscure and nothing should be obscure tonight
you will live half the year in a house by the sea and half the
year in a house in our arms
we peer into the future and see you happy and hope it is a
sign that we will be happy too, something to cling
to, happiness
the least and best of human attainments

1957

You at the Pump
(History of North and South)

A bouquet of zephyr-flowers hitched to a hitching post
in far off Roanoke

a child watches the hitch tense

here an Indian
there a bag of marbles
here a strange sunrise
there suffused with odors
and behind the restored door
a change of clothing
fresh as baking bread
the child sits quietly

with his nose stuck in a
rose in the village square
where the dust is

and a tall man comes along and spreads water
everywhere for the flowers to drink and enjoy us

it is a small mystery of America
how northerly the wind
sweeping into the square
what icicle of color
reaches the bag
of young sensibility
and makes him think
I love you, Pocahontas
where his feet are

Getting Up Ahead of Someone (Sun)

I cough a lot (sinus?) so I
get up and have some tea with cognac
it is dawn
                    the light flows evenly along the lawn
in chilly Southampton and I smoke
and hours and hours go by I read
van Vechten's *Spider Boy* then a short
story by Patsy Southgate and a poem
by myself it is cold and I shiver a little
in white shorts the day begun
so oddly not tired not nervous I
am for once truly awake letting it all
start slowly as I watch instead of
grabbing on late as usual

        where did it go
        it's not really awake yet
        I will wait

and the house wakes up and goes
to get the dog in Sag Harbor I make
myself a bourbon and commence
to write one of my "I do this I do that"
poems in a sketch pad
                it is tomorrow
though only six hours have gone by
each day's light has more significance these days

A True Account of Talking to the Sun at Fire Island

The Sun woke me this morning loud
and clear, saying "Hey! I've been
trying to wake you up for fifteen
minutes. Don't be so rude, you are
only the second poet I've ever chosen
to speak to personally

                      so why
aren't you more attentive? If I could
burn you through the window I would
to wake you up. I can't hang around
here all day."

                    "Sorry, Sun, I stayed
up late last night talking to Hal."

"When I woke up Mayakovsky he was
a lot more prompt" the Sun said
petulantly. "Most people are up
already waiting to see if I'm going
to put in an appearance."

                        I tried
to apologize "I missed you yesterday."
"That's better" he said "I didn't
know you'd come out. You may be
wondering why I've come so close?"
"Yes" I said beginning to feel hot
wondering if maybe he wasn't burning me
anyway.

               "Frankly I wanted to tell you
I like your poetry. I see a lot
on my rounds and you're okay. You may
not be the greatest thing on earth, but
you're different. Now, I've heard some

say you're crazy, they being excessively
calm themselves to my mind, and other
crazy poets think that you're a boring
reactionary. Not me.
                      Just keep on
like I do and pay no attention. You'll
find that people always will complain
about the atmosphere, either too hot
or too cold too bright or too dark, days
too short or too long.
                      If you don't appear
at all one day they think you're lazy
or dead. Just keep right on, I like it.

And don't worry about your lineage
poetic or natural. The Sun shines on
the jungle, you know, on the tundra
the sea, the ghetto. Wherever you were
I knew it and saw you moving. I was waiting
for you to get to work.
                    And now that you
are making your own days, so to speak,
even if no one reads you but me
you won't be depressed. Not
everyone can look up, even at me. It
hurts their eyes."
                      "Oh Sun, I'm so grateful to you!"

"Thanks and remember I'm watching. It's
easier for me to speak to you out
here. I don't have to slide down
between buildings to get your ear.
I know you love Manhattan, but
you ought to look up more often.
                        And
always embrace things, people earth
sky stars, as I do, freely and with

the appropriate sense of space. That
is your inclination, known in the heavens
and you should follow it to hell, if
necessary, which I doubt.

              Maybe we'll
speak again in Africa, of which I too
am specially fond. Go back to sleep now
Frank, and I may leave a tiny poem
in that brain of yours as my farewell."

"Sun, don't go!" I was awake
at last. "No, go I must, they're calling
me."
       "Who are they?"
              Rising he said "Some
day you'll know. They're calling to you
too." Darkly he rose, and then I slept.

              Fire Island 7/10/58

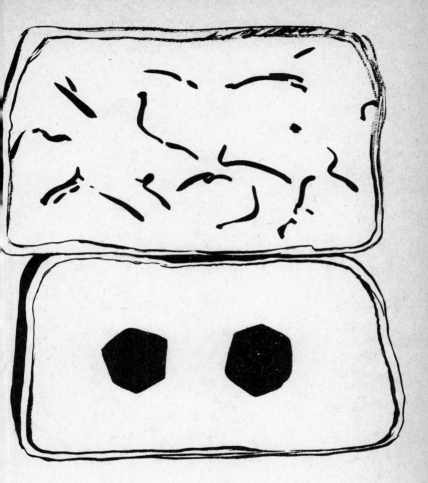

ARAM
SAROYAN

night
again
again

Had West followed up her fine opening lead by dropping the club king or queen on the second round of clubs, she would have been able to play the ten when Stayman tried to throw her in. Then East could have overtaken and returned a heart, wrecking the contract.

torgh

ly   ly

ly   ly

———————————

My arms are warm

Aram Saroyan

———————————

whistling in the street a car turning in the room ticking

car swerves,
injures 11;
driver held

oh oh oh oh oh oh oh oh oh

suggest bear

oh oh oh oh oh oh oh oh oh

crickets
crickets
crickets
crickets
crickets
crickets
crickets
crickets
crickets
crickets
crickets
crickets
crickets
crickets
crickets
crickets
crickets
crickets
crickets
crickets
crickets
crickets
crickets
crickets
crickets
crickets
crickets
crickets
crickets
crickets
crickets
crickets
crickets
crickets
crickets
crickets
crickets
crickets
crickets
crickets
crickets
crickets
crickets
crickets

aren't

ex-
track
coach
dies

a man stands
on his
head one
minute—

then he
sit
down all
different

French Poets

French poets are the greatest of all.
They arrive with different smiles.
They are used to the sun and to coffee.
They smoke
Incessantly.

If you tell them a joke they weep for joy.
If you tell them a
Sad story they weep for joy.
And if they only knew joy.

We others seem
Pained by comparison. We all smile
Less than we might, a lesson
In the great French movies:

Suddenly she is smiling. Suddenly she is
Smiling. Suddenly she is smiling. Sudden
Ly she is smiling. Suddenly she is smili

—while so often we seem lost in thought.
Our skin is dry.
We buy the wrong shirts.
Or we buy the right ones but we look tired.
Our eyes are often red
From thinking.

French poets are always smiling and watching
The sun spots on the coffee.
They are gay sons-of-bitches.

RON
PADGETT

After the Broken Arm

From point A a wind is blowing to point B
Which is here, where the pebble is only a mountain.
If truly heaven and earth are out there
Why is that man waving his arms around,
Gesturing to the word "lightning" written on the clouds
That surround and disguise his feet?

If you say the right word in New York City
Nothing will happen in New York City;
But out in the fabulous dry horror of the west
A beautiful girl named Sibyl will burst
In by the open window breathless
And settle for an imaginary glass of something.
But now her name is no longer Sibyl—it's Herman,
Yearning for point B.

Dispatch this note to our hero at once.

Homage to Max Jacob

Goodbye sting and all my columbines
In the tower which looks out gently
Their yo-yo plumage on the cold bomb shoulder
        Goodbye sting.

Goodbye house and its little blue roofs
Where such a friend in all seasons
To see us again made some money
        Goodbye house.

Goodbye line of hay in pigs
Near the clock! O! how often I hurt myself
That you know me like an apartment
        Goodbye line!

Goodbye lamb grease! hands carrying arteries
On the well-varnished little park mirror
Of white barricades the color of diapers
        Goodbye lamb grease!

Goodbye verges calves and planks
And on the sting our black flying boat
Our servant with her white hair-do
        Goodbye verges.

Goodbye my clear oval river
Goodbye mountain! goodbye cherry trees!
It is you who are my cap and tale
        Not Paris.

From *Some Bombs*

3.

The pied quarts of Chevrolets trim blent Sir her eyes on
The memo leg's knee asserts me with coo
Monday is a tent soused with covered fur
The fen beings brillo like the years

One of the arms pour rear
And a cur pours more rear

The General et an old monster
Sand's civil habits
A Blake blight a bone Blake blight at the fair
Ah a member of the fame isle
Says Louie Key a prissy toot he row is my parasol

The cur is a pre-sound without a rage where Lou too urns
                                                   without fins

Blue as a hurry
Monty "The Soup" Godzilla
His figuring is a negro Roy decorated with my soft age

He purrs Rye Anne

Chase the salvages
The music mews
New sums try and I sew O mildew
Where's Alley Ooops
The plays here at Mort author of *News*

Joe Brainard's Painting "Bingo"

I suffer when I sit next to Joe Brainard's painting "Bingo"

I could have made that line into a whole stanza

I suffer
When I sit
Next to Joe
Brainard's painting
"Bingo"

Or I could change the line arrangement

I suffer when I sit

That sounds like hemorrhoids
I don't know anything about hemorrhoids
Such as if it hurts to sit when you have them
If so I must not have them
Because it doesn't hurt me to sit
I probably sit about 8/15 of my life

Also I don't suffer
When I sit next to Joe Brainard

Actually I don't even suffer
When I sit next to his painting "Bingo"
Or for that matter any of his paintings

In fact I didn't originally say
I suffer when I sit next to Joe Brainard's painting "Bingo"
My wife said it
In response to something I had said
About another painting of his
She had misunderstood what I had said

December

I will sleep
in my little cup

The Ems Dispatch

Opening up a mud duck
The sin of the hearth had made him handsome
Don't ever give me what continues to be the tan arm of the
                                                    hero
As identical, these sums and the chance to disappear
By including the chamois
Though that's a fine mess, I wist
Titles, etc.   2. Two Veins.   followed, pursued, sought after
But the curse now
Laid you down in the patient tent
Where there are men, there are no men
Just what I wanted (lie) perfect (lie)
I cared for the boy's drawing of the horse to get going
Then the lovely shin quest
Into the untracked signal gun, flowers, birthdays, sonnets
Put the hot, sweet breath of your breath against mine enemy
Come with me the nurse ferocity
Streets streets and less equal streets
The sails being torn to pieces in the upstairs part
But in a few moments
Without themes space or the invisible table message
Under the legs "far" into the night our hut
Its flaming gates
And the invitation to commit bibliography
The proffered hand
Guessed we're on to each other
The lice looked up in astonishment
Didn't explain the available cardboard murder
Going on into the mail covered with rust and the box

The great shoe prediction sigh clock
No doubt about it the neighbor thought it over
The extra put on its countenance and clicked on off
Let my dog sleep
On the altar of girlhood
But polish around it, observing the priority of the bump
The close call packed away and sniffing at the edge

A Man Saw a Ball of Gold

A man saw a ball of gold in the sky;
He climbed for it,
And eventually he achieved it—
It was gold.

Now this is the strange part:
When the man went to the earth
And looked again,
Lo, there was the ball of gold.
Now this is the strange part:
It was a ball of gold.
Ay, by the heavens, it was a ball of gold.

The Sandwich Man

The funny thing is that he's reading a paper
As if with his throat
With the bottom half folded neatly under his chin
Which is, incidentally, clean-shaven
As he strolls absently toward us, toting a sewing machine
On the front
With delicate little gold lines curling and swaying below a
                        white spool in the afternoon
A dog barks—well, arf! you pull the cord attached to the
                                monastery
Bell that rings utterly somewhere else
Perhaps the cord is ringing
And you are a Russian
In some hideously small town
Or worst of all
You're listening to the story behind the bell
A history whose rugged but removed features
Resemble those of the sandwich man
Not the one that wandered off into the swamp
Cuffs filled with wind
And was never seen again
But this new one who overestimates his duty by teaching
School in a place that has as students
At best only a bunch of heavily panting dogs
Seated in rows of wooden and iron desks linked
Like slaves on a dismal galley, the Ship of Genius
Sailing for some points known and a few unknown
Caring little about either, huffing away
Toward the horizon destroyed by other students . . .
                             estudianti

One of these others, the head, is in fact the Infanta,
In reality only a very intelligent little girl

But beyond the immense corrugated brook we know of as this
earth
Covered with raving, a constellation in the shape of a bullet—
She always did love the sound of a ricochet—and I too
Can hear it often, at night, before I go to sleep
In my nose
In Spain, ah
In Spain there are the prune fields and the dark
Beauty of a prune now lowers a shade
Past the sewing machine, over which blow long, regular
waves of dust particles
In one of which a medium-sized boy in white sandals is
peddling up to
Offer you a worried rose

Rose . . . but I know nothing of this rose
Although I will draw it for you in words if you wish
Clockwise beginning at noon on the outer rim
On the first petal is a cave and the second a squiggle
The third a proper noun or else a common noun beginning a
sentence
Or even perhaps a noun capitalized for no reason at all, for
God's sake!

Japan! Penitentiary!
That's what we want!
To move and dance
With strangers, people we don't know
With lines and circles going through us
Who are the landscape

Whose clouds are really toots from the nearby factory
I love so much, the steam factory, making steam
For people to fall down on and permit their bodies to vibrate
Occasionally a straw hat is flung through the factory window
And sails spinning into the water

It is night

A dog barks outside the window
Either that or the window's silent in the dog
—You'll say I'm playing the overture

And finale off against each other, after all
There's no other way to locate the middle,
Which is more elusive than it might seem:
The fifty yard line does escape
The gridiron, extending itself through
Both grandstands, through you and me, plus
A parking lot now indistinguishable from the fog, backyards,
         dreams, washing . . .
And the large peanut that has come to stand for something
        beautiful and intelligent
In short, civilization.

No so! says a man in striped pants wheeled in out of the
         moonlight
You think this only because you associate this object with
         yourselves
. . . which is okay by me . . .
He was wheeled out and chucked over the balcony
Into the magnolia bushes.

At dawn, I find one other example, though nearly driven
         away
By the dust on it:
You are, say, six feet tall
Or six feet long,
In the first instance you are an active human being other
        than a baby
In the second you are either a very large baby or
A corpse or perhaps a bed-ridden invalid or
Two yardsticks placed end to end. What your six feet

Would be were you tilted at a 45° angle
I do not know
Doubtless a census taker's nightmare, in which bent
Horrible monsters jump out and bite him.

The next step is to know that this fuzzy angle is true in your
heart
But not to know what happens to it
When it leaves there, flowers gushing out . . .
It appears in Amsterdam always
City of extension cords
And ladies with boxes of rubber bands and
A truly horrible music washing the streets rushing below the
pigeons
That now seem to be following him as sure as iron
Follows a crook

I don't think I can stand it! the birds
Are swooping down in and out of a large design yes!
A police car is pulling itself together
In the skies, its headlights on now
Bearing down on the sandwich man, still reading,
Whose next step puts him behind
Us as we turn ourselves around to see his other board
And the horrible license plate on it

The Farmer's Head

At that instant there came a crash more terrific
than any that had preceded it, and the whole place
glared with intense light. Everyone was momentar-
ily stunned, and when they recovered their senses,
Ernest, looking toward the farmhouse, saw a sheet
of flame coming from the farmer's head.

"Fire! Fire!" she shouted. "Your head is afire!
It's been struck by lightning!"

"By gum! So it has!" yelled the farmer. "It's
blazing!"

He was rapidly shouting this as he ran from
the barn.

Detach, Invading

Oh humming all and
Then a something from above came rooting
And tooting onto the sprayers
Profaning in the console morning
Of the pointing afternoon
Back to dawn by police word to sprinkle it
Over the lotions that ever change
On locks
Of German, room and perforate
To sprinkle I say
On the grinding slot of rye
And the bandage that falls down
On the slots as they exude their gas
And the rabbit lingers that pushes it

To blot the lumber
Like a gradually hard mode
All bring and forehead in the starry grab
That pulverizes
And its slivers
Off bending down the thrown gulp
In funny threes
So the old fat flies toward the brain
And a dent on brilliance

The large pig at which the intense cones beat
Wishes O you and O me
O cough release! a rosy bar
Whose mist rarifies even the strokers
Where to go
Strapping, apricot

Strawberries in Mexico

At 14th Street and First Avenue
Is a bank and in the bank the sexiest teller of all time
Next to her the greatest thing about today
Is today itself
Through which I go up
To buy books

They float by under a bluer sky
The girls uptown
Quiet, pampered
The sum of all that's terrible in women
And much of the best

And the old men go by holding small packages
In a trance
So rich even they can't believe it

I think it's a red, white and blue letter day for them too
You see, Con Ed's smokestacks are beautiful
The way Queens is
And horses: from a pleasant distance

Or a fleet of turkeys
Stuffed in a spotless window
In two days they'll be sweating in ovens
Thinking, "How did I ever get in a fix like this?"

Light pouring over buildings far away

Up here when someone says "Hey!"
In the street you know they aren't going to kill you
They're yelling to a friend of theirs named Hey
John David Hey, perhaps
And even the garbage goes out
In big white billowy plastic bags tied at the top
Even the people go out in them
Some, now, are waiting
At bus stops (for a probably nonexistent bus . . .)
I thought it was garbage!
It's so pretty!

If you're classless or modern
You can have fun by
Walking into a high-class antique store
So the stately old snob at the desk will ask
In eternity
"You're going where?"
You get to answer "Up."

I like these old pricks
If you have an extra hair in the breeze
Their eyes pop out
And then recede way back
As if to say, "That person is on . . . dope!"
They're very correct

But they're not in my shoes
In front of a Dubuffet a circus that shines through
A window in a bright all-yellow building
The window is my eye
And Frank O'Hara is the building
I'm thinking about him like mad today
(As anyone familiar with his poetry will tell)
And about the way Madison Avenue really
Does go to Heaven
And then turns around and comes back, disappointed

Because up here you can sneer at a Negro
Or pity the man
And rent a cloud-colored Bentley and
Architecture's so wonderful!
Why don't I notice it more often?
And the young girls and boys but especially the young girls
Are drifting away from school
In blue and white wool
Wrapped in fur
Are they French? They're speaking French!
And they aren't looking for things to throw
Skirts sliding up the legs of girls who can't keep from
                                            grinning
Under beautiful soft brown American eyes
At the whole world
Which includes their plain Jane girlfriends
She even smiled at me!
I have about as much chance of fucking her as the girl at the
                                            bank

But I stride along, a terrifying god
Raunchy
A little one day old beard
And good grief I really did forget to brush my teeth this
morning
They're turning red with embarrassment
Or is that blood
I've been drinking—I ordered a black coffee
Miss

And then a black policeman comes in
Unbuttoning his uniform at the warmish soda fountain
While I pull the fleece over my teeth
And stare innocently at the books I've bought
One a book with a drawing
By Apollinaire called "Les fraises au Mexique"
"Strawberries in Mexico"
But when I open the book to that page
It's just a very blue blue sky I'm looking at

DICK
GALLUP

The Door to the Future

Just a little nudge, he said, and then
The Liner docked. You came down
The same gang-plank the Captain
Did. I wondered. You cried. I said
Hello and you said Hi! Later
In the city we found vast excitement
And several lumps of sugar and we had
Coffee with sugar and you left
For South Dakota. I felt that you
Had stayed for only a minute. Then
I knew it was finished. The lights
Of the city seemed to dim
As I took a few steps across
The airfield. You went up
The same ramp the pilot did. I
Wondered. You said you'd be back
In a minute but the speaker said
Chicago and the pilot had a big
Container of coffee. After that
I didn't see you anymore.

After Alcman

They sleep, eyeing the mountain peaks and clefts
the headlands and damp chasms,
so many creeping swarms thicken the black earth,
mountainous beasts and a house of bees
and the snakes in the depths of the dark gleaming sea:
they are still, the vultures,
the swarms of extended wings.

Ember Grease

There was no reason to go back now
They were in the storeroom nailing tacks
And the green rug nestled against the furnace
The few remaining traces were fading
Colors appeared and everything grew flat
Decayed quickly in its place

I looked around slowly trying hard to think
There were benches, or a chair I never used
The dust had covered all the tacks, the hammer
Had a striped handle and no claw . . .
The dirty yellow lawn, the movies fused
The lack . . . the endless chatter

Could there be no end to the beginning
The oil or grease surrounding slaughter
Coffee or tea in some cup of my own
At least new, or friendly?
Nothing was strictly the matter . . . yet
In this light everything turns to stone

A last glance finds the rug in the hall
The bare floor looks strange painted bronze
They are curled up in the kitchen hunting tacks
The dishes are washed, I think
The furnace grease is clogging up the lawn
A fading dust covering the hammer's tracks

Hygiene Sonnet

Every morning I hear the bells ringing
At six, and later, at seven, something goes
Chug, shuk-shuk-shuk, chug chugk, building
Pressure, driving . . . what? no one knows.
The bells though are certainly bells ringing, some
Church or other, and often I hear next door
In the bathroom, people shitting at random
Times, or just sitting, staring at the floor.
They grunt, moan, sometimes sing, or sigh,
They mumble and hum, and then they wipe their asses.
Shuffling their feet, they button or zip their fly,
And go back to their rooms, leaving behind their gases.
I'd rather they'd sing, or hum, or even chant high masses,
Than shit as they do, foully, and moistly give vent to their
                                                    asses.

Eskimoes Again

The scream of teeth is contortion tied
Down, a sack of many briny hides.
Why take again these dreams of Eskimoes
A fine yellow film follows where they go.
In the Arctic snows of time does time
Begin with dawn or end with a "bath?"
Or do the Eskimoes find "bath" sublime?
Knowing each bath is apt to be the last
My dreams of time have lost their feet
At night, where I see the ancient Eskimoes

In the russet folds of troubled sleep.
Though screams of trouble fleece the snow
A fine yellow film follows where they go
The ancient rugged Eskimoes

Some Feathers

"All calligraphy transferred onto cubes
Are an eye wandering thru avenues."

Is that a bottle-neck?
Darkness treading thru dry hair
Waving in airtight compartments?

I don't know
But

Although the car did not arrive
The war doesn't end anymore
And the highway spewing light
Treads down thru last week
There is someone there with hair
He does not breathe on the forest
In the vestibules
On the road
Repeating feather calligraphy avenue feathers

The blue bottle-neck
Feathers are waiting for the airtight feathers
In the vestibule compartment, but an eye
Sees only avenues repeating
Feather calligraphy avenue feathers

From the Beaumont Series

Age came not my conifer, O
Not my corral on the prairie:
The Navy, some Noël port,
In Voguelion collars.
Vase knee lop. Unguented an'
Interred d'old tram are:
O Me! Lasso dolent enter,
Come! O dig! So far!

A vase in Altrac, on the rate,
A knoll, remember? A deer:
For image knowing Anne, a tacked on
Tan—Tison, Lisos—Fire?
Chum, if Anne—O gran! goo! er
La notte, cold a day;
Nascent elan dint, er
Not my parch so see a.

O's antus and tus Deo,
Chain lever gin when is the
Tug guard all more me?
Boil da me dip ill art is to:

Oil tap or test ate
Then muted otta ate,
Idolize me more
Tisia! rack o man data!

    The crock salve agent,
" 'Em face dis weird:
The crock miff adolant,
No me well din opperage are—
O crock pall leg rind,
Perch me high if it is true!
O my lasso, Tapina!
Key or dough, send in the nut.

    Lo! Radar Imp Compass
The nut is Monad Man-Teen,
His a mug er rat-face,
Come a tole, Tamia, spin.
Oil, the pot est ate
The mute had otta ate,
Loam, idolize me more!
Vizor are comin', ain't 'at a!

    "Gwanda, Crock-pig lie I'm
Certain, no lamb in sight,"
Quatch ate and Tom's a mad
Dial it and Tom ache,
Neo-Fui bat up-a
'Em ass in purgatory.
And inch elate ten you too?
Purty stay it, Tamia.

    The Navy's so bellicose:
In bone or pose, Anne or air
Tell 'em oil am Orcon Ellen,
Elegant chee, ha!—wan deer.

O pad recriat ore,
Ah poor Tom's a lesson duce,
Cavern noa noa, Sir Widower
Of lotus and the crock!

    O Pear. Pre-Ego. Do let the
Chaise-aisle ape Namia.
Come and fetch me a sonnet
And mantle, Tensoria:
Chill on poss, so aberrant are
La notte 'n Ladia!
Interred ole tremor be,
List "a la vie," Tamia.

Building a House

Returning from the movies we find
An immense house called "Batter" has arrived;
With wires employed for hinges
We extricate the walls from the paste
Jewelry and set up the Kitchen
With three small hinges and a bolt.
Shall we go into the Sitting Room?
A few chairs and a table
Show the dominate mood

In the closet we find it is murky
That room is fetid and cool
Around the corner, and the yard . . .
What is that invertebrate squalor?!

The South-West Wing has a Pig Room
Full of sows and piglets.
Is infinity revealed here?
We do not know.

Someone knocks on the door to tell us
The true story of his arrival
In Agawam. He is a pedant and we show him
Into the library.
                    Elsewhere,
Attaching the last hinge
To the Observatory window, Tom
Bolt has discovered the heavens
In a moment of incineration.
The artistic furniture has been burned
Too, but the Borean Wing still stands.

Since the window lens is anathema
To one mistrustful of matter
 Some of the more fortunate visitors
Remove Tom to the Mortuary. One asks,
"What is that tree doing there?"
We tell him it is the Hinge Tree
And that ripe hinges needed
For the Solar Porch grow there.
He doesn't believe us and refuses
To don the hinge-guards we offer.

While the other visitors are out
We construct the Elevator Room
And run up the fore-stays of our own
Ample-boat Sea-scape
Drawing Room, where acres of Kansas
Wheat furnish the broad decor.

The guests were aroused to action
By some bones studded with hinges
Uncovered in the Statuary Room.
They demanded hinge-guards and huge
Repellent magnets to protect them
From the carnivorous Hinge Tree.
We refuse this request because we
Need hinges. Now an angry mob,
The guests retreat to the Cutlery
Just finished with two bolts and a hinge.

In the Ante-Diluvian Wing, where
Many a trophy of past victory
Is hung in a peplum alcove,
Saint Bilbous, or "The Hinge,"
Watches the hectic
Multitudes of his supposed followers
Devour the ancient Hinge-ist Archives.
Hundreds of Black Arm-Guards, Jackets,
Leatherette Satchels, Fountain Pens, Leatherette
Satchels, Rubber Stoppers, Cow Bells,
Moose Call Conches, Diseased Track
Coaches, and other of his many
Hinge-constructed products of
Utility perish beneath his futile gaze.
The humor drains out
Of his eyes to see such an
Anachronistic display of "consumption."

Assuaged in their troubled anarchy
The guests are leaving the visitors
Cowed by the Belliferous tones
Of returning Autumn Pageantry.
"Goodbye," they say, "to walls

"Offering gardens, and to the chomping Hinge
"Trees of Agawam, too. It's back for us
"To Pine Salons and Rosewood Dream
"Chambers above a hinge-less sea."
We watch them go up
Into the Hinge Trees of Finity,
A monument to the Autumn Harvest
Time colors, reared with innumerable
Hinges and a dozen bolts
For the Swift passing of our visiting guests."

Fits of Candor

It is only the orange light that brings forth the
orange in things. The eyes of the public will only
produce the small talk of pilots before action. Go
forth, then, into the air of the aerodrome that you
occupy, the trussed ceilings, the telephone in the
foyer, ringing briefly, the heightened contours of
social teas following hard upon the Spitkas and The
Somme. Go forth into the high life of novel languages, or into the lowly valleys to escape your
relentless fellows. Mix with the roarings of animals
your deft music or mingle amid the skies and de-
tours of quiet consuming fear, carrying into whatever the sense of your wings as you fill a prescription and you will radiate around you candor and a
vacancy, and leave behind you an orange bright-
ness of fearful aptitude.

Homer

We rejoin our hero at the edge of a vast impenetrable morass. His feet glitter as fishes darting in water. His arms are bathed in a milky light. His hands touch the fronds at the water's edge. With a gasp we realize that the temperature stands at 18 degrees.

The Return of Philista

Coming down the sluice of morning, Billy the Kid
Ignites a bitter cigarette, dreamy
Dreams fill his mind: she isn't in love.
Saddling his bronco, the rigamarole of buffoons,
Please, he says, making stratiations, making squawkings
In the quiet air of the rrible morning. A girl
Cometh to the Western water-tap: and she is in love.

It is morning, Billy says, and the morning and she is
                                                concocting
Something unpleasant for me and "Clumps,"
My sidekick. Where now is Ievski of Avila, and Alyosha?
Both just notches on the time-stick. The sly deviations
Of fate and a loose gun call him to memorising her gala
                                                occasions
Of communicating with his white love. A girl
Is more than her color, he thinks, as she is "in love."

It is a black morning and she is "in love""
With Franz Hals, theatrical
Bitch, says Billy, lern yr runcibles, Love. She murmurs

"Always skulking around, To be
Just so! a Paloma Negra . . . or some splendid king, all glory
In the flower, all honor is the love, was her dream, turned to
Shit. Alas! awaking she finds she's "in love."

On a kiddish morning and she is in love.
Kid love! Billy love! The love of morning is nothing but love,
Ravelled-sleeve love, jew love, prick love! oh! to waken so
                              shackled with love!
Billy the Kid wakes up in the morning and She is not in love.

Death and the Maiden

Travel gets us through the breach
Wearing it down   On the water
This picture comes back
The blue letter folded beside the bowl
You heard about it
Those lights on the water
It was a geographical joke
A big ugly antique
Good morning.   It was sky
In the English manner
It was by then a civilian

By which our hands return
Looking down in the mouth
Like the feelings of this rustic life
A field of earth plants
Where she was alive

In the goatskins
Standing out in an open field
When appearance reaches
And then leaves the story
Like a baked glistening afternoon
But only for a minute

Out-Dated Poem

A prelude sounded in a honky-tonk cafe
Ink glutted the white skein of the afternoon
Paper, that is history's footprints, black
Feet on the news now disappearing in the rain
On Second Avenue, Avenue of Dreams I had
In 1962 of immense beefsteaks when I was down
And out on the streets and too young to know
Better. Beautiful as an outline, hunger
Made my teeth ache as a handsome Lieutenant
Aches for a cold beer on a tropical island
In the topical year of 1942 which I can't
Remember like 1952 when I was much older
Without even trying, or cared much like I
Do today whether it rained or not.

Pretty Beads

1.
There is a lobster in the ocean

2.
A green lobster is saying his prayers

3.
A pebble drifts toward a monument

4.
The Violet State
                    (whose bed is the sea)

5.
Three granite indians do the bird

6.
The heart of a red rooster residing in Rhode Island

7.
A red gulley

8.
Busch Stadium looms in the distance like hope

9.
A Cardinal rounds third and heads for home

10.
The eyes look down under a pale moon

11.
Down the main street of Gallup, New Mexico

12.
Orange stars and peaches

    13.
Joy like a small train of thought

    14.
A fluid substance

The Furniture Man

The Supper Club meets in the evening
Beside the brand new image buster
Where we live with a hole in our shoe
Perhaps an elegant hole with the snow
Coming in

At the click of the meter
The Lunar Eye drops in
And enters the Age of Reason
Volume Eight, Number Four
Pigeons in the sky
As the Furniture Man comes down the street
And goes among the trees
The throes of sleeping books
The talky evenings and familiarity
Of another Century

He sits on a sofa
Thinking about the Canadian border
It is no secret
The rubber band he flexes
Just a prayer away
He sees, yes it is
The Canadian border
He holds in his hand

Relaxation

So gay on your lovely head
The hat cradles the specialty
Of the house brand new
And hedged with the flowers
Of the past we have somehow
Got through. If night
Should fold in on us
Here in the day dripping
Down the fire-escapes toward
The ground like poetry
In search of the common man
In all things smoky and
Vapid insight coming near
To what I can't keep my eyes
Off, the fragile jaws
Of antique life, a fretful
Crowd of messages delivered
Long ago in the pouring rain

Then night would find us
As we are, bright lives
Dancing in the somber light
Of history, shiny pencils
At the edge of things.

La Bohème

It will snow tomorrow
But today it is still Fall
In Union Square
Where New York City trees
Are dressed in the simple words
Of love in a coupé
On a street without stoops
Devoted this Thanksgiving Day
To Mrs. something Swopes
Dead at 77.

BERNADETTE
MAYER

The Port

We told them the myths about others
Sitting around the old and stately ship
And the ship's table, which had been shipped
From some faraway port.
The steward came to call for the mail
Hoping for a word from a nearby port
But, like the wine we had drunk too soon,
Our hearts were with the ship
Where after all our table had been set.
Part of our attention was placed
On the storm which flailed us about as if rain
Could outweigh the presence of others
And the old devotion of the captain's address.
The captain preferred ancient modes of opening
To those that were short
And had intercepted the steward's letter
In the course of his own first address,
Abbreviated with praise for the ship's company.
He accused us of being old and drunk
And of growing mustaches which caught
In the salt of the sea we were sailing
If only we could leave the port.

An Ancient Degree

Life was a thorough pool of restoration
Which she liked to compare to the councils of the
                              Elizabethans,
Making mazes in the fields and manners of the births

In which she could partake, thinking to tell good tales.
The way she was waxing in this difficult design
Could happen to anyone and in the morning sand,
The larger contest of her own life, it could be missed the
                                        same day.

A field is a useful article with which to tell the time—
To prepare the tales you tell and include new foreign countries
Which are beautiful and full of new designs.
In this way the landscape reformed her visions,
Like the battles underscoring their diffusion.
She did not seek counsel on the strength of these revisions,
An allusion of degree to the wife of sudden passion.

Index

a briar, a blunder, a
      bungalow

-awning

                                               Spelling is be-
briar   coming more
blunder   Steward
bungalow

                                           tawdry

                                           the blunder, a briar, a
                                               bungalow
                                           thigh

                                           Tradition

                                           tuck

America

As for me, when I saw you
You were in a tale
Thinking perhaps love is coming too
In America
Or perhaps as what is belated in a tale
May come true,
The scene is simply describing its use.

You had no hope
But the length of days, as in the sky
About which I already knew.

This gentle information
Comes as a prescription.

To notice a friend
Who is lettering a cloud
Which otherwise falls indifferently
Is no mark of distinction.
This is the difference
Between the past and dreams,
To dismiss an effigy
Which appears to be singing.

Sea

It's he, it's sea. The sea is continuous; a continuous body.
There was an Old Man of the Hague who is famous. What
color is it? As you are when he's ashore. Wind is a natural
motion of air. The numberless hues include grey, buff, slate,

brown, and russet. Some winds blow all year in the same direction. She came from the south.

With swords I am building an empire. Two drams borax, one dram alum, one dram camphor, one ounce sugar candy. The sea a continuous body of salt water covering three-fourths of the earth's surface. There was an Old Man of the Hague, whose ideas were excessively vague. Then when is a sailor like a beach? Hear when he's ashore, when he's aloft, when he's aboard, his diet, duties, and exercise. In atmosphere wind has speed, direction, and motion. The colors of salmon, faun, Esterhazy, lilac, green and maize, before the eyes. Winds of the same seasons and at the same hours of the day are periodic and never blinding. She came from the south, she arrived at her destination. It was winter.

One word follows the other with words. Repeat a ten minute stirring three times daily for two weeks. Sea and ocean are sometimes synonymous. A man from the Hague has built a balloon to examine the moon. There was an Old Man of the Hague. When is a sailor not a sailor? When else? If you want to know, when he was in the shrouds, since I've been at sea, they were riding the main, living on whale. The warmer air rose, the cold rushing in currents to fill the space. Full winds vary their directions change. She walked toward the house of the doctor who was singing.

With words you say and with pencils a drawing. Later a bell, a spill and a spell. Stir until clear and transparent. Hurricane winds blow sixty-four knots or more at sea. There was an Old Man from the Hague who built a balloon out of vague ideas. When is a sailor a corpse? Why are they always bad horsemen? The sailor muttered his health was better. The ship is adrift. The warmer air ascends. The Sargasso Sea is red and tints and shades of the same. Others are blue, green and Esterhazy all shades that vary. The doctor sang through the seasons. She broke the ice and threw it into the water, laying down a layer of blue earth.

A bell can't spell. We spell bell bell. It's he, it's sea. Strain, blot and bottle up for use. If too strong add water. The shore divides the land from the sea.

> There was an Old Man from the Hague
> Whose ideas were excessively vague;
> He built a balloon
> To examine the moon,
> There was an Old Man from the Hague.

When is a boat like a heap of snow? What makes a road broad? If you want to know my health is good though I diet, sail and exercise. The ship now rests in the bosom of a cove. The winds are regular, periodic, and variable. We study colors. Some have slight motion some violent velocity. The rest of the story goes:

She put down a second layer of blue earth and a third. But the water still ran inland. So she put strips of basketry along the shore's length. The water ran through and out and came no further inland than where she had placed the basketry along the beaches. The blue earth could be seen. The ocean had retired.

It is not true that: where a warehouse is further a redder one may be laughed at. It is true that returning. Laughed at, one may be redder; further is a warehouse where . . .

Laura Cashdollars

cut mats are even
come to rest when
cut mats securing
the parks bits to
poor Laura secure
as yet with still
less to neck than
the drink as four
corners the stick
to mix the fourth with.

Sermon

The sermon educates
the barrister of courts.
The women warming feathers sing.
A transom is a crosspiece, lets
in some light, this last sign—
Someone sent is humming
woman sum of something humming
this my guest and here
Is anyone there?
Next
the door is crumbling something flying in the dome
is tumbling forward.

Corn

Corn is a small hard seed.

Corn from Delft
Is good for elves.

White corn, yellow, Indian

Is this kernel a kernel of corn?

The corn they sought
Was sown by night.

The Corn Islands are two small islands,
Little Corn Island and Great Corn Island,
on an interoceanic canal route.

Any of several
insects that bore in maize is a corn borer.

Painting by Chimes

The buttocks of the ruffed grouse
        now hang aloft
supposing to engender
at first or with a knife
the certain duties of rehearsal
        as a ploy would.

The wing is a corporeal element
        akin to the divine
        and which by nature tends to soar.

And in the same conception
        a line without position
has brushed a stroke with its return.

It Moves Across

It moves across and over
across the ground
it moves across over the ground
under (by the bridge) the moss
over the moss
across the grass the
grass moves across crossing the
blades of grass into
larger fields
of grass crossing over the
mounds and hills of
nothing but grass on top of

roots of grass
it moves across slowly
slowly into
another field or further
through the forest still
moving by
and by emerging from
the forest small enough
moving
the same rate
under the bridge next to the
trees next through the
trees missing them moving
around them still
crossing like the trees
the trees over
like blades of grass the
grass over as a bridge goes over
bridges
bridges over the trees
it moves across the hills
like a field over the fields
like field on field
of a hill of a hill
as if the forest
into its forest
on the ground like the ground over
it
stopping over
near a patch of grass.

Steps

steps, shops   noses, ears, eyes   steps
           mouths, bills, beaks   shops
telephone   whiskers, horns, tufts   ships at sea
and telegraph   hair, fur, feathers   post cards
wires

           hair, fur, feathers   a   protecting
1. short   b   insulating
2. medium
3. long   black hair, blue black wigs, hairpieces
           brown hair, grey, light   (a) hoofs
           brown, platinum hair,   (b) hoofs
1. blondes   reddish brown, yellow hair   tons of steel
2. brunettes
3. redheads
           the palms of the hands   cleaning women
persons   soles of the feet   elevators
persons working

                               white space
microscopes   noses, ears, eyes
binoculars
telescopes   windows
crossed periscopes   black eyes, blue eyes are like cameras
eyes   brown eyes, grey eyes   i. blind
compound eyes   green eyes, red eyes   ii. color blind
floodlights   iii. myopic

           lids, brows, lashes   observatory

antennas

nails, claws, wings   limbs
antlers, antennae, arms   visitors
color vision   legs, feet, hoofs, paws
5. sex   fangs, teeth
television tower
shedding
molting
shells, torsos, trunks   1. height
2. weight
3. color of eyes
4. color of hair

miles of pipeline

Poem

I am beginning to alter
The location of this harbor
Which now meets with a channel
Joining one place with another.
Then it continues
As if in a town
The artfulness of a hand
Full of some things
And not others.
The eye rests
And we see
What is before
Everything else the same.
Though this implies a beginning
To which we ascribe no point
Nevertheless it has an end,

For no bishop of any importance
Constructs his tomb in a bad time.

The end which comes
Is not as important as the motion
Held in the air
Pausing in its course.
To switch then
Reverses the train
Of a running line,
And as before
May wheel and address
To a new location
To be seen beneath.
This flying conversion
Sets the scene
To a bell.

I have told more
Than can be seen.
The bell makes its trick
More than an opera.
If you have seen the world from a ship
Then you have not seen
What the ship lets fall into the sea
To blacken its top and make it grow.
To get out of this seaport
You must be a cutter of networks.

Wind Force

Sea like a mirror.
One. Ripples with the appearance of scales formed, but
 without foam crests.
Two. Light. Small wavelets, short but pronounced; crests
 appear glassy, do not break.
Three. Gentle. Large wavelets with crests beginning to break;
 foam appears glassy. Perhaps scattered white horses
 (white foam crests).
Four. Moderate. Small waves, becoming longer; fairly frequent white horses . . .
Five. Fresh. Moderate waves of a pronounced long form;
 many white horses, possibly some spray.
Six. Large waves begin to form; white foam crests more ex-
 tensive everywhere; probably some spray.
Seven. Strong. Sea heaps up; some white foam from breaking
 waves blows in streaks along the direction of the wind.
Eight. Moderately high waves. Edges of crests begin to
 break into spindrift. Well-marked streaks of foam blow
 along direction of wind.
Nine. Gale. High waves. Dense streaks of foam along direction of wind. Spray may affect visibility.
Ten. Very high waves with long overhanging crests; great
 patches of foam blown in dense white streaks along
 direction of wind. Sea surface takes on a white appearance. Visibility affected.
Eleven. Whole Gale. Exceptionally high waves; sea completely
 covered with long white patches of foam lying along
 direction of wind; edges of wave crests everywhere blown
 into froth. Visibility affected.
Twelve or more. Hurricane. Air filled with foam and spray;
 sea completely white with driving spray. Visibility very
 seriously affected.

EDWIN
DENBY

Aaron

Aaron had a passion for the lost chord. He looked for it under the newspapers at the Battery, saying to himself, "So many things have been lost." He was very logical and preferred to look when nobody was watching, as anyone would have, let us add. He was no crank, though he was funny somehow in his bedroom. He was so funny that everybody liked him, and hearing this those who had been revolted by him changed their minds. They were right to be pleasant, and if it hadn't been for something making them that way, they wouldn't have been involved in the first place. Being involved of course was what hurt. "It's a tight squeeze," Aaron was saying in his bedroom, and let us suppose he was quite right. He closed his eyes and shivered, enjoying what he did. And he went on doing it, until it was time for something else, saying, "I like it." And he did. He liked a good tune too, if it lasted. He once remarked to somebody, "Tunes are like birds." He wanted to say it again, but he couldn't remember, so the conversation became general, and he didn't mind. What was Aaron's relationship to actuality? I think it was a very good relationship.

The Silence at Night

(*The designs on the sidewalk Bill pointed out*)

The sidewalk cracks, gumspots, the water, the bits of refuse,
They reach out and bloom under arclight, neonlight—
Luck has uncovered this bloom as a by-produce
Having flowered too out behind the frightful stars of night.

] 509

And these cerise and lilac strewn fancies, open to bums
Who lie poisoned in vast delivery portals,
These pictures, sat on by the cats that watch the slums,
Are a bouquet luck has dropped here suitable to mortals.
So honey, it's lucky how we keep throwing away
Honey, it's lucky how it's no use anyway
Oh honey, it's lucky how no one knows the way
Listen chum, if there's that much luck then it don't pay.
The echoes of a voice in the dark of a street
Roar when the pumping heart, bop, stops for a beat.

The Climate

I myself like the climate of New York
I see it in the air up between the street
You use a worn-down cafeteria fork
But the climate you don't use stays fresh and neat.
Even we people who walk about in it
We have to submit to wear too, get muddy,
Air keeps changing but the nose ceases to fit
And sleekness is used up, and the end's shoddy.
Monday, you're down; Tuesday, dying seems a fuss
An adult looks new in the weather's motion
The sky is in the streets with the trucks and us,
Stands awhile, then lifts across land and ocean.
We can take it for granted that here we're home
In our record climate I look pleased or glum.

The Shoulder

The shoulder of a man is shaped like a baby pig.
It terrifies and it bores the observer, the shoulder.
The Greeks, who had slaves, were able to hitch back and rig
The shoulder, so the eye is flattered and feels bolder.

But that's not the case in New York, where a roomer
Stands around day and night stupefied with his clothes on
The shoulder, hung from his neck (half orchid, half tumor)
Hangs publicly with a metabolism of its own.

After it has been observed a million times or more
A man hunches it against a pole, a jamb, a bench,
Parasite he takes no responsibility for.
He becomes used to it, like to the exhaust stench.

It takes the corrupt, ectoplasmic shape of a prayer
Or money, that connects with a government somewhere.

Standing on the Streetcorner

Looking north from 23rd the vast avenue
—A catastrophic perspective pinned to air—
Here has a hump. Rock underneath New York though
Is not a subject for which people do care.
But men married in New York or else women
Dominate the pavement from where they stand,
Middle-age distends them like a vast dream
While boys and girls pass glancing to either hand.

Sly Carolina, corny California
Peculiar Pennsylvania, waiting Texas
You say what you say in two ways or one way
Familiar with light-reflecting surfaces.
Time in every sky I look at next to people
Is more private than thought is, or upstairs sleeping.

Summer

I stroll on Madison in expensive clothes, sour.
Ostrich-legg'd or sweet-chested, the loping clerks
Slide me a glance nude as oh in a tiled shower
And lope on dead-pan, large male and female jerks.

Later from the open meadow in the Park
I watch a bulging pea-soup storm lie midtown;
Here the high air is clear, there buildings are murked,
Manhattan absorbs the cloud like a sage-brush plain.

In the grass sleepers sprawl without attraction:
Some large men who turned sideways, old ones on papers,
A soldier, face handkerchiefed, an erection
In his pants—only men, the women don't nap here.

Can these wide spaces suit a particular man?
They can suit whomever man's intestines can.

People on Sunday

In the street young men play ball, else in fresh shirts
Expect a girl, bums sit quietly soused in house-doors,
Girls in dresses walk looking ahead, a car starts
As the light clicks, and Greeks laugh in cafes upstairs.

Sundays the long asphalt looks dead like a beach
The heat lies on New York the size of the city
The season keeps moving through and out of reach
And people left in the kitchen are a little flighty.

Look at all the noises we make for one another
Like: shake cake bake take, or: ton gun run fun,
Like: the weather, the system, the picture of his brother,
And: shake hands and leave and look at the sun go down.

One Sunday a day-old baby looked right at my eyes
And turned its head away without the least surprise.

13

Suppose there's a cranky woman inside me who
On the prettiest day rip! yanks down the window shade
But what a shade! no mote of light gets through
I breathe in pitchdarkness miserable and afraid.

She says she's Whistler's Mother. But I've heard her
Rollerskating down the hall when I'm sound asleep
Thundering in the dark and yelling bloody murder
She might as well be a subway I happen to keep.

At meals she eats like a wolf. Sometimes by mistake
Dives under the table and bites me too.
If I talk she makes noises like a hen or a snake
And if I don't she babbles, screw jew, screw jew.

She tore up your picture in one of her recent fits
But I felt around for and swallowed all the bits.

17

Thin air I breathe and birds use for flying
Over and through trees standing breathing in air
Air insects drop through in insect dying
And deer that use it to listen in, share—

Thickens with mist on the lake, or rain
Cuts it with tasteless water and a grey
Day colors it and it is the thin and plain
Air in my mouth the air for miles away.

So close it feeds me each second, everyone's friend
Hugging outside and inside, I can't get rid
Of air, I know it, till the hateful end
When with it I give up the insanely hid

The airless secret I strangle not to share
With all the others as others share the air.

A Domestic Cat

The cat I live with is an animal
Conceived as I, though next to me she's small.
More like each other, so our births assert,
Than either one is like a house, or shirt.
I nervous at my table,
She by the stove and stable,
Show what a gap lies between cats and men;
But shift the point of view to see again
Surrounding both of us disgusting death,
Death frames us then in this still room, each pumping breath.

Her white fur where she cleaned it smells like talc;
Her claws can tap the floor in a rapid walk;
Her shape in walking bulges up and down;
Jealous, she sits remote, but does not frown.
To sleep, she puts an eye
Upside down next a thigh
And lost the small snout grows a deeper pink;
To eat, above the neck her elbows shrink,
The outstretched neck, the head tilt when she chews,
They thrust, they gulp; and sated she rises to refuse.

Compelled, as men by God are, twice each year
Her look turned stony, she will disappear;
Exhausted, three days later, dirty and plain
She will creep home, and be herself again.
She cleans her young contented,
At one month they're presented,
Clear-eyed she hauls them out and on my bed;
Here, while they wolf her tits, she purrs, outspread.
She waves her tail, they look, they leap, they riot,
She talks. And later, when they've gone, she cowers quiet.

Graceful as the whole sky, which time goes through,
Through going time she wanders, graceful too.
Sits in the sun, sleeps rounded on a chair,
Answers my voice with a green limpid stare.
Modest in drooping furs
She folds her paws and purrs
Charmed by the curious song of friendly talk;
But hearing up the stair a stamping walk,
Under the bed she streaks, weakly disgraced,
As humble as an alleycat that's being chased.

We live through time. I'll finish with a dream:
Wishing to play and bored, so she did seem;
But said, she knew two kittens just outside
That she could play with any time she tried;
We went to see this thing,
But one hung by a string,
A kitten strung up high, and that looked dead;
But when I took it down, it was well instead.
All three then played and had a pleasant time.
So at war dreamt a soldier for him I made this rhyme.

Trastevere

Dear head to one side, in summer dusk, Olga
On her terrace waters potted azaleas
Thoughts of friends, their fine successes, their failures
Greek reliefs, Russian poets, all water with her;
The plants rejoice; across the street, the high wall

Reaches the decayed park of a long dead Pope
Urchins stole the sphinx near the fence up the hill
Where woods grow thick, sold it to a Yank I hope;
Now young priests smoke at the basin, by blurred sea-gods
Above them rises a hairy thicket of palms
That male in their joint green dusk yield Rome the odds
Returning with the night into primeval realms
As laughing Olga, feeding through the window cat-shadows
Then reading, then sinking into slumber, too does

Sant'Angelo D'Ischia

Wasps between my bare toes crawl and tickle; black
Sparkles sand on a white beach; ravines gape wide
Pastel-hued twist into a bare mountain's back
To boiling springs; emblems of earth's age are displayed;
At a distant end of beach white arcs piled
Windows, and in the sea a dead pyramid washed
As if in the whole world few people had survived
And man's sweetness had survived a grandeur extinguished;
Wonders of senility; I watch astonished
The old hermit poke with a stick the blond lame boy
Speaking obscenities, smiling weird and ravished
Who came from New York to die twenty years ago;
So at a wild farmer's cave we pour wine together
On a beach, four males in a brilliant weather

Forza D'Agrò

Leaving the bambino home, by bus, afoot
Past a wild sea-keep, we climbed to the viewed town
Got lost among pigs, at last unguided stood
Above roofs, steeps, the sea, under Etna in rain;
Cold poor town, more beasts live in it than people
Was their joke as the young priest showed us paintings
Who when I urged a hot-water bottle giggled
And took us to the cafe where all was wanting;
The gangster from New York was building his house
But sweetly priest and a youth leaping showed the path down
We ran down lost in sunset to make the bus
And in a black winter night got safely home;
The lithe girl watching her goats, sparkling and fifteen
Smiles her clear smile as sleep and tearing grief return

Ciampino

Flying from Greece to see Moscow's dancing girl
I look down on Alba Longa, see Jacob's house
And the Pope's, and already the airplane's curls
Show St. Peter's, and the Appian tombs' remorse;
But Jacob, a two year old American
Is running in the garden in August delight;
'Forum not a park, Forum a woods,' he opines
In November quiet there on days less bright;
Now in New York Jacob wants to have my cat
He goes to school, he behaves aggressively

He is three and a half, age makes us do that
And fifty years hence will he love Rome in place of me?
For with regret I leave the lovely world men made
Despite their bad character, their art is mild

A Postcard

Elaine, Nini, Sylvia, Marjorie, Theda,
Each sends you happy wishes for your birthday,
Red and black Frances, Frannie, and Almavida,
Louise, gay Germaine too who is far away,
Kind Maggie, and Pit, Martha who prays gladly,
Jeannie, Ruth, Ernestine, Anne, Billie Holliday,
Husky Patsy, Ilse they love so madly,
And straightfaced Teddy,—Dear Rudy, they all say.
And then Victor, and Bill, and Walter the mild,
And Frank, David, John, Aaron, Paul, Harry and
Virgil, the Photoleague, Oliver, Ebbie wild,
I and Gankie and the Shoe-man shake your hand.
Marieli and Susan come running at the end
And all of us send our love to you, our friend.

19

The size balls are saddens Lamarck
It's of no relevance to Marx
And Freud shoots his lunch at the fact
Dad's funny if he's just as small

July subway, meditate on
The decently clothed small male parts
Take their fabulous importance
Felt by homes, felt better by farts
They won't be missed, science will soon
Claim, parthenolatric more than
Religion, women left alone
To travel planets with women
In the lit subway gently shook
Imagine they've a goodbye look

20

The grand republic's Poet is
Brooklyn Whitman, commuter Walt
Nobody else believes all of it
Not Harvard, that finds him at fault
I have, but first he broke my heart
He points to the moon and breaks it
I look for him, twenty-first street
Sleep against the push of a cat
Waking stumble to start coffee
At my back Walt in underwear
His head slants from unaltered day
Strokes my cat, the cheeks streaming tears
Sits on a bed, quietly cries
While I delay turning round, dies

23

Heavy bus slows, New York my ride
Speeds up, on the hill Rudy waves
Then faster seize me, pivot, evade
A mien, step, store, lawn sliced from lives
A nap at dusk; entering night
Landscape threatens, no matter which
Caveman's faith, artificial light
A shack in the woods, the turned switch
One a.m. stop; drunk or sly strangers
Turnpike, the bus wheezes, slows, drives
And so Bronx, known Manhattan kerbs
Turned key in my lock, the door gives
Miserably weak, pour some shots
Don't look, make the bed, it's day out

24

New Year's near, glass autumn long gone
Daily done tasks that required it
Like a no trouble office man
One undone, scale from which I shrink
In my clean loft with the heat on
It's fifty, zero outside, gale
Banged sash, gust screams, gust rolled ashcan
Tonight the two stray cats here wail
I can't tell them the facts of life
The Cuban bomb, or cats in snow

But a ribbon takes their mind off
Fall asleep twined, later with me
Two, three nights, weather becomes soft
Awhile, and cozier the loft

30

Roar drowns the reproach, facing him
Quite near, subway platform, she heeds
Head tossing slow like a pony's
In the wrong, the pinto I rode
A boy of twelve, that lovely head
Quarrels I believed riders win
White-haired pass these lovers in luck
Hurry to ballet, its invention
Where there's no quarrel, but there's fate
A scream unhurried of music's choice
And we recognize the games played
In heaven, foreknowing they cease
The move, the pitch arrive, turn to air
Here, as if love said forever

32

Drenched saw Doris home, midnight gale
Later a hospital weak Helen
At five, coffee oatmeal alone
Dark union square, me light-headed

Two youths lope sullen, one; flood-lit
Penthouse, me walking to my bed
Walk cautious as if drunk up Sixth
Prowl car walk past at my corner
The night's end foreknown, furred room mate
Witty neuter with his beast fate
White-polled like me ghost grandfather
Reads in my sleep dreadfully
The grandeur of scene, of persons
Random safety, random city

DAVID

SHAPIRO

New World of Will

A black ear crawls on the window. It is
my own, my very own remarkable ear.
I hear little of the original spirit.

A piece of paper caught up in a tree
bearing the stationery marks of you and me.
If you were here in teeth and kisses, in NY,

How would you see these animals, the ants,
how they teem and murder, and they are driven too.
It is time for the pronunciation of the will.

So here among the dull and nightly rocks,
here where we first met, with philosophy,
upon a bank where oarsmen rowed them past,

receiving the strict letters and in the morning
on this same spot again I hinder you.

1964

Poem from Deal

I discovered the United Nations night building.
It was a low-slung bar.
News on an electric band ordered one to
DEFINE THE PLACE; DEFINE THE TIME.

Napoleon used to persuade me to shinny up
long poles that always drop back from heaven.
What is the pacifist nutrition?
RHYTHM AS MENTALITY; RHYTHM AS SENSORY CONTROL.

Why do we invent communities
in the clouds? their strictures against children
posted in the castles at Deal:
WALK ON THE MATTRESSES; DON'T WAKE THE BABIES.

The Idea of a University

To have even a portion of you is the highest
State to which a good article can aspire.
It puts me beyond chance, necessity, anxiety,
Suspense, and superstition, the lot of many.

Vaulters, whose hours are possessed by one pole,
Take exaggerated views of the importance of height,
Are feverish in the morning, and are
Startled and depressed when they happen to fall.

When I am in difficulties, I originate vast ideas
Or dazzling projects equal to any emergencies.
I can remember to whom I am speaking.
This is genius. Something really luminous,

Something really large. The earth smiles.
The rocks are deranged over the sequence of ideas,
Too violent to last before this giant fascination.
And the hand opens its ten thousand holds.

The Heavenly Humor

Light became audible, that is, a child, and took the empty
                                                    place.
Farther back, majesty was a leek to eat. Why make a younger
                                                    mom
The thunderbolt of something quick go the round of her
                                                    lover?
To themselves, they would guard it,
Fall upon a ray like the earless. Conquests or a new baby?
What has happened to Tommy, his violin and bow, must be
                                                    wedded soon.
You must strike a beam.
Since childhood I sat down, sleeve across mouth.
What cannot be streaked over corpse-grey in the land of
                                                    rectangles.

Drenched?
Before the fire? Among airmen, entrusted to slaves,
I hope the peril in the ice will "experience" him.
And he was angry, raised his eyes to the dangers of the
                                                    mountains.
My desire sings admirably well but the mail-pilot
His belt—the toll-gatherer—sometimes does.
What, they ask, is this science?
Up the dead lane are forty-seven wings. We withdrew, killed
                                                    his lift,
Sold olives, beans, unleavened paste.
They're all mad, leading me into the inappropriate feeling
                                                    range.

A gleam hangs on the lips of a warmer sea
Simple as Plato taught, to be forbidden dream
Noon-tide light, broad daylight, manipulating the pulleys,
Crying "All this fine talk is from my own party"
All about vibrating surfaces—oh yes!

To buy a sound mantle for every strong man
The gallery filled up with stony variations of the Main Cashier.
He endured until the next day when the longest lull occurred
My diagnosis suffered from an air of posing
He charged my toll "Why, good evening"
Very famous, he loves it, anything frantic with grief
It's noon-tide in Corsica
This is a woman's point and David's point, expecting to find
                                                    her husband.
Shut your eyes, furbish
Musical drums, post-horns, sourdines, all she was doing was
                                                    music.
More remote, living safely together
Girls often suggest men glance at the chalcography shop
Past times show bands—should in time be sunlight
Incurious, exclusive,
Today, a fade into the glare
With reference to a particular period.
And with sparkling desire expected to come crashing through
                                                    the floor.

1964

The Contribution

A dollar for Whitman, you are all stumbling.
Well in a field of malacostraca the child picks up
The claw which is still limber and open and king.
The child examines the claw for Abyssinian crap
But only lobster pimples pink the claw and the top
Is swollen like a popular mouth that's about to sing.

Furiously at the hedges the claw starts bouncing.
Then Cleopatra strides in with a check for Charmian,
Her famous maid, and almost faints meeting the striking
And voyaging claw, whose attraction will soon be gone
Like the purple member of a child nearly eaten
Thrown into the vestibule of a vagina in the ring.

1963

The Bicycle Rider

I see the winter turned around
like pleasure make the cabinet wail
when I open it, make the girls go
through the curtains again
and fold the shiny parts

The shiny roots are fired, the balls
in the sycamores
are swinging.
A talented bicycle rider
flew out of the winter for a sad party.

I'll stick that man in a tree,
especially without hooks,
without the jocks to meet those horrifying spooks,
like the bicycle rider
irrationally dropping his books.

1961

Two Poems on the Emotions

1 *Dust*

They commune at 7:30 where I walked my arid hands
This woman, she forces me to notice bloody lambs
While she selfishly contrives to the word is arouse me on the
snow-dunes
you realize in a few moments she is going to smash it

Other small people scrawl in their journals about vacations
They escape thinking lust is a withered thing
Whereas on one hand I have the withering complex
they get excited by dismembered chickens and dance up and
down

2 *Love*

As on the Greek island of Corfu, at sunup,
we saw the dying woman posing nude for the
kittenish photographer who was, for example,
her own father—it demolishes desolation
it makes one feel in the company of erections
or the stiffer tenderness of green jade or
the glossy tenderness of blue marble
No longer in the realm of "personal feelings" but
Beauty, as in Keats——Only the word exists for
ten thousand Roman soldiers slaughtered at Cannae
this involves much light in the mystery while
Juliet has her hand on my door

1963

Four Stories

1. The Children of Scotland

Once children in Scotland contracted the throbbing foot disease of horses. Formerly, only cut-throats and ruffians were infested. But in weaving a metallic prickle around a Think Plant, from end to end of Scotland the germ twisted. This character was frustrated; this one had dirty thumbs; this one was closed, suffocated, throttled. Finally he picked his way open at both ends. The pure-bred animals crossed the wood in the thundery evening.

2. Walking

Mike went walking in finely-cut grooves one day in the Milky Way. I supplied him with the occasion: October. At the raffle, he sold her undies and the straight bar with teeth on its edge. What could make it clearer? In psychoanalysis this process is known as the duplicating process. Breathe in— a large thrush eats the mistletoe.

3. Water Collects

Jerry was a human being of super-human size. He laughed in a suppressed way, liable to hump out of the brighter part greater than a semi-circle. Australia trusted him to give a serious, dull present. He succeeded in coming meaningless. Four Georges, then only semi-transparent speech and mildness. Gibber gunyah—I'm heating up this stone for your toy. Water collects and then the writer's name appears on the saucer: a fine gift.

4. Girl In Her Teens

"I love a faithless telephone-pole blown out by a storm.

"I was frightened into singing, singing is saving.

"I called up your state: it tears them where it can.

"You are the best.

1963

Five Songs

With Debra

1 *The King of the Elephants*

We won't favor you
For supper
We won't call you in
To eat lunch

But we love you
Come when we don't call
You have white pearls
And blue stones

2 We Are Ugly

You don't know my sister
She has white teeth
I commend her
You don't know my sister
Who is named the purple pearl

She goes under a bridge and gets lost
She doesn't come home till she dies

3 Now About God

God is help
And his name is softer too
Than the arm flesh of a baby
Who sleeps in the zoo

4 Like Mushrooms

Let's talk about love pats
Even if I kill you it's a love pat
Even if you fall down and hurt yourself
And bleed it's a love pat

5 Us Tasting the Air

For all I know
In twenty years
The tiger and the cougar
And you and I
We will all be
In Colorado
The best friends of the world

In Memory of Your Body

Your body has narrow slits instead of
windows. And inside, your brain turns
around, silent. The more mouth you
have the more pleasure. Your eyes look
like dungeons, look like stables,
though they are hard and white as
your legs. Nor are those legs without
ornament: two chains of great size and
rotundity keep you prisoner. Loitering
on the beach, one common night, they
were recognised and stopped. In another
corner of your body, a fountain spouts.
Then there are your breasts, which,
carved in stone, would be thought wonderful for miles. Everything around
appearing a little abstract! I loved
you, so I carved your hands small and
perfectly clean. And here I beg
permission to close a chapter of still life.

Elegy to Sports

Orestes pointed out what was despotic
        In youth and stingy hunger.
From his golden injuries he got
        What he wanted from you.

The key used to dial was at last in place,
    The house asbestos.
And he dressed up as a piece of human candy
    With great hustling.

Last stop! Your clothes fill up the trunk
    With a pitful hand.
The seer in old age follows the raindrops,
    Touring an inhuman scene.

The Swiss have no wars, though they lose combats,
    The English are hemmed in by waves,
Those who drink the rivers Po, Tagus, and Danube,
    Are found on the river bottom.

And so the vaulter, who rebounds into gravel
    Dragging his pole behind,
Like gasoline sets the hurdles on fire
    Jumping and jumping again.

The pianist whistles during the accompaniment;
    Mrs. closes her eyes;
She retires from us, seeing you dislike her
    And her rowboat collection.

Now you are happy, and you are more than happy,
    You swan of Lancaster.
Don't complain about the dull apartment life
    A thousand times a day.

A gnome brought suit against the cedarwood,
    And Libya owes money to a tree.
Your father has received the gems amber and garnet
    For a year's work on his bed.

You beat your hand, you jump out of line,
    And you say among yourselves:
"This is what Italy and Greece dumped on us
    In a thousand poems."

So you give away your violin, the other his trumpet;
    The girl gives you away.
And the women, the pedestrians, and the detective
    Desert the champ.

Master Canterel at Locus Solus

I

And nothing was missing
Introduced into the brain
The family is now watching
The scene that's produced

The scene that's produced
Might be several different scenes
Once the muscles are loosed
With vitalium and resurrectine

With vitalium and resurrectine
They dress as they need to
Outside the cooling machine
Inside the grieving family

Inside the grieving family
Covered with heavy sweaters
And the wig they wear is heavy
Then they leave the ice-box

Then they leave the ice-box
And the laboratory technician
Takes a key and locks
After the end of the cycle

After the end of the cycle
There is no putrefaction
But that invariable cycle
Of the animated corpse

Of the animated corpse
He must document everything
He identifies the corpse
And he surrounds the corpse

And he surrounds the corpse
Puts walls where it falls
Puts stairs and chairs
Using originals if possible

Using originals if possible
He repeats indefinitely
The same scene in his skull
Chosen once forever

Chosen once forever
His eyes, working lungs, words
Actions, walk, as ever
And nothing is missing

II

For perfection in prognostics
I imagined an apparatus
That the sun and wind would fix
The sun and wind combined

The currents of the atmosphere
But how they could give birth
To an art work was not clear
Only a fine mosaic would do

I searched for a material
That would engage the sun
And disengage my own will
And used multicolored teeth

Which I had learned to attract
As you attract the breath
Attract rather than extract
Like wind to a balloon

Almost bloody roots
Immense molars and monstrous canines
And a milk tooth that shoots
An imperceptible light

A brusque and powerful magnet
That the world obeys
And the sick tooth drawn to it
Leaves the mouth without torture

Thus the tooth aches stop
And the inferior maxillary
And tooth filling drop
Down the unwooded esplanade

At times bleeding, then brilliant
From the roots and cavities
I have furnished a monument
Where I found myself

Beyond this region of teeth
There is a single red root
The dove made of white teeth
Graciously flies to it

Mornings the mirror turns east
Dawn it contemplates the south
Nights the mirror shines west
And directly receives the sun

For the Princess Hello

Bridges that, a little because of absence,
Have like circuses changed their sites,
And the wood rots due to circumstance,
And, I believe, because of their engagement
To light, and something like light,
Whose voltage will run dry,
These bridges come like all bridges
To change and be re-painted.

Stone cries when it spans a void,
The wood thinks about the last century,
Both hate each other by custom,
And can't contain their mountainous
Duality, like a turkey with two feathers
Pushed by the wind, turning
Into feathers of nothing without sweat:
A turkey's definition of change.

The old bridges faint under caresses
Discovering the constant in a circle
Around forty-seven plane figures
Which they invented in foreign ports;
The liar and his lie
Win over a racially mixed city!
And these bridges come like all bridges
To change and be re-painted.

It's sweet to follow the trace of a bridge
And get angry without knowing why
Which one of the architects will succeed
In vaulting, character, and facing.
All the days of nine committees
Have been concerned with city bridges!
Now you will see the proof
That each has been re-painted.

Both stone and wooden bridges promise
Elevated above us, to separate
The hardened student from the breaths
Of a young girl, mouth open:
Each conserves the advantage
Of forces despite everything you say
In each of your false languages:
In its turn will be re-painted.

Biographies and Bibliographies

JOHN ASHBERY

Was born in Rochester, N.Y., July 28, 1927, and grew up in Sodus, N.Y. He attended Deerfield Academy and Harvard (B.A., 1949), did graduate work at Columbia (M.A., 1951, thesis on Henry Green) and N.Y.U., specializing in French literature. He worked in publishing with Oxford University Press and McGraw-Hill, 1951–1955. He received a Fulbright to France (Montpellier) in 1955, renewed in 1956 for Paris, where he later became an art critic for the European Edition of the *New York Herald Tribune* and for *Art International* (Zurich), as well as Paris correspondent for *Art News* (New York). He returned to New York in 1965 to become Executive Editor at *Art News*. He returned to Europe in 1968 on a Guggenheim grant.

His collections of poems are *Turandot* (Tibor de Nagy, 1953), *Some Trees* (Yale Series of Younger Poets, 1956), *The Tennis Court Oath* (Wesleyan, 1962), *The Poems* (Tiber Press, 1960), *Rivers and Mountains* (Holt, Rinehart & Winston, 1966), *The Double Dream of Spring* (E. P. Dutton, 1970). He is also the author of several plays, among which *The Heroes* (1950) was performed by the Living Theater (1952) and the Artists' Theater (1953) and published in *Artists' Theater* (Grove Press). *The Compromise* (1955) was performed by the Poets' Theater in Cambridge in 1956. His translations of French poets, such as Roussel, Jacob and Reverdy, remain uncollected.

His poems have appeared in many magazines and anthologies, among them *The Harvard Advocate, i.e., Poetry, Har-*

] 545

per's Bazaar, Locus Solus, "C," Art & Literature, Angel Hair, Semicolon, Tel Quel, Partisan Review, Kenyon Review, Evergreen Review, The Yale Literary Magazine, Location, The London Times Literary Supplement, The New American Review, Big Table, The Paris Review and The Hasty Papers.

BILL BERKSON

Born August 30, 1939, in Doctors Hospital, New York City. Son of Seymour Berkson (journalist) and Eleanor Lambert Berkson (publicist). Baptized in Presbyterian Church: William Craig Berkson. Grew up in New York, East 80's. Trinity School 1944–55. Communicant of the Church of the Heavenly Rest (Episcopalian) 1952–56. Summer jobs: International News Service 1954–55 (Sports Desk) and Newsweek 1956–57. Lawrenceville School 1955–57: fictitious sports columns give way to Serious Verse ("Love as an Idol of the Flesh" and "Threnody in Dust"); first readings of English literature with Dr. Thomas H. Johnson, Emily Dickinson scholar, very gentle and informative; private studies (with Johnson's encouragement) of Eliot and his background (Dante, Elizabethans, some modern French); introduced to Pound's Personae by John Silver and to Stein and Petronius as well as Graham Greene by Frank Rouda; period of half-assed "existentialism," analytically bent; "Threnody" got the Fifth Form Prize for Best Poem and an Eliot study swept the field for Long Essay—the prizes included Frankenberg's Introduction to the Pleasure Dome and The Collected Poems of T. S. Eliot.

Brown University 1957–59: Versification with S. Foster Da-

mon, short story with John Hawkes, tragedy with Gerald
Weales (a course, that is); an attempt at musical comedy
with Al Curran; sudden awareness of works by Ginsberg,
Corso, O'Hara and others of "the men of '56" and reviews of
them in the *Brown Daily News*; "re-invented" cyclical theory
of history, presented to a little club we had in Professor
Workman's classroom. Travels in Europe (mostly France,
mostly Paris) summers 1958–59. Left Brown, January 5,
1959.

Study with Kenneth Koch and William Troy, The New
School 1959: greatly influenced by Koch's sense of humor and
beauty (he presented their connection clearly) and through
his teaching, by Williams, Reverdy, Auden, Stevens, Mi-
chaux—then, of course, O'Hara and Ashbery, and Koch's
own work, or more exactly, his way of seeing funny details.
Translations of Cendrars and Aretino. Dylan Thomas Memorial Poetry Award 1959. Involvement in atmosphere of New
York painting and sculpture from about this time (de Koo-
ning's show of landscape-abstractions that spring). General
"cultural" education through friendship with Frank O'Hara:
the Stravinsky-Balanchine *Agon* (and Edwin Denby's essay on it), Satie (we created four-hand "annoyances" at
various apartments, once played for Henze in Rome), Feldman, *Turandot*, a certain Prokofiev toccata, Virgil Thomson (I
had heard a recording of *Four Saints* at Harry Smith's, Providence, 1957), movies . . . we read Wyatt together, recited
Racine, skipped through galleries, collaborated on *The Hymns
of St. Bridget* 1961–64, a note on Reverdy for *Mercure de
France* 1961. Columbia College 1959–60. Editorial Associate
Portfolio & Art News Annual 1960–63. First book: *Saturday
Night: Poems 1960–61* (Tibor de Nagy Editions, John Myers,
ed.). Included *10 American Poets* (Koch, ed., lithos by An-
gelo Savelli). Film Editor, *Kulchur* 1962–63. Lived in Paris
1963–64.

Associate Producer "Art New York" series WNDT-TV, New
York, 1964–65. Participated in "Settimano di Poesia," Festi-
val of Two Worlds, Spoleto, Italy, June 1965. Reviews and

articles for *Art News, Arts,* museum catalogues, 1965–66. Instructor at The New School 1964–70. Free-lance editorial work for The Museum of Modern Art 1965–68. Writers/Teachers Collaborative sessions at Benjamin Franklin High School 1968. Edited *In Memory of My Feelings* (by Frank O'Hara, illustrated by 30 U.S. artists), The Museum of Modern Art, 1967. Grant from The Poets Foundation, 1968. Guest at Yaddo summer 1968. Editor: *Best & Co.,* 1970. *Shining Leaves,* book of poems written at Yaddo, *Angel Hair,* 1969.

Published in: *Big Table, Poetry, Locus Solus, Art & Literature, The Floating Bear, Nomad, The Paris Review, LVII* (Belgium), *"C" Comics, The World, Angel Hair, Nadada, Kulchur, Art in America, Adventures in Prose,* etc.

Present height: 70". Weight: 154. I live in New York.

TED BERRIGAN

Born in Providence, R.I., 15 Nov. 1934, Scorpio, where my father was Chief Mechanic for Ward's Baking Company. Went to Catholic Schools for 13 years, with one year out to work in a factory. Member in good standing of the United Electrical Workers Union. Quit Providence College in 1953 to join the U.S. Army. 3 years in Army including 18 months in Korea. Released from service in 1957 in Tulsa, Oklahoma. Attended Univ. of Tulsa, 1955–60. A.B., M.A. (Thesis on GBS). Moved to NYC in 1960 and lived there until 1968, mostly on the Lower East Side. Founded *"C" Magazine* with Lorenz Gude in 1963. 13 issues, 2 edited by Ron Padgett, 2 Comic Strip issues edited by

Joe Brainard. *"C"* Books by myself, Ron Padgett, Dick Gallup, Tom Veitch, Kenward Elmslie, Joe Ceravolo, Michael Brownstein. Collaborations with painters Joe Brainard & George Schneeman were the most eye-opening things that happened to me in NYC. Aram Saroyan's *Lines,* Peter Schjeldahl & Lewis MacAdams' *Mother,* Ed Sanders' *Fuck You,* and Anne & Lewis Warsh's *Angel Hair & The World* magazines provided plenty of energy, excitement & annoyance during my years in NY. In 1967–68 I taught a poetry workshop at the St. Mark's Arts Project. Earlier I had done a similar workshop at the Free University of NY. For a brief period in 1964–65 I helped run the poetry readings at Le Metro Coffee House. Also worked in 1966–67 as a reviewer for *ArtNews* magazine. Presently I am teaching a poetry workshop & Form of Poetry class at the University of Iowa. I am married & have two children, a boy and a girl.

Bibliography:

The Sonnets (*"C"* Press, 1964, Grove Press, 1967)

Seventeen, plays, with Ron Padgett (1964)

Living with Chris, illustrated by Joe Brainard (Boke Press, 1965)

Noh, w/Ron Padgett (*Lines* Broadsheet #1, 1965)

Many Happy Returns (*Angel Hair* Broadsheet, 1967)

Bean Spasms, w/Ron Padgett & Joe Brainard (Kulchur Press, 1967)

Many Happy Returns, poems (Corinth Press, 1968)

3 Silkscreens, w/George Schneeman, edition of 20 (1968)

Assorted Collages w/words, w/Joe Brainard (1961–8)

Tambourine Life, a long poem, edited by Duncan MacNaughton (Mother Press, 1969)

Etc.

JAMES BRODEY

Born Brooklyn NY November 30, 1942. Blue (eyes) Blond (hair) 165 (weight) 6' (high). Two small scars on left thumb, one on chest. Grant from Poets foundation 1967. Dylan Thomas Poetry Prize, New School, 1966.

Works appeared in: "*C*," *Lines*, *Elephant*, *City Lights Journal*, *Mother*, *Art & Literature*, *Kulchur*, *LA Free Press*, *LA Oracle*, *Ear*, *Bluebeat*, *Clothesline*, *Angel Hair*, *The World*, *Adventures in Poetry*, *Vice*, *Splice*, *Nadada*, *5 Summer Poets*, *Intransit*, *Wild Dog*, *Wormwood Review*, *The Paris Review*, *San Francisco Earthquake*, & various non-profit ($) spiritual broadsides.

Books: *Fleeing Madly South* (Clothesline Editions, NY, 1967)
Identikit (Angel Hair Books, NY, 1967)
Long Distance Quote (Mustard Seed Press, LA, 1968)
Head-Waters, New and selected poems (LA, 1969)
Editor: *Clothesline*, a One-Shot Magazine (NY, 1966)

MICHAEL BROWNSTEIN

I was born in Philadelphia and grew up in New Jersey, Tennessee and Ohio. I went to school; Antioch College and New School in New York City. I have lived in New York City, northern California and Paris, France. Now I'm living in New York City. I received a Poets Foundation Grant in 1966 and was Fulbright scholar in France in 1967–68, translating Max Jacob. Won the Frank O'Hara Foundation Award in 1969.

Books: *Behind the Wheel* ("C" Press, 1967)
Overjoy (Spine Wind Press: Paris, 1968)

Magazines: *The Paris Review, Angel Hair, The World, "C", Mother, Get That, Spice, Nice, Blue Pig, The Floating Bear, Adventures in Poetry, Ronald Reagan*

Anthologies: *The Young American Poets* (Follett, 1968)
The World Anthology (Bobbs Merrill, 1969)

JOE CERAVOLO

was born in 1934.

He is a civil engineer as well as a poet. He lives in Bloomfield, New Jersey, with his wife, Rosemary, and their two children. His poems have appeared in *Locus Solus, "C," Lines, Mother, Art & Literature, The Paris Review,* and other magazines, and in *The American Literary Anthology/1.* Two pamphlets of his poetry have been printed: *Fits of Dawn* ("C" Editions, 1965); and *Wild Flowers out of Gas* (Tibor de Nagy Editions, 1967). His first book, *Spring in This World of Poor Mutts* received the first Frank O'Hara Foundation Award and was published by Columbia University Press in 1968 as the first Frank O'Hara Award Book.

TOM CLARK

Born in Chicago in 19 and 41.

Went to high school, etc. Worked for three years as an Andy Frain usher, the kind they had at the recent Chicago Democrat convention. Mostly digging the ballparks, etc.

Went to U. of Michigan, wrote some poems, won two Hopwood awards, got a degree in 63, got a Fulbright to England.

Fulbright at Cambridge (Caius College) 1963–65.

1966–67 taught American poetry at U. of Essex. Edited the *Once* series of magazines and books from Brightlingsea, Essex, 1966.

Traveled around Europe & N. Africa, etc. Poetry editor of *The Paris Review* since 1963.

Co-founder and -editor of *The Wivenhoe Park Review*, 1966.

Publications: *Airplanes* (Once Press, 1966), *Sand Burg* (Ferry Press, 1966), *The Emperor of the Animals* (Goliard Press, 1967), *Bun,* with Ron Padgett (Angel Hair, 1968), *Stones* (Harper & Row, 1969).

Author of an unpublished novel, *The Riot at the Garrick Theatre.* Went back to America and lived on L.E.S. of NYC 1967–68.

Wrote book reviews for *New Statesman, The Review* (England), *Kulchur,* the *New York Times, Poetry* (Chicago).

Published poems in *New Statesman, Encounter,* the *Times Literary Supplement, The Listener, Art & Literature, The Nation, Poetry* (Chicago), *Coyote's Journal, Mother, Angel Hair, The Paris Review,* etc. etc. Won Bess Hokin Prize, given annually by *Poetry* (Chicago), 1966.

Gave poetry readings in London, Cambridge, Colchester, Bristol, Nottingham, Newcastle, New York, Ann Arbor, San Francisco etc.

Awarded a grant for poetry by Rockefeller Foundation 1967. Awarded a grant by the Poet's Foundation 1966.

Married the former Angelica Heinegg of Wellington, N.Z., in St. Mark's Church, 2d Ave & 10th St, NYC, March 22, 1968.

Moved to Bolinas, Calif., where he lives on a mesa over the Pacific Ocean with his wife and daughter.

CLARK COOLIDGE

Bio Note:

Born: February 26, 1939 in Providence, Rhode Island.

Height: 6'3". Weight: 200 lbs. Eyes: hazel.

Schools attended: John Howland Elementary School, Nathan Bishop Junior High, Classical High School, Brown University (all in Providence, R.I.).

Jobs held: Engineering Lab Technician, "society" "jazz" "rock" drummer/Classical Percussionist, Disc Jockey, Library Searcher, Cave Explorer.

Wife: Susan. Daughter: Celia Elizabeth (born 26:IV:68).

Current Residence: San Francisco, California.

Biblio Matter:

Books: *Flag Flutter & U.S. Electric* (Lines, Aram Saroyan, 1966)

Clark Coolidge, 20 poems (Lines, Aram Saroyan, 1967)

Magazine Appearances: *Hubris, Brown Review, Lines, Insect Trust Gazette, Thrice, Nice, Coyote's Journal, Wild Dog, Elephant, Change, O'er, Patterns, Drainage, Joglars, Art & Literature, The Paris Review, o To 9, Angel Hair, The World, The Floating Bear, The*

Anthologies: *The American Literary Anthology/1* (Farrar, Straus, & Giroux, 1968)
The Young American Poets (Follett, 1968)

Tape Recording: 14 poems, approx 20 minutes–Poetry Room, Lamont Library, Harvard University–14 January 1967.

STATEMENT:
This is a sentence.

EDWIN DENBY

Biographical data: b. 4 Feb. 1903, Tientsin, China; current res.: N.Y.C.; have shrunk to 5'10", 126 lbs.

Publications: *In Public, In Private* (Prairie City, Ill.: Decker Press, 1948) *Looking at the Dance* (Farrar and Cudahy, 1949; Horizon, 1968)
Mediterranean Cities (N.Y.: Wittenborn, Inc., 1956)
"C" Magazine, Entire issue No. 4 devoted to Denby's poetry (N.Y., 1965)
Dancers Buildings and People in the Street (N.Y.: Horizon Press, 1965)

KENWARD ELMSLIE

was born on April 27th, 1929 in New York City. He was raised in Colorado Springs, Colorado, & educated at Harvard, graduating in 1950. Three collections of his poetry have been published—*Pavilions* (Tibor de Nagy Editions, 1961), *Power Plant Poems* ("C" Press, 1967) and *Album* (Kulchur Press, 1969), and in 1968, Black Sparrow Press bought out *The Champ*, an epic poem illustrated by Joe Brainard, with whom he collaborated on *The Baby Book* (1965) and *The 1967 Gamebook Calendar*, both published by Boke Press. His poems have appeared in: *Folder, New Folder, Poetry, Wagner Literary Magazine, The Beat Scene, The Hasty Papers, The Literary Review, Locus Solus, Nomad, Set, "C," "C" Comics, Art & Literature, Nadada, Lines, Mother, The Paris Review, Tzarad, Angel Hair, Wild Oats, The World, Juillard, Via Roma, Cicada, Adventures in Poetry,* and *Poetry Pilot,* and in the following anthologies: *The Beat Scene* (Corinth Books, 1960), *The American Literary Anthology/1* (Farrar, Straus and Giroux, 1968), *The Zodiac* (Brownstone Press, 1968), *The Young American Poets* (Follett, 1968) and *The World Anthology,* (Bobbs Merrill, 1969). Translations, written in collaboration with Ruth Yorck, are included in *An Anthology of Medieval Lyrics* (Modern Library, 1962), *Medieval Age* (1963) and *Leopardi: Poems and Prose* (Indiana University Press, 1966).

He has written three opera librettos, published by Boosey and Hawkes: *The Sweet Bye and Bye* (1966), composed by

Jack Beeson and produced by the Juilliard Opera Theatre in 1957, *Lizzie Borden* (1967), composed by Jack Beeson and produced by the New York City Opera in 1965 and revived in 1967, and *Miss Julie* (1968), composed by Ned Rorem and produced by the New York City Opera in 1965. A one-act play written with James Schuyler, *Unpacking the Black Trunk,* published in *"C,"* was performed by the American Theatre for Poets in 1965, and in 1967, *The Grass Harp,* a musical play based on the novel by Truman Capote, with music by Claibe Richardson, was performed by the Trinity Square Repertory Company, in Providence, R.I.

He is 6'1", weighs 190, and lives in New York City and Calais, Vermont. He is Scotch-Irish-English-Hungarian-Jewish-German, and became an American citizen in 1946.

DICK GALLUP

Born Greenfield, Massachusetts, July 3, 1941. Youth spent in Tulsa, Oklahoma (1950–1959). Educated at Tulane University (1959–1962) and Columbia University (1964–1968, B.A.). He has lived in New York City since February 1962. Married 1964 to the former Carol Jean Clifford; children, Christina Danielle, b. 1965, and Samuel Sabine, b. 1969.

Author of *Hinges* ("C" Press, 1965) a book of poems, and *The Bingo* (Mother Press, 1966) a play in five acts.

Poems etc. have appeared in the following magazines:
Lines, "C", Angel Hair, Columbia Review, Wagner Literary

Magazine, Mother, Poetry, The Paris Review, The Censored Review, Tom Clark's English Magazines, *The World, Adventures in Poetry, Blue Pig, First Issue, The East Side Review, The Poet's Home Companion.*
And Others.

JOHN GIORNO

Biographical Note:

singer, actor, b. Tupelo, Miss., Jan. 8, 1935; s. Vernon John and Gladys Giorno; grad. high sch., Memphis. Truck driver Crown Electric Co.; recorded for personal use My Happiness, also That's When your Heartaches Begin, 1953; first commercial recording That's All Right Mama, also Blue Moon Of Kentucky, for Sun Record Co., 1954; personal appearance tour as Hillbilly Cat, weekly performances on Louisiana Hayride, radio sta. KWKH, Shreveport, LA.; recordings popular music for RCA Victor, 1955, include Blue Suede Shoes, Hound Dog; appeared TV, Jackie Gleason's Stage Show; actor films Love Me Tender, 1956, Loving You, 1957, Jailhouse Rock, 1957, King Creole, 1958, Kid Galahad, 1963, Blue Hawaii, Girls! Girls! Girls!, others. Numerous personal appearances. Served with U.S. Army, 1958. Address: care Colonel Tom Parker, Box 417, Madison, Tenn.

Bibliographical Note:

The poems selected were originally published by: *Mother, Spice, Clothesline, The World.*

A book, *Poems by John Giorno,* was published by Mother Press.

An LP stereo record *Raspberry and Pornographic Poem* was brought out by The Intravenus Mind.

Poems have appeared in *The Paris Review, The World, Angel Hair, "C," Mother, Spice, Clothesline, Manifestos* (A Great Bear Pamphlet/Something Else Press), *Do-It, OU, Adventures in Poetry, Poet's Home Companion.*

KENNETH KOCH

was born in Cincinnati, Ohio, in 1925, and has degrees from Harvard and Columbia University. He has received Fulbright and Guggenheim grants and has spent three years in France and Italy. His first collection, *Poems,* with prints by Nell Blaine, was published by the Tibor de Nagy Gallery in 1953. His mock-epic poem *Ko, Or a Season on Earth* was published in 1959. Tiber Press issued his *Permanently* as one of a four-volume boxed set, the other three volumes being devoted to the poetry of John Ashbery, Frank O'Hara, and James Schuyler, the volumes illustrated, respectively, by Al Leslie, Joan Mitchell, Mike Goldberg and Grace Hartigan. His other book publications include *Thank You And Other Poems* (Grove, 1962), *Bertha and Other Plays* (Grove, 1966), *Poems from 1952 and 1953* (Black Sparrow, 1968) and *The Pleasures of Peace and Other Poems* (Grove, 1969). Several of his plays have been produced off-Broadway, most

recently *Bertha* at the Cherry Lane and Living Theater, and
George Washington Crossing the Delaware at the Maidman
Playhouse. He was editor of *Locus Solus*. He is currently
teaching at Columbia College.

Mr. Koch's work has appeared in the following magazines:
*Poetry, "C," Art & Literature, Mother, Partisan Review, The
Paris Review, ArtNews, Evergreen Review, Angel Hair, Semi-
colon, i.e., Folder, Big Table, Yugen* and *First Issue.*

FRANK P. LIMA

PHOTO
UNAVAILABLE

Born December 27, 1939, of Mexican
parents in New York City, where he
grew up and now lives and works as a
photographer's assistant. In 1962 he won
the Gotham Bookmart Avant-Garde
Poetry Prize at the Wagner Literary
Conference. He has several grants from
the Poets Foundation. His first collec-
tion of poems, *Inventory,* was published in 1964 by Tibor de
Nagy Editions; the same year he won the John Hay Whitney
Award. His work has been anthologized in *Introduction to
Poetry* (Dade College, Florida) and in the forthcoming *New
York Poets,* edited by John Bernard Myers. His poems have
appeared in the following magazines: *Floating Bear, "C,"
Evergreen Review, Provincetown Review, Signal, Angel Hair,
Wagner Literary Magazine, The Plumed Horn* and *Art &
Literature.* He stands 5 feet 11 inches and weighs 160 pounds.

LEWIS MacADAMS

Bio

I was born on the clean high plains of of West Texas, 1944, October 12, 7:04 A.M. Raised in Dallas, had a normal boyhood, except I was a switch hitter. Thought I wanted to be a clown or do some other kind of religious service. Still do. People grow up so young, and it's hard to stop. Went to college. Was in Buffalo two years watching folks dig out from where the Charles Olson River broke through its banks, learning lessons from other refugees, one of whom, Jack Clark, is my teacher, another of whom is John Weiners. New York has been nearby for years, Frank O'Hara and Ted Berrigan, especially Berrigan, who gave me my first pill and showed me how to write words down. My wife is asleep so I better type softer. Grace I dig special. Magic doesn't interest me at all. Right now I work as a switchman on the Southern Pacific all around S.F. Write rock songs, put tapes together and watch the words shiver up and burn. Have one book out, *City Money* (Oxford Burning Water Press, 1965) and another, a selected poems, coming out in Rome. Another, *U.S. 40 West,* is just waiting for the right man to come along. Was Peter Schjeldahl's co-editor on *Mother No. 5, 6, 7* and co-edited in Buffalo with Duncan McNaughton, *Mother 8* and *Mother 9 (the record).* I intend to do more records, if I stay in the country, but this here draft is about to eat me up.

That's all I want to say. Magazines I've been in are few: *Eggs, The World, Angel Hair, The Ant's Forefoot, Audit* (Fall, 1968), *Mother, Carroll Anthology, Intransit* (Warhol-Malanga superish), *Paris Review 42, Presence, Conditions, Slice, The Magazine of Further Studies, Intrepid.*

HARRY MATHEWS

was born in New York City on February 14, 1930, and lives in Paris. Publications: two novels—*The Conversions* (Random House, 1962) and *Tlooth* (Paris Review Editions: Doubleday, 1966); and poems in these magazines: *Locus Solus*, *"C,"* *The Paris Review*, *Lugano Review*, *Art & Literature*, *Mother*, *Quarterly Review*, *Hudson Review*, and, in England, *Icteric* and *Juillard*.

BERNADETTE MAYER

Born in New York, May 12, 1945. B.A., New School for Social Research, 1967. Co-editor of *o TO 9*. Living in New York. Published works: *Story* (o TO 9, 1968); poems in *Angel Hair*, *Ice*, *Joglars*, *Lines*, *Mother*, *The Paris Review*, *Tzarad*, *The World* and *o TO 9*.

FRANK O'HARA

Born June 27, 1926 in Baltimore, Md. (Full name: Francis Russell O'Hara.) Musical studies (piano and composition): 1933–1943; 1946–1950 (mostly private, then at New England Conservatory and Harvard). U.S. Navy: 1944–1946. Harvard 1946–1950 (B.A. English Literature, after first majoring in Music). University of Michigan (M.A. 1951 and Avery Hopwood Major Award in Poetry the same year). Settled permanently in New York City, 1951. Part-time job as secretary to Cecil Beaton, briefly, and prepared John Latouche's *The Golden Apple* for publication. Part-time, then full at the Front Desk of the Museum of Modern Art, 1951–1953. Editorial Associate (monthly reviews and occasional articles) *ArtNews,* 1954–1956. In 1955 joined staff of Department of Circulating Exhibitions (International Program) of the Museum of Modern Art; selected numerous exhibitions for circulation abroad (*Jackson Pollock 1912–1956, Franz Kline, David Smith,* etc.) and participated in the selection of others (notably *The New American Painting of 1959* and *United States: XXth Century Sculpture* in 1965). Also selected exhibitions for circulation in this country (*Gaston Lachaise, Arshile Gorky Drawings*). Director of *New Spanish Painting, Motherwell* and *Nakian* exhibitions at the Museum, 1961, 1965 and 1966 respectively. Named Associate Curator in 1965 and then Curator, confirmation of which was to have been in September, 1966. Ford Foundation Fellowship to the Poets Theater, Cambridge, Mass. as playwright-in-residence, January-June 1956. Contributed to musical comedy *Undercover Lover* by Arnold Weinstein and John Gruen (produced at Adelphi College). Various poems set to music by Ned Rorem, Morton Feldman, John Gruen. Collaborated with Larry Rivers on a series of lithographs, *Stones*, 1957–1958, and on other poem-painting projects with Grace Hartigan, Norman Bluhm, Jasper Johns, Franz Kline, Michael Goldberg and Joe Brainard. Created a double-scenario (with subtitles) for Alfred Leslie's film *The Last Clean Shirt* and provided the musical background (a Satie, Poulenc and Scriabin recital) for Rudy Burckhardt's *The Automotive Story*. Acted in the Living Theater production of Picasso's play *Desire Caught by the Tail*.

Travels: South Pacific and Japan (during Navy tour of duty 1944–1946); Europe (Spain and Paris) 1960; Europe again (Rome and Paris) 1961; and again (Amsterdam, Copenhagen, Stockholm, Warsaw, Paris, Vienna, Prague, Belgrade, and Zagreb, Rome, Milan, Turin, Milan) 1963. Died July 25, 1966, in an accident at Fire Island.

Publications:

Poetry:
A City Winter (Tibor de Nagy Gallery Editions, 1951)
Oranges (Tibor de Nagy Gallery Editions, 1953)
Meditations in an Emergency (Grove Press, 1957; second edition, 1967)
Odes (Tiber Press, 1960)
Second Avenue (Totem/Corinth Press, 1960; second edition undated)
Audit magazine, Frank O'Hara issue, 1964
Lunch Poems (City Lights, 1964)
Love Poems (Tentative Title) (Tibor de Nagy Gallery Editions, 1965)
In Memory of My Feelings, commemorative volume illustrated by 30 U.S. artists and edited by Bill Berkson (The Museum of Modern Art, 1967)

Drama:
Try! Try! included in *The Artists Theater*, Herbert Machiz ed. (Grove Press, 1960)

Art Criticism:
Jackson Pollock (Braziller, 1959)
The New Spanish Painting (The Museum of Modern Art, 1961)
Robert Motherwell (The Museum of Modern Art, 1965)
Reuben Nakian (The Museum of Modern Art, 1966)

Dramatic Productions:
Try! Try!, Poets Theater, Cambridge, 1951
Change Your Bedding, Poets Theater, Cambridge, 1952
Try! Try! (2nd version), Artists Theater, New York, 1952
Love's Labor, The Living Theater, New York, 1959
Awake in Spain, The Living Theater, New York, 1960
The General Returns From One Place to Another, New York, 1964

Introductions:
A. B. Spellman. *The Beautiful Days* (Poets Press, 1965)
Edwin Denby. *Dancers, Buildings and People in Streets* (Horizon Press, 1965)
Erje Ayden. *The Crazy Green of Second Avenue* (Canyon Books, 1965)

Art Editor: *Kulchur Magazine,* 1962-64.

His poems, plays, and criticism have appeared in the following magazines and anthologies: *The Harvard Advocate, Semicolon, Accent, Measure, Horizon, Evergreen Review, Folder, Yugen, ArtNews, Kulchur, Poetry* (Chicago), *New World Writing, Partisan Review, Nomad, Nugget, City Lights Journal, Big Table, "C," Art & Literature, The Hasty Papers, i.e.* (*The Cambridge Review*), *"C" Comics, Signal, The World, The Paris Review, Locus Solus, Nadada, It Is, Fuck You/A Magazine of The Arts, Fuck You* (German Anthology), *LVII* (Belgium), *Metro* (Italy), *Mercure de France* (Pierre Reverdy memorial volume), *The New American Poetry 1945–60, A*

Controversy of Poets, Second Coming, The Floating Bear, The Beat Scene, School of New York.

An edition of O'Hara's collected poems will be published sometime in 1969; a selection of essays, memoirs and other documents may be found in *Frank O'Hara 1926-66*, edited by Bill Berkson and Joseph LeSueur, Paris Review Editions, 1969.

RON PADGETT

Born Tulsa, Oklahoma, 1942. B.A. Columbia College 1964. Gotham Bookmart Avant-Garde Poetry Prize at Wagner Literary Conference 1964. Grants from Poet Foundation 1964 and 1968. Fulbright to Paris 1965–1966. Currently living in New York City with wife and son and sister-in-law on the uptown fringe of the Lower East Side. Books and pamphlets: *Some Bombs* (1963). Translations and mistranslations of poems by Pierre Reverdy. Covers by Joe Brainard.

In Advance of the Broken Arm ("C" Press, 1964). Poems. Cover by Brainard.

Two Stories for Andy Warhol ("C" Press, 1965). Prose. Cover by Warhol.

Sky (Goliard Press, London, 1966). Prose poem.

Tone Arm (Tom Clark's Press, 1966). Poem. Cover by Clark.

100,000 Fleeing Hilda (Boke Press, 1967). Short poems. Cover and drawings by Brainard.

Bean Spasms (Kulchur Press, 1967). A play, sections from a novel, poems, stories, cartoons, interviews, collaborations by Ted Berrigan and Ron Padgett and others. Covers and pictures by Brainard.

Bun (Angel Hair *Books*, 1967). Poem by Tom Clark and Ron

Padgett. Cover by Jim Dine.
The Poet Assassinated (Holt, Rinehart & Winston, 1968).
Translations of Guillaume Apollinaire's *Le Poète Assassiné*.
Cover and pictures by Jim Dine.
Great Balls of Fire (Holt, Rinehart & Winston, 1969). Poems
1963–1968. Covers by Joe Brainard.

JOHN PERREAULT

Born Aug. 26, 1937, New York City.
Occupation: Art Critic (*The Village
Voice, ArtNews*, etc.). Pre-occupation:
Poetry. Books: *Camouflage* (Lines Press,
1966), and *Luck* (Kulchur Press, 1969).
His poems have appeared in the fol-
lowing magazines: *"C," Mother, Locus
Solus, Art & Literature, Chelsea Re-
view, The Paris Review, Slice, Cothesline, Nomad, o TO 9,
Bones, Angel Hair, The World,* and *Extensions.*

ED SANDERS

was spewn from the Chaoma in 1939 Kansas City Missouri. He left the midwest in 1957 as a direct result of the following events:

One: reading *Howl* in shop class in 1956.

Two: the hideous probability of being stuck with an Eskimo Pie franchise

Three: purchasing Pound's *Cantos* at the Cokesbury Bookstore

Four: breaking up w/his high school sweetheart while watching Wilt Chamberlain & the Kansas Jayhawks defeat Missouri University.

He graduated from N.Y. University. He is editor of *Fuck You/A Magazine of the Arts*, owner & head maniac at the Peace Eye Bookstore, leader of The Fugs, a chromosome-damaged assembly of musicians & pussy addicts. His books are *Poem from Jail, Peace Eye, King Lord/Queen Freak, The Toe Queen Poems, F.G.I.A.*, and *Duck Butter*.

ARAM SAROYAN

Born September 25, 1943. Attended many private and public schools in New York and Los Angeles. Graduated from Trinity School in Manhattan in 1962. Attended—briefly, in quick succession —the University of Chicago, N.Y.U., Columbia General Studies. Started *Lines* in fall 1964—edited and published six magazines and eight books—stopped in spring 1967. Numerous little press books of his own work, two books with Random House: *Aram Saroyan* (1968), *Pages* (1969). No longer writing. Still to be published: *Poems* (1962-66), *Prose* (1964-68), *New Poems* (1967), *Letter* (1968).

PETER SCHJELDAHL

was born March 20, 1942, in Fargo, North Dakota, and raised in various Midwestern places. He attended Carleton College (three years), dropping out to get married (in New York) and spend a year (in Paris). Before leaving Carleton he co-founded *Mother* magazine, a journal of art and literature that expired after eight issues in 1967. Since returning from Paris (in 1965), he has lived on the Lower East Side and written art criticism for *The New York Times*, *The Village Voice* and *ArtNews*. Recently he worked as an editor for *Avant-Garde* magazine. His first book of poems, *White Country*, was published in 1968 by Corinth Books. His poems have appeared in these magazines: *Mother, The Paris Review, Art & Literature, Angel Hair, Tzarad, Epoch, Nice, The World, Intransit, Promethean, Ronald Reagan,* and *Bones.* And in these anthologies: *The American Literary Anthology/1* (Farrar, Straus & Giroux, 1968) and *The Young American Poets* (Follett, 1968).

JAMES SCHUYLER

James Schuyler was born in Chicago in 1923, grew up in Washington, D.C., Buffalo, and East Aurora, N.Y. He attended Bethany College in West Virginia. He lived in Italy 1947–1949, after which he lived in New York City. He currently lives in Southampton, N.Y. He has worked at the Museum of Modern Art and as an editorial associate on *Art News.*

His novel *Alfred and Guinevere* was published by Harcourt, Brace and Company in 1958. He is the author of several off-Broadway plays, among which are *Presenting Jane, Shopping and Waiting,* and (with Kenward Elmslie) *Unpacking the Black Trunk.* His text for Paul Bowles' *A Picnic Cantata* has been recorded by Columbia Records. A selection of his poems, *Salute,* was published by the Tiber Press in 1960, as one of a four-volume set (the other three were by John Ashbery, Kenneth Koch and Frank O'Hara). Another selection, *May 24th or so,* was published by Tibor de Nagy Editions in 1966. *A Nest of Ninnies,* which he co-authored with John Ashbery, was published by Dutton in 1969, the same year Paris Review Editions published his first large "public" collection of poems, *Freely Espousing.* He has received awards from the Longview Foundation, Poets Foundation and National Council of Arts.

His work has appeared in the following magazines and anthologies: *The New Yorker, Accent, Poetry, Partisan Review, New World Writing, Locus Solus, "C," Art & Literature, Mother, Angel Hair, The World, Get That, Semicolon, The New American Poetry 1945–1960* (ed. Donald Allen), *The World Anthology* (ed. Anne Waldman).

DAVID SHAPIRO

Curriculum vitae:

January 2, 1947, Newark, N.J.; Deal, N.J.; 1964–8, Columbia, N.Y. 1967 Merrill Fellowship, U.K., France, Italy. 1968 Kellet Fellow at Cambridge. *Art and Literature* #1. 1965, *JANUARY. Location*, Summer, 1964. *The Young American Writers. Minnesota Review*, Spring 1963. Antioch, summer '61. *Poems of our Moment*, 1968. *Floating Bear*, 1962. *"C," The World, Bones, Nice, Spice, Mother. The Paris Review* 39. *Harpers, The Nation, Chicago Review, Beloit Poetry Journal, Ergo, Davar, Columbia Review* (1964–8), *Wagner Literary Magazine, Paris Magazine, XbyX, Bones. Poetry* (Chicago), June '66, May 1968. *Elephant, Sundial, First Issue, Time, Life, Newsweek, Possibilities of Poetry*, 1969. Dell. Book of poems, *Poems from Deal*, (E.P. Dutton, 1969). *Tri-quarterly*. N.Y. Poets Foundation award, 1967. Robert Frost fellow to Bread Loaf, 1965. Gotham Book Mart award, 1962. Book-of-theMonth Club Fellowship, 1968. Voice of America, 1956; WEVD, TV. *Art News*, May, 1969. *Learn Something, America*, Bedford-Stuyvesant Muse, 1969, co-edited with Kenneth Koch.

TONY TOWLE

was born June 13, 1939 in New York; grew up in Queens and Westchester County; began writing poetry in 1960; lives in New York with his wife and daughter.

Books: *Poems*, Hand set and printed by the poet (1966)
After Dinner We Take a Drive into the Night (Tiber de Nagy: New York, 1968).
Anthologies: *Poems Now* (Kulchur Press: New York, 1966)
The Young American Poets (Follett: Chicago, 1968)
Magazines: *Lines*, *"C,"* *The Paris Review*, *Spice*, *Mother*, *"C" Comics*, *Elephant*, *Clothesline*, *Wagner Literary Magazine*, *Nadada*, *Art & Literature*, *The Cardinal*, *The World* and *Angel Hair*.

TOM VEITCH

a boy role in life born 1941 over Bellows Falls, Vermont. You can see him in the way he writes, especially from behind. Twelve unpublished novels, most no longer extant. Lately in San Francisco undergoing various love torments and the painful emergence of God in his flesh. Hi folks.

Books: *Literary Days* ("C" Press, 1964)
Toad Poems (Once Press, 1966)
Das Luis Armed Story, trans. Peter Behrens (Kiepenheuer & Witsch, Cologne, 1970).

Anthologies: *The Young American Writers,* ed. Kostelanetz (Funk and Wagnalls, 1968)
The World Anthology, ed. Anne Waldman (Bobbs Merrill, 1969)
Acid, ed. Rolf Dieter Brinkmann (Marz Verlag, 1969)
Magazines: *"C," Angel Hair, Once, The Paris Review, The San Francisco Earthquake, Lines, The World, Mother, Drainage.*

JOE BRAINARD

Illustrator.

Index of First Lines

VINTAGE HISTORY AND CRITICISM OF
LITERATURE, MUSIC, AND ART

A free catalogue of VINTAGE BOOKS *will be sent at your request. Write to* Vintage Books, 457 Madison Avenue, New York, New York 10022.

VINTAGE POLITICAL SCIENCE
AND SOCIAL CRITICISM

A free catalogue of VINTAGE BOOKS *will be sent at your request. Write to* Vintage Books, 457 Madison Avenue, New York, New York 10022.